TILTED

TILTED

THE TRIALS OF **CONRAD BLACK**

Second Edition

Steven Skurka

DUNDURN
TORONTO

Editor: Jennifer McKnight
Design: Jennifer Scott
Printer: Webcom

Library and Archives Canada Cataloguing in Publication

Skurka, Steven
    Tilted : the trials of Conrad Black / Steven Skurka. -- 2nd ed.

Includes index.
Issued also in electronic formats.
ISBN 978-1-55488-934-1

1. Black, Conrad--Trials, litigation, etc. 2. Trials (Fraud)--United States. 3. Hollinger International Inc--Corrupt practices. I. Title.

KF225.B53S59 2011   345.73'0268   C2011-901180-8

1   2   3   4   5   15   14   13   12   11

We acknowledge the support of the **Canada Council for the Arts** and the **Ontario Arts Council** for our publishing program. We also acknowledge the financial support of the **Government of Canada** through the **Canada Book Fund** and **Livres Canada Books**, and the **Government of Ontario** through the **Ontario Book Publishing Tax Credit** and the **Ontario Media Development Corporation**.

Care has been taken to trace the ownership of copyright material used in this book. The author and the publisher welcome any information enabling them to rectify any references or credits in subsequent editions.

J. Kirk Howard, President

Printed and bound in Canada.
www.dundurn.com

Dundurn	Gazelle Book Services Limited	Dundurn
3 Church Street, Suite 500	White Cross Mills	2250 Military Road
Toronto, Ontario, Canada	High Town, Lancaster, England	Tonawanda, NY
M5E 1M2	LA1 4XS	U.S.A. 14150

TO RANDI, MONTANA, JORDANA, AND DYLAN

CONTENTS

"You never really understand a person until you consider things from his point of view ... until you climb into his skin and walk around in it."

— Harper Lee, *To Kill a Mockingbird,* 1960

FOREWORD

I often have the privilege of commenting for international television, radio networks, and print media, including the wire services, about high-profile criminal and civil corporate fraud cases, capital markets regulatory issues, and corporate governance. Media commentary comes with tremendous responsibility, to bring experience and shed light on the dynamics of the cases and the issues, and ensure that the public is correctly informed. The perspective that the media invites me to bring is 26 years practising law as a former Securities and Exchange Commission enforcement lawyer, a former state criminal prosecutor, a former United States federal criminal prosecutor, and as a defence lawyer and advisor to corporations and their officials. So, the Conrad Black case perfectly fit the profile of another such opportunity for commentary for my friends in the Canadian media in particular, with whom I also have discussed Enron, WorldCom, Lucent, Bernie Madoff, Alan Stanford, insider trading, international investigations, public corruption, and more. Little did I know at the time that I would meet and become friends with a prominent, articulate, successful, and quick-witted Canadian criminal defence lawyer, Steve Skurka, with whom I came to share many a microphone and printed page as the fate of Conrad Black and his C-Suite colleagues at Hollinger International wound its way into and along the roller coaster of the United States federal courts.

When Steve and I first met in person in Toronto during one of my periodic trips to Canada to speak at a securities law conference, he gave me a copy of the first edition of *Tilted: The Trial of Conrad Black*. Over the years, I have started to read books about various criminal trials, and typically put them away unfinished, as they were little more than a comprehensive but lifeless diary of a case. I found reading *Tilted* just the opposite — not only an entertaining and informative read, but a most insightful critique of the American federal criminal justice system. In fact, I have come to highly recommend this book to many American and international lawyer colleagues and non-lawyers to gain a valuable and different perspective on the American justice system and the criminalization of corporate misconduct in America. Just as important, Steve brings to life the relevance and dynamics of a trial that captivated Canada and the United Kingdom, but, to the frustration of Conrad Black, was a non-event in the United States. To this day I still wonder whether the championship game of the Canadian Football League had a greater real-time following in the United States than the Conrad Black trial outside of Chicago. Nevertheless, Steve's close following of and ability to humanize and retell the case reflects that we "south of the border" missed a fascinating drama while it played out.

A number of times, while commenting for Canadian television on the case, I asked a producer to permit me to correct misinformation provided by another commentator. That never happened when I shared a segment with Steve. While Steve and I may not always have agreed on the approaches adopted by the attorneys or our expectations as the case worked through the appellate process, Steve's analysis of the goings-on in court and the dynamics of the case always were well thought through, with fully supportable and justifiable strategies and outcomes. And, where I always limited my commentary to an arm's-length perspective of a former prosecutor and a defence lawyer, Steve was up close and personal with all the parties and the lawyers. Steve watched critical motions and the trial day-in and day-out, ran through his mind the analysis of what might he have done differently and why, and observed first-hand the reactions of the judge, lawyers, defendants, and the jury. This provides a rare and valuable perspective on a criminal case that most outside the United States questioned as to the existence of criminality, and those inside the United States recognized as the further over-extension of a legal theory of corporate boardroom prosecutions that the United States Supreme Court ultimately rejected.

For me, as an American lawyer and commentator, there are several facts that are undisputable about the case. Twelve American citizens heard all of the evidence and convicted Conrad Black on several, albeit not all, charges. The judge who presided over the trial upheld the conviction. So too did the first level appellate court with a stinging opinion by one of America's preeminent jurists. Benefiting from the United States Supreme Court's displeasure with federal prosecutors' misapplication of the deprivation of honest services statute under federal criminal law in the corporate prosecution and conviction of Jeffrey Skilling, Enron's Chief Executive Officer, Conrad Black received a second chance in the courts. Although the first level appellate court ultimately threw out two more charges, Conrad Black remained a convicted felon, and the trial judge sent him back to jail to complete a reduced sentence. Steve superbly and clearly walks you through each step of the trial and the appellate process.

Regardless of whether you agree or disagree with the charges and the outcome, whether you are or are not a Conrad Black fan, and whether you believe Conrad Black deserved to sit twice in an American jail, you will find Steve's book a most satisfying read. You will smile at Steve's humour and dry wit. You will share outrage in his perceived excesses and injustices in the American judicial system. And, you may even come to understand why American prosecutors investigated and tried Conrad Black and his confidantes. After reading this book you will come away with a thorough understanding of the Conrad Black case, and considerable food for thought about the federal criminal justice system in the United States.

JACOB S. FRENKEL
Chair, Securities Enforcement, White-Collar Crime
and Government Investigations Practice
Shulman, Rogers, Gandal, Pordy & Ecker, P.A.

ACKNOWLEDGEMENTS

I am reminded of the *All in the Family* episode in which Edith Bunker is attending her high school reunion and is asked by a former classmate to recount what has happened in her life since high school. Edith then proceeds to explain, in painful detail, the precise vicissitudes of her life from her teenage years to the present.

I shall resist any temptation to follow Edith Bunker's example and thank my bar mitzvah teacher. I would, however, like to highlight two English teachers who shaped my writing skills in my formative high school years, Mr. Moore and Mr. Woolard. Howard Engel, a prominent Canadian writer, was the first person who told me that I had some writing talent and urged me to pursue it. I studied with Martin Amis at the Humber Summer Workshop in Creative Writing and he was very encouraging.

I interviewed a myriad of sources for this book and only a few requests were denied. Socrates remained unavailable to explain the Socratic Method. Conrad Black, by contrast, was always helpful and accommodating in our exchanges.

Kirk Howard had faith in this book, and I am grateful to him as well as everyone else at Dundurn Press. Jennifer McKnight, my editor, provided me with expert guidance. My agent, Margaret Hart, was a reliable source of support.

The timeline used throughout the book is reprinted with the permission of *Maclean's* magazine. In a couple of instances, the first names of individuals unrelated to the trial were altered to protect their identity.

The sketches from the courtroom were prepared by Cheryl Cook.

Finally, I would like to make special mention of my parents, Fred and Rene Skurka, and my grandparents, Morris and Annie Levitt and Jack and Clara Skurka, who greatly influenced my life.

INTRODUCTION

> For my part, I believe I have made it clear to fair-minded observers and will continue to do so that I committed no illegalities, I made the most I could of my time in prison, enjoyed teaching there, and my career as a writer has flourished. My financial condition is quite satisfactory. I have responded as well as I could to Radler's treachery and other unbidden events ...
>
> — Conrad Black in an email to the author, May 23, 2011

Conrad Black's final opportunity for vindication in his costly legal struggle[1] that deprived him of over two years of his freedom took place in the Dirksen Federal Building in Chicago in a ceremonial courtroom. The courtroom was reserved for special occasions and a hearing was set to proceed before a panel of three judges from the Court of Appeals for the Seventh Circuit. Black had already secured his place in American legal lore with the United States Supreme Court's decision in his case. The decision of the Supreme Court to hear the appeal was regarded by Black's own lawyers as an "unbelievable" achievement. The odds of obtaining a Supreme Court review were calculated to be about one in one hundred.[2] Black had managed to overcome such daunting odds to subsequently obtain a ruling from the nation's highest court that placed his three remaining convictions for mail fraud and his obstruction of justice conviction into jeopardy. The showdown would unfold in Chicago with the Court of Appeals acting as the arbiter of Black's legal fate.

Conrad Black was recognized as a celebrity figure in the Dirksen Federal Building. His status was confirmed on a mounted board adorning the wall immediately outside of the ceremonial courtroom. There in bold lettering was an outdated, and slightly inaccurate, account of Conrad Black's case. The inscription on the board read as follows:

> The world's media came to Dearborn Street in 2005 when U.S. Attorney Patrick Fitzgerald brought eight criminal charges against international newspaper mogul Conrad Black, Baron Black of Crossharbor. Four new charges were added later that year, alleging racketeering, obstruction of justice, money laundering, and wire fraud. Under the racketeering count, the government sought forfeiture of more than $92 million. A media circus erupted on the streets surrounding the Dirksen Building with photographers jostling one another for shots and staking out all four corners of the city block. After 12 days of deliberation, the jury found Black guilty of three counts of mail and wire fraud and racketeering. On December 10, 2007, Black was sentenced to 78 months in jail. A subsequent appeal to the Seventh Circuit was denied; Lord Black has appealed to the U.S. Supreme Court.

Conrad Black was likely the first British Lord ever tried in the courthouse. Black's Chicago-based veteran attorney, Ed Genson, had announced to the local media that he had never defended a Lord before.[3] Perhaps the novelty of the lordly designation explained the inclusion of Baron Black recorded on yet another board in the hallway capturing the "famous faces" that had graced the courthouse as trial litigants in the past. Notably, Al Capone wasn't among the group. Conrad Black featured prominently on a list of such notable historical figures as Thomas Edison, Charlie Chaplin, Marcus Garvey, John D. Rockefeller, Joseph Smith, and Alexander Graham Bell.

The atmosphere in the courtroom in the moments leading up to the hearing was cordial and had the feel of a reunion. It was homecoming week for three of the trial prosecutors in Conrad Black's case as they hugged each other in warm embraces on the side of the courtroom. Two of them, Eric Sussman and Jeffrey Cramer, had left the U.S. Attorney's Office shortly after the trial concluded, a feature of a lucrative revolving door for American prosecutors in high-profile cases. Sussman, the former lead prosecutor, had secured a partnership and was head of regulatory enforcement and white-collar litigation practice at the Chicago law firm of Kaye Scholer. Cramer became the managing director at the Kroll consulting firm, a corporate fraud and internal investigation company.[4]

Sussman recognized me from attending the trial of Conrad Black and was quite gracious as he greeted me in my seat in the front row of the gallery. He referred to the book that Conrad Black was reportedly writing and was curious to learn if it was still being published. Black's book was also the topic of discussion on the appellants' side of the rectangular courtroom. Richard Greenberg, Jack Boultbee's counsel, asked a member of Black's legal team if either he or Gus Newman, Boultbee's trial lawyer, received mention in Black's forthcoming book. The cheerful response was that "it's a great story. It has great potential."

Michael Schachter was acting as the attorney for another of the co-defendants, Peter Atkinson. Schachter was formerly a federal prosecutor in New York and had played a key role in the successful prosecution of Martha Stewart for making false statements and conspiracy. During the trial, Schachter was confronted by Rosie O'Donnell, who asked him if he wanted his children to grow up knowing him "as the man who took down Martha Stewart."[5]

It required a measure of legal acumen on Schachter's part to even permit Atkinson to be included in the appeal in Chicago. After the initial disappointing result in the Court of Appeals, Atkinson, with roots in Toronto, had abandoned any effort to appeal his case further. Peter Atkinson suffered more than any of his co-defendants at the loss of reputation after the trial and had become increasingly fragile. It was decided that Atkinson would focus on being transferred to a Canadian prison and seek early release on parole. The U.S. government wouldn't consider his transfer to a Canadian prison until his appeals were resolved. When the U.S. Supreme Court agreed to review Black's petition, the first telephone call that Eric Sussman received was from a frantic Michael Schachter. He shouted into the phone with the startling news of the development in the Supreme Court. Sussman attempted to calm his adversary with a few soothing words about Atkinson's impending prison transfer to Canada. Schachter refused to be placated. He later discovered an obscure provision in the Supreme Court rules that allowed his client to join the appeal in the nation's highest court.

Conrad Black's final co-defendant was Mark Kipnis. Ron Safer was Kipnis's lead counsel at both the trial and series of ensuing appeals. Safer, the managing partner of a national law firm, Schiff Hardin, was a former chief of the Criminal Division in the U.S. Attorney's Office and supervised one hundred U.S. Attorneys in the division. He was very familiar to the prosecutors in the case. Sussman described him as an outstanding advocate and later conceded that it would have been beneficial not to have him in the courtroom as opposing counsel.

Ron Safer was carrying an additional burden as he strode into court for the appeal. He genuinely believed that Kipnis was an innocent man. He rued his miscalculation at trial of ignoring common sense and following the advice of a jury consultant by remaining firmly in the background of the case. A low-key approach plainly was a horrible plan when 90 percent of the witnesses at the trial dealt with his client who had prepared the paperwork as in-house counsel. Safer had "zero doubt" that Kipnis's convictions were a miscarriage of justice. It marked a hollow victory that the government had sought a twelve-year sentence against Mark Kipnis, but Safer had secured probation for his client. The jury's verdict was devastating, and Safer was left feeling depressed after the trial and experienced difficulty getting up to go to work.

Conrad Black's venerable counsel at the hearing was Miguel Estrada, a former assistant to the U.S. solicitor general and part of an emerging breed of lawyers who specialized in Supreme Court advocacy.[6] His law firm of Gibson Dunn in Washington had attained a seminal victory in the case of Bush v. Gore that became a decisive factor in the outcome of a presidential election. Estrada had played a critical role in the hastily prepared winning argument before the U.S. Supreme Court. Conrad Black referred to Estrada as "brilliant" and to his legal writing as "completely rapacious."

The judge who sat imposingly at the centre of the panel in the Court of Appeals was Richard Posner. Posner, a Reagan appointee and law professor, had been a federal Court of Appeals judge for more than a quarter of a century. In some quarters of the legal community, he was revered. Albert Alschuler, a criminal law professor at Northwestern University School of Law, described Posner's standing as the most prominent legal scholar of the past sixty years. He was also the most prominent judge in America not sitting on the U.S. Supreme Court.

Judge Posner was the author of a number of wide-ranging books on law, economics, and literature, including one book devoted to the regulation of sexuality. It was motivated by his "belated discovery that judges know next to nothing about sex beyond their own personal experience, which is limited."[7]

The hearing before the Court of Appeals represented the second appeal for Conrad Black before Judge Posner. The first round was marked by a series of caustic exchanges during oral argument between Posner and Black's appeal counsel, Andrew Frey. The ultimate dressing down came with Judge Posner's claim that a portion of the evidence had to do with "pretty naked fraud." Judge Posner also exhibited a palpable disdain for Conrad Black. The reasons were unclear, but Posner had once disparaged Conrad Black in one of his judgments, noting that he wasn't as well known or as colourful a figure as the former governor of the state of Illinois, Rod Blagojevich, who had been accused of participating in a political corruption crime spree.[8] Judge Posner's characterization of Black's colourful status was debatable. Blagojevich hadn't even rated as one of the famous faces on the mounted hallway board. His place, however, was secure for another board in the courthouse highlighting the fact that six Illinois governors had been indicted during their administration or after. Even a Lord couldn't qualify for that board.

> The U.S. prosecutors have the ability to poison the wells with a media trial; they have huge procedural advantages in delays, notice periods, and their ability to discourage the appearance of defense witnesses by their ability to expand the range of questions where appearance is voluntary. The great majority of judges are former prosecutors, the prosecutors speak last to the jury, and the Fifth, Sixth, and Eighth Amendment rights of due process, the grand jury as a guarantee against capricious or malicious prosecution, of no seizure of property without just compensation, of prompt justice, an impartial jury, access to counsel (of choice), and reasonable bail, have all been put to the shredder, and I didn't receive any of it.
> — Conrad Black in an email to the author, May 23, 2011

Sketch by Cheryl Cook

Conrad Black with his lawyers Miguel Estrada, Carolyn Gurland, and David Debold at his resentencing hearing.

American justice is very different than the justice meted out at the Old Bailey or in a Canadian courtroom. Justice isn't blind in America. It perennially favours the side of the government. It is also a system of justice that is desperately in need of reform. The current U.S. Attorney General, Eric Holder, acknowledged that "too much time has passed, too many people have been treated in a disparate manner and too many of our citizens have come to have doubts about our criminal justice system."[9]

The unfairness is evidenced by the rampant over-criminalization that infests the American justice system. There are over four thousand federal crimes with thousands more regulatory provisions that allow for criminal sanctions. A significant number of federal crimes lack any meaningful requirement for the culpable mental state of criminal intent.[10] According to Jim Levine, the president of the National Association of Criminal Defense Lawyers (NACDL), the largest group of criminal lawyers in America, the proliferation of criminal sanctions has led to profound and disturbing consequences:

The hallmarks of enforcing this monstrous criminal code include a backlogged judiciary, overflowing prisons, and the incarceration of innocent individuals who plead guilty not because they actually are, but because exercising this constitutional right is all too risky. This enforcement scheme is inefficient, ineffective and, of course, at tremendous taxpayer expense.[11]

The honest services fraud statute, one of the two alternative theories of mail fraud that were presented to the jury at Conrad Black's trial, was a prime example of a legal code that had become "a vast, vague, and unpredictable invitation to selective enforcement."[12] This over-reaching fraud statute that was zealously relied upon by government prosecutors for over two decades failed to limit the key phrase in the statute of "intangible right of honest services." Gerald Lefcourt, a leading white-collar defence lawyer from New York, outlined the law's potential for abuse:

With the power that prosecutors already had with unlimited resources and leverage, the addition of the impossible to define, intangible 'honest services' fraud statute made prosecutors all powerful and god-like with the ability to indict or threaten anyone who remotely did something unappealing or unethical. It was the kind of law that totalitarian governments would embrace, enabling them to put anyone in their cross hairs at any time.

The introduction of honest services by prosecutors in Conrad Black's case was the catalyst to his successful appeal in the Supreme Court. The honest services law widely expanded the roadmap for the jury to convict. During the oral argument at Black's appeal, one of the Supreme Court justices, Steven Breyer, stated that people sometimes joke that it would be simpler to have only one criminal law: "It is a crime to do wrong." Sometimes adding, "in the opinion of the Attorney General."

America is the empire of illusion where many of its inhabitants cling to the reassuring message that they live in the greatest nation on earth, a mythical narrative that is given the aura of uncontested truth.[13] An extension of this insular belief is that the United States, a country that continues to harbour the odious spectacle of the death penalty,[14] is endowed with a superior system of justice. It is a facile conclusion.

America is a nation where currently about one in every hundred of its inhabitants is behind the bars of a prison cell. The "rough justice" in America has resulted in overcrowded prisons, and never in the civilized world have so many been locked up for so little.[15] With less than 5 percent of the global population, the United States has almost one quarter of the world's prisoners. Canada's incarceration rate, by contrast, is less than one-sixth of the U.S. rate, despite sharing a relatively similar economic and political system.[16] The U.S. Supreme Court recently ruled that the state of California had to reduce the disturbing pattern of overcrowding in its prisons or, alternatively, tens of thousands of inmates could be released. As one commentator noted, "a majority of the justices decided that when a state approaches Stalinist standards of barbarity, something has to be done."[17]

In his majority opinion, Justice Anthony Kennedy cited the unsanitary and unsafe prison overcrowding: "To incarcerate, society takes from prisoners the means to provide for their own needs ... A prison's failure to provide sustenance for inmates may actually produce physical torture or a lingering death."[18]

The Supreme Court of the United States cited Canada as a suitable model to emulate for prison reform. Statistics demonstrated that the prison population of Canada had been lowered without sacrificing public safety.[19]

Ed Genson spoke candidly of devoting his professional life to a system of justice in Midwestern America that was very heavily weighted in favour of the prosecution. It is essentially a terrible system, he acknowledged, that is pro-prosecution from the introduction of the indictment to the conclusion of the case. His experience in the Conrad Black trial exposed him to the Canadian justice system for the first time. Canada was an "eye-opener" for him. "You don't have more crime in Canada," he shared with me. "It can't be that pro-prosecution rules in my country are beneficial."

Patricia Holmes, one of Mark Kipnis's lawyers, vividly described the injustice of the guilty verdicts against her client as something that "makes me hurt." She pointed to the prosecutors in the case as overzealous. It is more important to do justice than to win, and she believed that they lost sight of this basic principle. Their decision to go after Kipnis's assets in a forfeiture hearing exposed the prosecutors' heavy-handedness.

Prosecutors are vested with remarkable power in America and it is exemplified by their control over the information provided to the defence. There is a significant risk that prosecutors are withholding relevant evidence. A featured *USA TODAY* investigation identified 201 cases since 1997 in which federal judges overturned convictions or faulted federal prosecutors, "the nation's most elite and powerful law enforcement officials," for misconduct. The failure to turn over evidence favourable to defendants represented the most common problem among those cases.[20]

The United States federal system gives prosecutors the power to hold back the statements of witnesses until their evidence-in-chief is completed. Ellen Yaroshefsky, the head of Cardozo Law School's Jacob Burns Ethics Center, described the discovery process as playing a high-stakes poker game where the prosecutor, with remarkable power, possesses all the cards and the defence is left guessing. The failure to turn over evidence is a serious issue in documented wrongful conviction cases, although a comprehensive study of the problem can't be conducted because 95 percent of defendants plead guilty. The Justice Department, Yaroshefsky noted, very strongly opposes open-file discovery, a process where prosecutors disclose all of the material gathered during an investigation.

One senior prosecutor offered the following justification for resisting open-file discovery: "I have found in the past when you have information that is given to certain counsel and certain defendants, they are able to fabricate a defense around what is provided." The statement was made at a hearing before a federal judge in Virginia who threw out a murder conviction and death sentence as a result of prosecutorial misconduct that included withholding tapes of critical government witness interviews from the defence.[21]

The restrictive scope of discovery of the government's case was only marginally modified in Conrad Black's case. Ed Genson described situations in other cases where a judge would afford him five to ten minutes to read a witness's statement before he had to embark on a cross-examination. At some point an unwritten rule developed that a minimum of thirty days notice would be provided. When Judge St. Eve extended the notice period to sixty days in the Black case, Eddie Greenspan, Black's counsel from Toronto, noted with bewilderment that his American colleagues were thrilled. It was described as a "minor miracle." He also confirmed that the statements, which were actual summaries prepared by an FBI agent, routinely arrived precisely as directed by the judge and never a day earlier.

Greenspan described the disclosure process in this fashion: "They throw every piece of paper at you. You receive millions of pieces of paper that aren't collated or indexed. The disclosure can't be presented in the Japanese language. That is what it seemed like. In Canada the Supreme Court of Canada set out a series of rational and highly principled rules surrounding disclosure in Stinchcombe.[22] They have absolutely no principles in the U.S." According to Greenspan there were seven million pages of documents in the Black case, which were several million more than he managed to read personally. He added that during the trial, the prosecution kept turning over more discovery through their case-in-chief.

In Canada, witness statements that are actually statements of witnesses are routinely provided to the defence. Video or audio tapes of a material witness's statement under oath and the original notes of the law enforcement officials involved with an investigation are basic components of the disclosure package that a Canadian prosecutor presents to the defence in a timely fashion. In America, such a practice would be construed as overly generous and a mistake. It would only provide a defendant in a criminal case with a level playing field. It is more laudable to corrupt the process than to promote its integrity. The overwhelming culture created in the American criminal justice system permits the prosecutors to punish defendants who exercise their right to go to trial and reward the legion of defendants who accept responsibility, plead guilty, and, most significantly, point fingers at others. Justice is effectively bartered in the prosecutor's office, not fought for in the courtroom.[23] As one American defence attorney noted, "Practicing criminal law has become draining, dispiriting, and completely unsatisfying."[24] In one case in Tampa, Florida, a lawyer bothered to have his fraudster client's staggering sentence reduced to 835 years from 845 years with the tangible benefit of moving the sentence farther beyond the next millennium.[25]

The injustice begins with the manner in which indictments are instituted by grand juries under the federal system. Prosecutors decide what evidence will be submitted to a grand jury and are not obligated to inform the grand jurors about evidence of innocence. "The notion was that [grand juries] protects defendants-any defendants-against prosecutorial abuse is a fraud."[26] The injustice is then compounded when the prosecutor packs the indictment with as many counts as possible. According to Ellen Podger, a law professor at Stetson University College of Law, "what may have once been a single white collar offence can become a multi-count indictment with charges of mail fraud, obstruction of justice, false statements and money laundering."[27]

Several defence lawyers spoke to me about the built-in advantage that loading of counts in the indictment provides the government. Carmen Hernandez, a former president of the NACDL, emphasized that it is much more difficult to secure an acquittal with so many counts.[28] There is a psychological barrier for jurors to repeat a not-guilty verdict twenty times. This became a tangible hurdle for the defendants in the Black trial. Loading an indictment with a barrage of counts also serves the purpose of forcing guilty pleas.

The defendant who dares to accept the risk and conduct a trial is faced with the dismal prospect of a crushing sentence. Hernandez related to me the example of a defendant found guilty of distributing fifty grams of crack cocaine with a prior felony conviction for simple possession of marijuana. The sentence that would be imposed in such a case would be life imprisonment with no chance of parole. The defendant would die in prison.

Even an old trial warrior like Ed Genson felt trapped by the system's plea inducement scheme. He shared with me a case that was scheduled for the following week. His client had been in a fight after being punched in the face. The client maintained that his assailant brandished a gun during the struggle. At that point he took out his own gun and shot his assailant once in the heart, instantly killed him. Genson had assessed his chances of winning the trial at about 80 percent. If his thirty-two-year-old client were convicted, he would serve a forty-five-year sentence of incarceration without a reduction of a single day. The prosecutor came with a generous offer that would leave his client serving about four and a half years in prison.

"What choice did my client really have?" he asked me. I had no suitable reply.

The sentencing guidelines that still retain a lot of force[29] were devised over twenty years ago, in theory to normalize the range of sentences imposed by judges and to infuse the process with some sense of due process. With hundreds of amendments added (almost invariably enhancements), the guidelines were used politically to increase sentences. The guidelines presently read like an elaborate tax code.

It is these sentencing guidelines that allowed the prosecutors in the Conrad Black trial to seek with straight faces a twenty-nine-month prison sentence for the star witness and co-operator David Radler, who pleaded guilty (premised on a fraud amount exceeding $30 million), and a dozen years for a minimal player like Mark Kipnis who dared to proceed to trial. The currency of co-operation in "the criminal justice flea market" has vitiated the very uniformity that the sentencing guidelines sought to achieve.

Why didn't Mark Kipnis testify at his trial? Many, including Eddie Greenspan, believe that he should have. As Patricia Holmes explained to me, the decision began with an assessment of the risks involved under the guidelines that inhibit a defendant's testimony. If Kipnis took the witness stand and was convicted, then it follows that he must have lied to the court during his testimony, and he would face a two-point enhancement of his sentence under the guidelines. Kipnis potentially would have faced three to five more years in prison. Even belated pangs of remorse offered to a probation officer after conviction could not expunge an enhanced sentence.[30]

Incredibly, the guidelines also permit prosecutors to rely on acquitted or uncharged conduct by a defendant, even for a charge as a serious murder.[31] As Greenspan observed, "If George Orwell were alive today he'd be hitting his forehead and wondering why he didn't think of that one." Genson described the unprincipled practice of artificially resuscitating a jury's not-guilty verdicts as "disgraceful." For instance, in a situation where a defendant charged with two separate sales of cocaine, one involving a single ounce and the other involving three kilos, a conviction on the lesser charge for the one-ounce sale permits the prosecutor to invite the judge to find on a preponderance of evidence that the defendant was involved in the three-kilo sale. The jury's verdict becomes moot at that point and any sense of double jeopardy or due process is discarded.

If any Canadian prosecutor were to make a similar submission, he would be ordered to return to law school to relearn the basic rules of fairness and procedure. In America such a shameful practice of "acquitted conduct sentencing enhancement" is *de rigueur*, and the prosecutors in the Conrad Black trial eagerly attempted to hitch their cart to it.

More than 90 percent of criminal cases end in guilty pleas, magnifying the significance of the sentencing process.[32] Patricia Holmes, who is in the unique position of having been both an assistant United States attorney and a judge before becoming a defence lawyer, offered her opinion that the prosecutors just don't lose. That is the justice system in America. It is a "tyrannical" system weighted heavily in favour of the prosecution, according to the former president of the NACDL, and it is left to the prosecutor or judge to exercise moderation.

It is tempting for prosecutors to unfairly exploit the leverage and power placed in their hands. Ron Safer made reference to its frightening influence in the Black trial in his closing address:

> Pressure from the government is a truly awesome thing ... You saw the response that several witnesses in this case had to that enormous pressure that the government can apply. [For] some witnesses it was dramatic ... For David Radler, at a certain point he started confessing to everything the government asked him about, even though he had vehemently and vigorously denied these same exact points time and time and time again.

In Canada the trial of Conrad Black would have been a bench or judge alone trial. Eddie Greenspan suggested that the decision in those circumstances would have been a "slam dunk." He believed that Judge St. Eve would have acquitted the defendants of all the charges they faced.

There are several reasons that the case was well suited to be tried by a judge sitting alone. Firstly, none of the defendants testified, and there is always a genuine concern that a jury will interpret that as a conspiracy of silence.

Secondly, the premise of the defence was that the vast millions of dollars of non-competition payments the defendants received were lawful and approved by the audit committee, but ultimately the defence conceded that no direct economic benefit to the shareholders resulted. That is not an attractive argument to make to a jury.

The final reason that a judge should have heard the trial was the incredible zeitgeist that lingered from the high-profile corporate fraud trials in America such as Enron, Tyco, and WorldCom. A new crime wave shook the public's faith in corporate America and Wall Street, and business leaders became the new fodder for the prosecution mill as attitudes towards corporate governance hardened. The criminal charge of racketeering was being applied without discretion against corporate defendants.

A bench trial in America, however, requires the government's consent. I was advised that in a high-profile case like the Black trial, consent would never be given because it would improve the defendant's chances of winning.

Does anyone care that the American system is slanted in favour of the prosecution? Politicians boost the vast powers invested in American prosecutors. Judges are elected on get-tough-on-crime platforms exploiting a dire fear among Americans that the nation ever be considered soft on crime.[33] Prisoners are inhibited from using DNA evidence to support wrongful convictions while voters continue to reward prosecutors who are well known for locking up innocent people.[34] Congressional hearings are ordered for pressing issues like the use of steroids by professional athletes but never for the nation's plague of miscarriages of justice.

Segments of the media openly favour the side of the prosecutor and vilify the presumption of innocence.[35] The most striking example is Nancy Grace[36] with her popular nightly show on HLN, an affiliate of CNN. She has been appropriately been described as a former prosecutor "turned broadcast judge-and-jury."

"Working with a contingent of experts who have all the independence of a crew of trained seals, Ms. Grace races toward judgment, heedlessly ignoring nuance and evidence on her way to finding guilt."[37]

Nancy Grace, however, isn't the media's sole offender. During the Michael Jackson trial, Tim Rutten, a respected columnist with the *Los Angeles Times*, commented on the secession by an entire segment of the news media from mainstream American journalism. He cited most of the commentator/personalities on FOX News (with the notable exception of Greta Van Susteren), the prime-time segment of CNN Headline News, and Court TV. He added the following: "These operations no longer feel constrained by even the minimal requirements of fairness, balance or dispassion required to practice American-style journalism. Instead, they operate as an apologetic cheering section for the prosecution."[38]

It was Conrad Black's naïve assumption that he could successfully navigate the turbulent stream of American justice and emerge unscathed with his liberty intact. He will have the experience of three years in a Florida federal prison to reflect on his grand miscalculation. David Radler, who pleaded guilty and in Black's words "was exposed as a double-dealing cheat and liar and perjurer,"[39] served about nine months of his twenty-nine month prison sentence before he was paroled in Canada.

Conrad Black's case, however, did help to expose the systemic failings of a severely flawed U.S. justice system. Despite the obstacles, only fragments of the government's original case against him and his three co-defendants remained. Ron Safer described the final result as a huge defeat for the government given where the case started. Black was left in the end with a single fraud conviction and an additional conviction for obstruction of justice for a crime committed wholly under Canadian jurisdiction. He overcame 99 percent of the total fraud alleged in the indictment. His share of payment in the proven fraud amounted to of $285,000. Black overcame a tilted prosecution that included the testimony of a watchtower audit committee that portrayed itself as the cast of MTV's *Jersey Shore*.

Eddie Greenspan described "everyone talking in terms of forty years" if Conrad Black was convicted of every charge he faced. He certainly would have died in prison. Greenspan wryly observed that "we now know that there were no witches in Salem and there was no corporate kleptocracy."

Barbara Amiel being attended to by court officials at Conrad Black's resentencing hearing after reacting to the judge's pronouncement of her husband's sentence.

For Conrad Black, the final chapter in his case has not been written. As Jacob Frenkel concluded, Black will not be content with such an outcome. "He will go to every president in his lifetime until he gets a pardon."

TITAN ON TRIAL

THE CASE AGAINST CONRAD BLACK

On the eve of his criminal trial, Conrad Black was staring down a crushing blow to the media empire he had devoted forty years of his life to build. Beginning with the purchase of a series of small Canadian newspapers in the 1960s, Black, along with his cohort, David Radler, grew his empire steadily, eventually becoming the world's third-largest media publisher. Influential newspapers such as *The Daily Telegraph*, *Chicago Sun-Times*, and *The Jerusalem Post* were part of the stable of newspapers under Black's control.

Conrad Black's gradual rise to the pinnacle was contrasted by a relatively swift downfall, culminating in a series of felony convictions in a federal courtroom in Chicago for mail fraud and obstruction of justice. Lord Black was transported from the austere surroundings of a Palm Beach mansion to a Florida federal prison, Coleman FCI, with the ignominious title of inmate number 18330-424. The enigmatic entrepreneur's collapse was set into motion during the late 1990s when Hollinger International, a publicly traded Delaware company with Black as its chairman and controlling shareholder, began selling its pool of American community newspapers to eliminate a portion of the corporation's mounting debt. This was accompanied by the sale to CanWest, a Canadian media company, of some of Hollinger's major Canadian assets, including *The National Post*, for $3.2 billion.

In May of 2003, at an annual meeting, alarming concerns were raised about particular details of these commercial transactions by a group of shareholders of Hollinger International led by the New York investment firm, Tweedy Brown. A feature of their complaint related to the claim that several million dollars from the sales proceeds had been improperly funnelled to Conrad Black, his associates, and to affiliate companies under Black's control (Ravelston and Hollinger Inc.) in the guise of fictitious non-compete payments. Under the terms of a legitimate non-competition agreement (which was common in the publishing industry), part of the purchase price in a transaction would be allocated in return for the vendor's contracted promise not to compete with the new owner.

By the end of 2003, Conrad Black had resigned as Hollinger's chief executive and David Radler resigned as the president and chief operating officer of the company. The Hollinger board of directors established a special committee to investigate the allegation made in the complaint by the disgruntled shareholders. The Special Committee Report was prepared by Richard Breeden, a former chairman of the U.S. Securities and Exchange Commission, and appointed by George H.W. Bush. The voluminous Breeden Report was issued in August of 2004 and concluded in scathing language that Conrad Black had led a "corporate kleptocracy" at Hollinger that aggressively looted the company of hundreds of millions of dollars that included over $200 million of unauthorized management payments. Black was accused of orchestrating together with his associates "an entity in which ethical corruption was a defining characteristic of the leadership team." Hollinger was tapped as a piggy bank for the Blacks. The non-compete payments totalling more than $90 million were cited in the report as a potent device for funnelling a portion of the sales proceeds into the hands of Conrad Black and other officers of the company. The report also highlighted a lengthy list of personal expenses improperly charged to the company including a "Happy Birthday Barbara" dinner party in Manhattan for Black's wife, Barbara Amiel, that featured Beluga caviar and lobster ceviche. The lavish party was noted to be less expensive than Dennis Kozlowski's party for his wife in Sardinia that was charged in part to Tyco.

The audit committee of Hollinger was blamed for its inadequate scrutiny of Black and Radler's financial scheming. The three member committee chaired by a former governor of Illinois and U.S. Attorney was found to have operated deferentially as a rubber stamp and was characterized in the report by an "inexplicable and nearly complete lack of initiative, diligence, or independent thought."

In the period following the release of the Breeden Report, American prosecutors closely followed the script of the play written for them by counsel for the Special Committee and pursued a criminal investigation of Conrad Black's misconduct at the helm of Hollinger. It was an ominous sign for Black when the indictment of David Radler was announced.

As part of his plea deal, Radler had agreed to co-operate with the U.S. prosecutors in their continuing investigation of Black; he also agreed to accept a twenty-nine month prison sentence that could be served, with an approved transfer, in a penitentiary in the province of British Columbia where Radler resided. David Radler loomed at the upcoming trial as the government's undisputed star witness and the ultimate insider who could expose Black's complicity in a fraudulent scheme.

In November 2005, approximately one month after Radler's guilty plea was entered in court, Patrick Fitzgerald, the high profile U.S. attorney for the Northern District of Illinois supervising the case, held a press conference in Chicago to report the indictment of Conrad Black on eight federal charges of mail and wire fraud relating to his participation in an alleged scheme to illegally divert funds away from the shareholders of Hollinger. Other senior executives of the company, Jack Boultbee and Peter Atkinson, along with the in-house counsel for the company, Mark Kipnis, were also indicted. A superseding indictment with additional charges, including racketeering and obstruction of justice, was brought later against Conrad Black. The obstruction count resulted from Black being videotaped removing thirteen boxes of documents from the Toronto office of a holding company of Hollinger at a time when a grand jury investigation and criminal proceeding were brewing against him and the Securities and Exchange Commission (SEC) had made an imminent production request for documents to Black's counsel in the U.S.[1] There had been five previous document production requests from the SEC that resulted in Black turning over 112,000 pages.[2]

Conrad Black maintained a defiant position about his list of criminal charges as he publicly proclaimed his unwavering belief in his innocence. His legal team was in place for the upcoming courtroom battle and consisted of two legal luminaries in Canada and the U.S.: Eddie Greenspan and Ed Genson. Teams of attorneys from Chicago and New York represented Black's co-defendants. Patrick Fitzgerald assembled a relatively youthful and energetic prosecution team for the case. The trial judge overseeing the case was Amy St. Eve, who had been appointed to the federal bench by George W. Bush. In March of 2007, the jury trial of Conrad Black began in downtown Chicago in an overflowing courtroom. It would mark the beginning of a legal struggle that would occupy over four years before reaching its surprising ending. The trials of Conrad Black were set to commence.

THE JUST US DEPARTMENT

My grandparents arrived at Halifax Harbour in 1930 with the prescient sense that Canada might be a marginally more inviting place to raise a family than Poland. It was only a scarce few years before Adolf Hitler's dutiful soldiers invaded the hapless eastern European country and brutally savaged its people. When my father was born on Oxford Street in Toronto several years later, my grandparents were so enamoured with the relative comfort of their new surroundings that they decided to name him after the ship that had safely carried them across the Atlantic. It was called *The Frederick*. My father remained eternally grateful that the ship's builders hadn't christened it *The Matilda*.

My dad became a chartered accountant, and I was taught from an early age that life is a balance sheet, with good deeds and corresponding rewards. I inherited my dad's somewhat infuriating habit of obsessively planning each day with meticulous detail. I have daily planners, weekly planners, and even monthly planners. I purchase them from a stationery store in the chic Yorkville area of Toronto that imports them especially from Italy. I am therefore able to celebrate *Giorno del Canada* (Canada Day) and expand my vocabulary simultaneously. I never have the misfortune of missing the birthday of a good friend or relative. The dates are neatly sorted in a designated area of one of my planners in a section titled "*date da ricordare*" (dates to remember).

It was therefore with some pleasure that I stumbled fortuitously on a store that devoted itself exclusively to selling products that are associated with the name "Fred." The unique boutique was located on one of the charming main streets in Charleston, South Carolina. I was there attending a legal conference sponsored by the NACDL.

The affable saleswoman showed me the various cups, T-shirts, and hats all adorned with the name "Fred." I pondered my father's gleeful reaction several months hence at receiving such personalized gifts and ultimately purchased them all. I was feeling quite satisfied as I contemplated checking off the birthday purchase in my bright orange calendar. I then noticed that the saleslady's face had suddenly turned rather stern.

"What's that?" she asked as she pointed to my identification tag for the conference. I replied that I was a criminal lawyer visiting Charleston for a conference at a nearby hotel. I was promptly told that I was going straight to hell for my flawed career choice. There would apparently be no detour to Baskin-Robbins for one last cup of pistachio almond ice cream. I must confess that I never inquired if the jarring comment was made playfully or in earnest. The tone certainly conveyed that she was perfectly serious, but in the true spirit of my profession, I was prepared to give her the benefit of the doubt. I left the store, however, in haste and downcast with the gained knowledge that as a criminal defence lawyer I was destined to spend eternity charting my way through a maze of smouldering flames.

I was reminded of my hellish fate each time I set out on my regular trips between the cities of Toronto and Chicago during the protracted proceedings of the Conrad Black trial. At O'Hare Airport outside Chicago, there are a series of moving sidewalks that over the course of several minutes would take me from Area B to Area C, where the gate for Air Canada flights was situated. The moving sidewalks were surrounded on top by multicoloured lights that looked like they had been designed by a couple of ambitious Grade 7 students for their middle school's science fair. My travel mates on the moving sidewalks were a group of numb, expressionless strangers. The only sound that echoed in the corridor was the intermittent blare of a recording by an official with the Department of Homeland Security warning travellers of the current colour-coded state of terror alert at the airport.[3]

I had a recurring nightmare that I was trapped forever on a moving sidewalk that would never reach its ultimate destination. I would be a moving sidewalk castaway. This must have been precisely what the nice saleswoman in the Fred store had contemplated when she foretold my assignment to hell.

The Conrad Black defence team had their own version of hell. Prior to the trial, they booked a series of rooms at the historic Palmer House Hotel near the courthouse. There was no work room available and they spent sleepless nights listening to the clanking trains pass through the Loop. The beleaguered group fortunately experienced a renaissance when they moved their quarters to a hotel of that name.

In actual fact, I was quite looking forward to covering the Conrad Black trial. There have been other great Canadian trials to rival it, but the case certainly stood as one of the most significant in the country's history. In typical Canadian fashion, it had a distinctly American flavour. Conrad Black was indicted in the State of Illinois and his trial unfolded in a Chicago courtroom. I had my media credentials with a rather sickly green card that bore a dark, shadowy photograph that made me appear to be one of Al Capone's henchmen. Only someone genuinely affiliated with the case would dare to show that ID to gain access to the courtroom.

The trial had riveted people in the streets of Canada and England, but in America it had registered only a faint, distant blip on the radar screen. A search of Conrad Black on the CNN website revealed far more hits for the All Blacks rugby club in New Zealand.

I am somewhat uncertain of the reason that Chicago was chosen for the site of the trial. It seems to be linked to the *Chicago Sun-Times* building, owned at the time by Hollinger International and where David Radler was stationed and oversaw the company's media empire. A case could certainly have been made for Conrad Black to be prosecuted in a Canadian courtroom. The head office of Hollinger International's parent company, Hollinger Inc., was located in the austere surroundings of 10 Toronto Street in downtown Toronto, built originally in the middle of the nineteenth century as a post office. The premises were a most auspicious location for a mail fraud case.

Three of the four defendants, Conrad Black, Jack Boultbee, and Peter Atkinson, worked in the Toronto Street office. The proceeds of the various contentious non-compete payments were wired to the senior executives through a Canadian bank. Indeed, Hollinger Inc., a company largely controlled by Conrad Black and his media cohort, David Radler, was the recipient of a portion of the non-compete payments as well. Finally, 10 Toronto Street is destined to become a valued stop on future bus tours of Canada's largest city. It is the spot where Conrad Black was notoriously caught on videotape loading thirteen boxes into a limousine, in apparent defiance of the SEC's request for production and an Ontario court order not to move them. The obstruct justice charge was tied to that *Candid Camera* moment.

Indeed, two senior prosecutors assigned to the Public Prosecution Service of Canada, Rob Goldstein and Rick Visca, attended three days of the Conrad Black trial to monitor the proceedings. I was familiar with both of them as colleagues and worthy adversaries in their former positions with the Department of Justice. I fortuitously caught sight of them one evening during the cross-examination of David Radler. They were gracious enough about being spotted; they preferred to remain incognito during their stay.

"I didn't see you in court today," I stated.

"That's because we were watching from the overflow courtroom," Rob replied.

Apparently Goldstein had called Jeffrey Cramer prior to attending the trial and asked for a small favour. He had heard that it was crowded in the courtroom and wondered if a couple of seats could be set aside for the two Canadian prosecutors. They weren't sure when they would be coming to Chicago.

Cramer's response startled Goldstein. In a fairly brief phone call, he was advised in no uncertain terms that he would receive no favours from Conrad Black's prosecutors. Cramer was clearly upset at the lack of co-operation extended by the Canadian government to the American prosecutors. I had heard from one senior Canadian prosecutor that the reason Conrad Black was even charged with obstruct justice was related to the frustration the American prosecutors felt about the perceived indifference of Canadian officials to pursuing Conrad Black. As it was explained to me, the prevailing attitude was "Screw you, Canadian government — if you guys can't enforce your own laws, then we're going to do it for you."

Goldstein and Visca were left to their own devices to acquire courtroom seats. It was duly noted by them that there was a series of empty seats in the government section. They watched a portion of Eddie Greenspan's cross-examination of David Radler from a large video screen in a second courtroom on the seventeenth floor reserved for the overflow of spectators.

Will Conrad Black ever be prosecuted in Canada? My personal view is that the only realistic avenue is the tax evasion route. That would place Canada in the unusual position of extraditing a man desperate to acquire a Canadian passport. Of course David Radler's fragrant agreement with the U.S. Attorney's Office couldn't cover any Canadian prosecution. The prospect therefore remains that one day Conrad Black and David Radler will be reunited in a Canadian courtroom.

MR. BLACK GOES TO WASHINGTON

Proceedings at Sidebar:

Mr. Sussman:　　*Your Honor, at this point, Mr. Greenspan has called the witness a liar. It was not a question.*

	He just called him a liar to the jury. I think he has been over this line of questioning. At this point now he is commenting on counsel's objections directly to counsel; and, I think, we are far afield from the question and answer that should be — that, in my view, is appropriate for cross-examination. I know your Honor's the one that makes that decision. I object to this way of conducting cross-examination. I think it is hostile and is argumentative and is inappropriate.
The Court:	*Mr. Greenspan? …*
Mr. Greenspan:	*Mr. Genson, my counsel.*
Mr. Genson:	*Your Honor, basically, the man said, "I reviewed it." I told Mr. Greenspan that he had said he had reviewed it. Then he said, "I hadn't reviewed it." Then he said Mr. Greenspan was unclear when he used the word "review" one time, but evidently not that unclear when he used it a second time. And he is inquiring as to which of these statements is a lie.*
Mr. Greenspan:	*He spent, your Honor — unless you care to rule, he spent — an hour on Thursday making sure that I couldn't ask a question because he said, "I can't — I haven't read it. I haven't read it. I haven't read it." Quite frankly, I would have put it to him on Thursday if anybody at our table had remembered what happened Wednesday. But it was that night, when we went back and reviewed it and found that. I think it's, in my respectful submission, very important.*
The Court:	*I think the line of questioning about the apparent inconsistency certainly is appropriate. The problem is you are crossing over from asking him questions about did he say this,*

	what did he mean, to saying, "Which one are you lying about?" That crosses over, under our system, into argument. You are free to argue that to the jury —
Mr. Greenspan:	*I see.*
The Court:	*— at the end of the case. But when you say to him, "Which one are you lying about," or —*
Mr. Greenspan:	*You can't do that?*
The Court:	*— "You are a liar, aren't you?" That crosses over into argument. Similar to the question you asked about, "Isn't this going to lead the jury to believe that you're lying?" You are crossing over into the jury's province there.*
Mr. Greenspan:	*I must tell you only —*
Mr. Genson:	*Is it possible to say, "Which one is true and which one isn't"? I don't see why —*
Mr. Greenspan:	*I must say this to you: that, in Britain, the great cross-examiners can't wait to get to where I just got —*
The Court:	*And —*
Mr. Greenspan:	*— only to find out the rule is you can't do it.*
The Court:	*You can certainly argue that. I think it is fair to say, "Which one is accurate?" But you are — you have crossed over the line.*
Mr. Greenspan:	*I apologize.*
The Court:	*There is no need to apologize. I am just —*
Mr. Greenspan:	*I am going to work very hard —*
The Court:	*— indicating.*
Mr. Greenspan:	*— to change the rule.*
(Laughter.)	

Whereas Barbara Amiel described her husband's defence team as "the help," for Conrad Black they were the military commanders with whom he entrusted his fate. He once sent Ed Genson a congratulatory note during the trial that read, "That reminded me of the salvo of the *Bismarck*." In another case, he sent other words of support to Genson: "That was very strong. Barbara agreed."

43

For all of his public outbursts and bombastic nature, in many ways Conrad Black was the ideal client. He was gracious and polite and always respectful in discussions with his lawyers. Only once during the trial, during the testimony of a member of the audit committee, Richard Burt, did Black genuinely panic. Even after the verdict, when Eddie Greenspan was vilified in many quarters, Black resolutely stood behind his chosen general.

Greenspan maintained that the source for the scorching article that appeared in *Maclean's* magazine after the trial about his abject performance and "disastrous defence" was Barbara Amiel and not his client. He telephoned his good friend George Jonas to complain that Amiel, who was Jonas's ex-wife, had only succeeded in increasing her husband's sentence. Greenspan was confident that the trial judge would read the article and be particularly perturbed by the disparaging comments made about Ed Genson. Genson was by far the judge's favourite attorney in the case.

How did Conrad Black come to retain "two fat Jewish guys," as Greenspan amusingly described the Black legal team?

Greenspan first became involved in Black's tangled legal affairs in November of 2003 as an independent legal advisor. Black had signed a restructuring agreement that essentially removed control of Hollinger International from himself. Greenspan would later refer to this "baffling act" as the single moment that unravelled Conrad Black. He was uncertain if Black had obtained any legal counsel before taking such drastic action.

Black continued to conduct the company's affairs as if there had been no transfer of control. He maintained that he had been lied to and the agreement was therefore of no force and effect. He had retained a Washington law firm, Sullivan Cromwell, partly on the basis that John Foster Dulles was associated with the firm. Greenspan had flown into Washington before and was aware that one of the airports was named Dulles Airport. "Don't they name airports after dead people?" he asked Black.

The pressing legal question confronting Black at the time was a subpoena to testify at the SEC. Black's counsel at Sullivan Cromwell was urging him to testify in Chicago. Greenspan spent a couple of days with Black listening to his version of the facts. While heartened by what he heard, Greenspan was adamant that there could be no advantage for Black in testifying. A testy exchange then ensued with Black's Washington lawyer.

"I've never had a client refuse to testify before the SEC," he advised Greenspan.

"Well I've never agreed to ever have my client testify," was the brusque reply from Greenspan. Black eventually asserted his Fifth Amendment right to remain silent before the SEC.

Conrad Black's civil actions continued in the early months of 2004. One of them was disastrous. In Delaware, the sale of Hollinger International assets to Barclays Bank in England was halted in Commercial Court. Black's credibility was shredded by the presiding judge, Leo Strine. Black's confidence in Sullivan Cromwell was gone and he was ready to bring on new counsel to represent him. By this time a grand jury had been established to proceed with a criminal indictment against Black. Criminal charges were a virtual certainty.

Black had watched the Iran Contra hearings on television and was particularly enthralled with Oliver North's lawyer, Brendan Sullivan. On the strength of that sole appearance, Black selected him as his new attorney. Sullivan agreed to take on Black's file.

On March 19, 2004, Conrad Black met Sullivan in Palm Beach, Florida, to retain him to handle his civil and criminal matters. Greenspan was linked to the meeting by speaker phone. During the discussion, Sullivan told Black that he never had a client go to jail. Greenspan later commented that either Sullivan was lying or he was not a criminal lawyer. However, if Sullivan's claim was true, Greenspan promised to send him all of his clients.

Sullivan's firm was hired; the Palm Beach meeting was the only time that the two men ever met. Greenspan spoke to him a few times, and all of Black's contact occurred with lawyers at the firm who made few critical decisions without first checking with Brendan Sullivan.

Greenspan had considerable misgivings about one law firm representing Black on both his civil and criminal matters. During discovery, it would be impossible for the law firm to block disclosure of a document connected to the criminal case. Greenspan told Black that having a civil firm acting on both ends of his case was "nuts."

A competition began among law firms for the millions of dollars at stake in Conrad Black's civil file. They wooed him with highly sophisticated demos and PowerPoint presentations. Black attended each of the presentations on his own and regularly reported back to Greenspan. Greenspan was personally contacted by a number of prominent attorneys from the white-collar bar in the U.S. actively seeking the case. The winner of the law firm pageant was the Washington firm of Baker Botts.

Greenspan was impressed with Bill Jefres in particular, who came highly recommended by Brendan Sullivan. Jefres would eventually act as co-counsel for Scooter Libby at his high-profile trial in Washington. Sullivan continued to act as Black's criminal lawyer while Greenspan remained in the background as a legal advisor.

Greenspan was teaching for one week at Hebrew University in Jerusalem when a fees dispute arose between Black and Sullivan's firm. Although Black had paid the firm millions, Sullivan asked for a further $25 million to represent him in his criminal matter. Greenspan told Black on the phone that "this is a fuck-off fee" and that Sullivan wanted to be removed from the file. There was some further discussion about one of Sullivan's partners, Greg Craig, taking over the file for a significantly lower fee, but ultimately it was agreed that new criminal counsel would be sought.

Greenspan had already concluded that a criminal case was inevitable. Radler had pulled out of the joint defence agreement and was turning to become a prosecution witness. Certainly the disaster in Delaware had been closely watched by Radler's Chicago attorney, Anton Valukas, a former United States attorney. The trial for Conrad Black would not be in New York as many suspected but rather in Chicago, the headquarters of Hollinger International. Chicago was an idiosyncratic town with its own character and personality. Black entrusted Greenspan with the task of choosing his Chicago counsel. "You pick the team," he instructed him.

For Greenspan there was only one viable choice. The attorney with the best reputation in the city, Dan Webb, was out of the running because he was a law partner of Governor Thompson's. Thompson was the chair of the audit committee at Hollinger International and would be a key witness in the case. That left Ed Genson, whom Greenspan knew because his daughter Juliana had worked for Genson for several years. The two men had dinner together every time Greenspan was in Chicago. Genson talked a great deal about himself at these dinners but Eddie found him to be colourful and amusing.

Genson was part of the Chicago fabric as much as Studs Terkel or Wrigley Field. In Genson's own words, "everyone tries to hire me in Chicago." In fact, Ravelston, the management company once controlled by Black and Radler, had earlier approached Genson to take on their criminal case.[4] Greenspan suggested he decline the case but made it clear that he wasn't promising anything.

Greenspan met with Genson to discuss the parameters of his involvement in the case. Greenspan wanted to handle the case in Chicago and he would be the undisputed "boss." If the two men differed, Greenspan would command the deciding vote. The second rule was that Greenspan would cross-examine Radler and the entire audit committee. Greenspan added Henry Kissinger, a Hollinger board member, to the list as well — the opportunity to cross-examine a former secretary of state was too alluring to pass up. Genson readily agreed to the terms. "Can we work together?" Greenspan asked Genson. "Absolutely," replied Genson. "We'll make a wonderful team. You're the boss, Eddie."

The two men shook hands. All that remained was for the client to meet Genson and approve. Genson's office was located in the Monadnock Building in Chicago's Loop. He kept a railroad spotlight from 1933 in the reception area. When the U.S. Attorney's Office had been across the road he had occasionally shone the spotlight directly at them as a prank.

Genson's introduction to Conrad Black reminded Greenspan of a scene straight out of *Bonfire of the Vanities*. Black walked in with his nose in the air. He was the "Master of the Universe [who] took a masculine pride in the notion that he could handle all sides of life." The thought must have passed through Black's aristocratic mind at that instant that he could have any big-firm guys he desired and was now settling on a character straight out of the world of the beleaguered defendant in Tom Wolfe's classic novel: "How could he let any decision affecting his life be made by this sort of person in this sort of atmosphere? He had called in sick — that lamest, weakest, most sniveling of life's small lies — to Pierce & Pierce; for this itching slum of the legal world."[5]

Black accepted Greenspan's recommendation for his co-counsel, and the key players in the defence team were in place. Genson never conducted any of the pre-trial motions in the case. That task was delegated to the "law guy" in the office, Marc Martin. Martin was regarded as having a keen legal mind and reminded Greenspan of his former partner, Marc Rosenberg (now a justice of the Ontario Court of Appeal).

Eddie Greenspan was the first person to let Conrad Black know that he would be charged criminally. Greenspan described it as a winnable case, but Black was "mad as hell." The indictment against Black was announced on November 17, 2005, and was accompanied by a detailed press release from the U.S. Department of Justice. Robert Grant, from the

Chicago office of the FBI, summarized the case in the release in the following fashion: "The frauds in this indictment were blatant and pervasive:
they extended from back rooms to the boardroom, and from Park Avenue
to the South Pacific. Our job is to protect investors from Wall Street to
LaSalle Street and in other global financial markets."

The indictment was bulky, which is a typical feature of indictments
in high-profile fraud cases in America. As one attorney noted, it serves
the purpose of telling the story from the prosecutor's point of view. The
press receives the public document with all of the intended sound bites.
That represents half the battle for the government. The other prominent
feature of the indictment was that it contained vague charges like mail
fraud where the actual criminal component was less than clear.[6]

As Greenspan observed, the case came down on Black "like a ton of
bricks." He put on a brave face in public but he was shocked at the severity and number of the charges. The racketeering charge seemed particularly mean-spirited to him and his attorneys. Greenspan and Genson both
wondered what the Racketeer Influenced and Corrupt Organizations
Act (RICO) had to do with non-competition agreements.

The prosecutors had the blueprint for their case in the investiga-
tive report prepared by Richard Breeden, the former head of the SEC
who led the special committee that was appointed to look into the non-
compete payments. They relied heavily on it. Their target was Lord Black
of Crossharbour, a newspaper mogul connected to the *Chicago Sun-Times*
who was much disliked in some circles. Both Genson and Greenspan
worried that that their client would become the prosecutors' ticket to a
major law firm and the case would evolve into a crusade.

Bail was carefully negotiated before Conrad Black surrendered to
the Chicago authorities. Greenspan left from Toronto with Black and
Juliana on a private plane the morning of the surrender. Prior to the trip,
Greenspan insisted that Black meet with him to discuss the consequences
of surrendering to the U.S. authorities. There was never any thought of
Black fighting extradition. When Greenspan told him about his possible
sentence if he was convicted, Black stared at him as if he were crazy.

When they arrived at the federal courthouse in Chicago, they were
greeted at the probation office by Genson and Martin. Black was never
handcuffed, but in accordance with standard procedure, he provided a
urine sample and a couple sets of fingerprints.

When they entered Judge St. Eve's courtroom, the mood was serious and the bail hearing was all business. Martin presented Greenspan's application to act as counsel in a Chicago courtroom and the application was granted with little fanfare. Greenspan was surprised, as he had believed it might be a contentious issue. Greenspan would later come to joke that he would never even fly over Chicago again because of the ordeal of the trial. But for now, he still loved the city.

A PICTURE IS WORTH A THOUSAND CONVICTIONS

Over the course of a legal career that has spanned almost forty years, Eddie Greenspan has formed a symbiotic relationship with the media. It has resulted in his achieving a degree of fame in Canada that is likely unmatched in the country's history. Just as Wayne Gretzky and Sidney Crosby have attained superstar status in hockey, Greenspan has reached the same lofty heights in the legal sphere.

The Conrad Black trial would bring Eddie Greenspan to the American stage for the first time. As Genson noted, Greenspan really wanted to do this trial. He revered legendary trial lawyers from America such as Edward Bennett Williams and Clarence Darrow. Indeed, Greenspan modelled the beginning of his closing address on Williams's famed closing statement in his successful defence of Governor John Connally.

A certain group of attorneys in Chicago watched with disbelief as Greenspan was featured in the media as the Black trial approached. They happened to be Conrad Black's prosecutors. They had devoted months to researching the case, poring over the Breeden Report and conducting multiple interviews with witnesses in both Canada and the United States. They emphatically resented all of the ink that some Canadian lawyer was attracting.

Their deep resentment towards Greenspan would bubble to the surface repeatedly during the trial and eventually would develop into a seeming obsession for some of them.

"Where's the great Eddie Greenspan? Where's Canada's Clarence Darrow? Huh!" Eric Sussman would rhetorically ask a Canadian journalist. Jeffrey Cramer declared at one point during the trial that "if Greenspan is the best lawyer in Canada, you guys are screwed."

A decision was made about one week before jury selection to take a staged photograph of the four prosecutors and distribute it broadly to various news organizations. The photograph was prominently featured in newspapers in both Chicago and Toronto. All four prosecutors posed like actors in *Law & Order* or the more dated *Mod Squad*. Eric Sussman's arms were firmly crossed while Julie Ruder's hair appeared to be blowing with the assistance of a fan.

Mark Kipnis picked up his local Chicago paper and was devastated. "Who do these people think they are?" he wondered. "Don't they know that I'm a husband, a father, a real person?"

This team photo of Black's prosecutors generated a lot of discussion among the lawyers in the city of Chicago. As far as anyone could recall, no prosecutors had ever posed for a publicity photo before a trial. Even some members of their own U.S. Attorney's Office began to poke fun at the four prosecutors.

When the trial concluded, Eddie Greenspan was invited to address the American College of Trial Lawyers on the subject of the Black trial. When he placed the prosecutors' photo on an overhead, it was greeted with laughter by the elite group of trial lawyers. Greenspan shared his view that the photo depicted the prosecutors posing as crime fighters. If any prosecutor in Canada attempted a similar stunt, he would immediately be reported to the Law Society for conduct unbecoming a barrister and solicitor.

BLACK "I"

He had a tendency to look down at us, like he couldn't believe people so beneath him were responsible for his freedom. He didn't portray any warmth, any emotions at all. It looked like he thought the whole trial was a big waste of his time.[7]
— juror Jean Kelly speaking about Conrad Black

It is very refreshing to have a system in America that allows jurors to speak freely after a trial and admit to drawing impermissible inferences that weren't based on a shred of evidence called. Jean Kelly further commented that other jurors felt that because Conrad Black was arrogant, "we have to nail him on something."[8]

While it is true that Black's mouth sometimes acted like an uncapped fire hydrant outside the courtroom, with his words gushing freely from the spout, his conduct in front of the jury betrayed none of his imperious traits (although Greenspan did have to remind him on occasion not to sit with his arms crossed). Any notion that he believed the case was an excessive waste of his precious time was drawn from thin air and exposes the grave danger of jurors relying on their subjective impressions of courtroom demeanour.

Black's greatest failing in the case was a profound lack of insight. His co-defendants accordingly were considered to be ingrates and hypocrites for daring to complain about his strident public outbursts. While his lawyers desperately tried to keep the Breeden Report out of the case, Black wanted it in. The jury should know about Breeden's hollow accusations of a corporate kleptocracy, he told them. When he persisted in pointing out to Genson that his successors had taken over Hollinger International and ruined it (the stock had plummeted from $20 a share to $4), Genson flatly asked him what that had to do with fraud. Black also wanted to advance a position that all of the buyers in the various American community newspaper deals genuinely wanted non-competition payments with Hollinger Inc. Greenspan viewed this as an overly risky and unnecessary strategy.

Black's lack of insight did not, however, extend to the decision not to testify. He knew that he had fared poorly in his mock cross-examination with Earl Cherniak, a leading Toronto litigator brought to Chicago to interrogate him in the privacy of a law office. Greenspan had earlier cross-examined Black for only a few minutes on his comment to the press about the prosecutors being a bunch of Nazis. It was pointed out in Greenspan's questioning that all four of them were in fact Jewish. Black fully supported his own lawyers' recommendation that he not take the witness stand. He also believed that the government's case was flimsy and remained optimistic of winning the trial. At the conclusion of Greenspan's cross-examination of Radler, Black leaned over and whispered to him at the counsel table, "Thank you. Now I won't have to testify."

It must be said that not once during Greenspan's lengthy cross-examination of Radler did Black's confidence in him waver. Greenspan had

started this most important cross-examination of his life believing that
Radler had made it easy for him, but Radler proved to be more resilient
and elusive than he could possibly have anticipated. By the end of the
first couple of days of cross-examination, even a member of his own team
began to turn on him. Greenspan had been telegraphing his planned
method of cross-examination for months in the media, the team member
pointed out, and what else could he expect the result would be. In other
words, Radler could anticipate Greenspan's strategy, a fact that foretold an
impending disaster inside the courtroom.

It would have been sorely tempting to follow the onslaught of criticism from the media, but Black resisted. He had chosen Greenspan and
would stand by him to the finish. By this point in the case, Greenspan
felt under siege from a number of quarters. Some of the media reports,
including one from a journalist in his hometown of Toronto, were disparaging and scathing. He complained that during the trial not one of
his co-counsel had lifted a finger to help him and left him "to twist in
the wind." Nothing changed during his cross-examination of Radler to
alter that perception.

There were occasional group meetings of all of the lawyers on the
case in a large boardroom at Safer's law firm. Greenspan didn't even bother
to attend all of them because he thought it was the enemy camp. He was
aware that both Kipnis and Atkinson had been approached by the prosecutor with deals that were still on the table during the trial. (Boultbee
had been offered a deal weeks prior to the trial with the stipulation that
his sentence could not be less than Radler's, at twenty-nine months.)
Greenspan was concerned that some of the other defendants' attorneys
"didn't know what being a defence lawyer means" and believed that they
still harboured the perspective of prosecutors. It wasn't the task of the
defence to prove anything but only to raise a reasonable doubt. Patrick
Tuite, Jack Boultbee's affable Chicago attorney, considered it unfortunate
that Greenspan had to learn the U.S. system while he was defending the
case. Ron Safer's view was somewhat harsher. He would never presume
that he could try a case in a Canadian courtroom.

The unfortunate conflict reached its zenith with the testimony of the
central witness in the case, David Radler. Safer, who had serious misgivings about Greenspan's approach to the witness, wanted to rely on Radler's
telling the truth in his statement to the Breeden committee (which he

renounced at trial) when he denied that there was any fraudulent scheme. It was captured in this portion of his cross-examination of Radler:

> Q: You discussed earlier a letter that your committee — your lawyer — wrote to the special committee. The letter addresses all of the non-competes that you testified about, except for CanWest, *American Trucker*, CNHI [Community Newspaper Holdings Inc.] I and II, Forum and Paxton, Horizon and APC. The letter states that it was your understanding and belief that International's audit committee and board of directors approved each of these transactions that was the subject of the inquiry and the letter says that, doesn't it?
>
> A: Yes.
>
> Q: With regard to non-competition payments, I refer you to the section about non-compete payments to the individuals. You address all $15.6 million?
>
> A: Yes.
>
> Q: And you state that you understood and believed that those payments were fair and reasonable, that full disclosure was made to the audit committee and the board of directors, and that the audit committee and the board of directors approved those payments?
>
> A: That's right.

For Greenspan, the case was very simple. Black never approached a single purchaser in the sale of the American community newspapers. He never negotiated a deal or had a single conversation with any of the buyers about the sale of the papers. David Radler was a liar and the members of the audit committee were all liars. A fraudulent scheme was singularly devised and put into operation by Radler. Radler performed the operatic parts of tenor, baritone, and soprano on his own and only used Mark Kipnis as his alto dupe.

By the time final argument arrived, a confused jury had three competing theories from the defence:

1. There was no crime committed by anyone and all of the $60-million proceeds of the non-competition agreements received by the senior executives and the parent company, Hollinger Inc., were legitimately obtained.
2. Conrad Black and the other senior executives were duped by David Radler, who kept them in the dark about an illicit scheme that he orchestrated to insert them into a variety of non-competition agreements.
3. What happened at Hollinger International wasn't a theft by Conrad Black but rather a theft *from* Conrad Black. There was a crime but Black was the victim.

The problem with the first theory was the perplexing question of the reasons behind David Radler's guilty plea. The jury was expressly instructed not to take the plea into account during their deliberations, but it must have confounded them. The jury was never informed that Radler faced up to twenty years under the sentencing guidelines if he risked going to trial and lost everything. The figure was calculated by a leading American sentencing expert, Jeffrey Steinbeck, retained by the defence. It takes a fluid legal mind and an abacus to decipher the sentencing guidelines, and Steinbeck was familiar with the various downward and upward adjustments. He prepared a memo that was available for the attorneys to use during Radler's cross-examination. Radler eventually worked out a deal for twenty-nine months. Would the dramatic difference in punishment entice an innocent man to forego a trial? You bet it would. According to Murray Richman, a veteran defence attorney from the Bronx, "Even innocent people often aren't willing to risk fifteen or twenty years or more in jail by going to trial. Not when they can get it down to one to four if they plead."[9]

Only in America would someone seek immunity when there is no legitimate basis for being charged. In the event you might attribute this proposition to the wild imagination of a Canadian lawyer feasting on Havana cigars, let me point out that it actually happened in the Black trial. Paul Healy, Black's former subordinate, received immunity from the prosecutors. Why? Ed Genson, who cross-examined Healy, couldn't explain it but happily pounced on the unexpected gift to undermine Healy's motives.

Angela Way, Mark Kipnis's assistant and a peripheral witness at the trial, was scared to death of the prosecutors. She had been interviewed by them several times before she testified. She wouldn't even look at her former boss on the witness stand during her examination.

The members of the audit committee were accused by the defence of remembering only what they chose to remember and disregarding the rest. Why would they do that? Ron Safer answered this puzzling question in his closing: "Because of embarrassment, because of liability. You know they were threatened by the SEC. They were investigated by the SEC. *They got together and they put together a story.* Ambassador Burt told you he was beginning to have a fear of being embarrassed as the controversy grew. Mrs. Kravis [another audit committee member] said the SEC enforcement proceedings were embarrassing."

There was a broad consensus among observers of the trial that the worst witness was Black's former executive assistant, Joan Maida. The decision to call Maida was foisted on the Black legal team by the client and his wife. By this point in the trial, Barbara Amiel was at the end of her rope with the poor collective judgment exercised by her husband's lawyers. It didn't matter that Genson's law partner, Terry Gillespie, along with Jane Kelly,[10] had interviewed Maida in Toronto and warned of the danger to the case of calling her as a defence witness. Black absolutely insisted that she be called.

Conrad Black's most critical lack of insight was demonstrated by his unrelenting strident public comments during the trial. At one point he approached me, stating, "I understand that you think that loose lips sink ships." He didn't need my answer to see the folly of his ways. He had repeatedly ignored the admonitions of several of his own lawyers to quell his outbursts.

The judge demonstrated incredible patience with Black's conduct during the trial. She really wanted Black's legal fate to be decided on the evidence and not on extraneous reasons. Her respect and compassion was most evident when the jury returned with its verdict. She understood instantly that the prosecution had succeeded with only morsels of its case. Eddie Greenspan, over time, shifted his harsh view of Judge Amy St. Eve. He ultimately believed that she was a fair judge and that any failings he had accused her of were really failings of the system that she was part of. "We've all thought she was a good person," he concluded.

MY KIND OF TOWN

"You win the case in the opening, Eddie."

Eddie Greenspan listened intently as Ed Genson implored him to open to the jury with some flourish, and he instantly made a decision about the case.

"Then you're doing the opening statement," he informed his Chicago-based co-counsel.

Greenspan's experience with opening statements in Canada was dramatically different. Beyond saying hello to the jury and reminding them of the standard of proof in the case, there was little utility to an opening. Not a single thing that you say actually lingers in the jurors' minds. I must admit that I generally shared Greenspan's cynical view. The idea that a jury might recall what a lawyer had told them months ago seemed far-fetched.

Both Greenspan and I forgot one essential factor in the Black trial: the jurors were permitted to take copious notes. One of them knew shorthand, which likely meant that the jurors had the equivalent of a transcript of the opening statements of all of the attorneys.

The prosecution proceeded first, and the very first thing that Jeffrey Cramer told the jurors was this: "You're sitting in a room with four men who stole $60 million. Four men that betrayed the trust of thousands of public shareholders. Four men who decided amongst themselves that their six- and seven-figure salaries were simply not enough."

In plain speak, the prosecutor was describing the case as a grand-scale theft by a group of four rich and greedy men. Genson understood the prosecutor's tactics. "He wanted to dumb down the case for the jury," he told me.

Was Cramer's tactic effective? Consider that he focused his sights on only three allegedly fraudulent transactions in his opening statement: Forum, Paxton, and APC.

The jury returned guilty verdicts against all of the defendants on only three transactions: Forum, Paxton, and APC.

It was during the days leading up to Genson's opening that Greenspan realized that there was a significant clash of styles that he wasn't certain could be overcome. Genson refused to show him the draft of his opening statement. There was a very good reason for this: Genson didn't have one. His practice was to jot down a few major points and then proceed to deliver some extemporaneous thoughts in front of the jury. He felt that it created a more natural, free-flowing rapport with the jury. Greenspan, by contrast, was meticulous in his preparation and had detailed scripted notes for every aspect of the trial. Like any accomplished advocate, he could react to surprises and adjust his questions accordingly.

Genson attributed the difference to their particular experiences in their own countries. If the Black trial had proceeded in Canada, there would have been an extensive preliminary hearing where the key witnesses would have been challenged in cross-examination under oath. The notion of preliminary hearings has almost vanished in the U.S. In Canada there would have been a body of discovery material to test the case and the attorneys at trial would not have to guess what the witness would say. Genson's own experience in obtaining statements from the grand jury a month or two before trial meant burying himself in preparation every day, including working on weekends and late into the night.

"You can be a trial lawyer until you're ninety in Canada," Genson observed with some degree of envy. I didn't want to disappoint the Chicago attorney by sharing with him that I wasn't familiar with a single trial lawyer in Canada over the age of seventy-five.

With the benefit of a preliminary hearing, for example, Ron Safer wouldn't have been surprised by David Radler's testimony. He was fully expecting Radler to get into the witness stand and claim that he had lied to the FBI when he distanced Kipnis's $150,000 bonus from the fraudulent scheme. Hadn't Jeffrey Cramer implied that was the case in his opening? Until the very moment the prosecution closed its case, Safer believed that the prosecutors had some mysterious evidence in their treasure chest to buttress Cramer's damaging claim.

Greenspan also understood that he would have to abandon one of his key strengths at the trial. He was a very funny man with a sharp wit and the exquisite timing of a great comedian. He once introduced Jackie Mason at a charity benefit in Toronto and Mason complained onstage that Greenspan was funnier than he was. It was the truth. Eddie Greenspan's speeches before lawyers and judges were regularly laced with warm and endearing humour. He had the ability to make people laugh from the centre of their belly and he exploited this skill to great advantage during his criminal trials.

No Canadian jury would ever get the impression that Greenspan was a rude and arrogant man.

This was Genson's town, however, and he would be the kibitzer in the courtroom. There could only be room for one of them. Greenspan knew they had to avoid any chance of their lawyer tandem coming across as Abbott and Costello. This sacrifice was an unfortunate setback for Conrad Black.

MARCH 14–19, 2007

Jury selection begins in Chicago for the trial of four former Hollinger executives — CEO Conrad Black, executive vice-president Peter Atkinson, former CFO Jack Boultbee, and general counsel Mark Kipnis.

David Radler reaches a $28.7-million settlement with the SEC and a $63.4-million (all figures U.S.) settlement with Sun-Times Media Group (as Hollinger International is now known). Defence attorneys argue jurors may have been tainted by the news. Judge Amy St. Eve agrees to question jurors individually about their knowledge of the settlements.

JURY OF MY FEARS

The Canadian jury is selected with the utmost courtesy and respect for the privacy of its members. Questions are rarely permitted during jury selection and the slightest hint of a personal question is immediately frowned upon by the presiding judge.[11] It is not a jury of twelve angry men but rather twelve unknown men (and women) that is ultimately chosen. I discussed the rather anonymous method by which Canadian juries are chosen with a noted criminal defence lawyer from Los Angeles, David Elden. He surprised me with his considered view that probing jury questioning invariably benefits the prosecution. Liberals proudly display their civil liberties credentials, whereas law-and-order conservatives are far more reticent to expose their pronounced views.

I recall a case in which I was defending a young man charged with criminal negligence causing bodily harm. In an attempt to take his own life, he had filled his home with gasoline and intended to set it aflame while he sat inside. As his painful moment of reckoning approached, he stumbled to the phone and called 911 to outline his lethal plan. As the dispatcher purposely delayed my client with protracted questions about his background, police rushed to the scene. Alas, at the very second that my client flicked his lighter, a police officer was at his front door. The ensuing explosion sadly caused the poor officer severe injuries, while my incredibly fortunate client left his kitchen chair without a bruise or scratch to his body.

As I perused the list of prospective jurors, I noticed that one man had listed his occupation as a director. I wondered if he was a director sitting on a board or perhaps more glamorously a movie director. Of course the distinction was meaningless to my selection, but my acute curiosity forced me to probe the matter further.

"May I ask you, sir, what type of director you are?"

"A funeral director," was the surprising response.

I chose to exercise one of my permitted twelve peremptory challenges. I haven't the foggiest idea why I did so other than perhaps that I unfairly chose not to associate myself for two weeks with someone in the morbid business of death. He might have been a delightful and gregarious fellow, but with the paucity of information in my possession, I could only resort to the worst form of stereotyping.

It was therefore striking for me to observe the elaborate jury selection process in the Conrad Black trial. All of the potential jurors had completed lengthy written questionnaires before they joined the panel in the courtroom. The trial judge, Amy St. Eve, was clearly a prodigious worker (the barista at the Starbucks by the federal courthouse related that the judge was there faithfully at six every morning) and meticulously read every word of the responses. In a warm and cheerful voice, she began to quiz the panel members individually as they were called forward. There were a few embarrassing moments. When asked if someone close to him had been arrested or charged with a crime, one man answered that his son was in jail for selling drugs.

A few common themes began to emerge. Canada fared poorly in some instances, with opinions of the country ranging from socialist to anti-union.

An unsettling number of prospective jurors had experience with identity theft in their family. A number of them had signed non-competition agreements at work. Enron merited repeated mention; one man spoke of a good friend losing his retirement savings in the Enron debacle. It was clear that the dots were being connected from Enron to the allegations of corporate pilfering by Conrad Black. The comparison was unwarranted. As Peter Henning, a law professor and former U.S. securities lawyer, noted, "What will handicap the government ... to a degree is [that it's] not the Enron/WorldCom type situation where you had people losing their jobs and the company collapsed."[12]

It was actually to Conrad Black's advantage that very few potential jurors professed the slightest bit of knowledge about his identity. Unlike many Canadians, they could start the trial without sharply negative views about the man already firmly embedded. The front page of the business section of the *Chicago Tribune* carried a column, titled "Black's trial no big deal for city," that described Conrad Black as "more than a nobody and not quite a somebody." I was interviewed by four local Chicago television stations, including FOX for *FOX Chicago Sunday*, and I was repeatedly pressed to explain to their viewers: who is this guy Conrad Black and why do people in Canada and England care so much about him?

One member of the jury panel commented that she couldn't see anyone making tens of millions of dollars legally unless they happened to be Donald Trump. The judge reminded her that there are many people who make lots of money through legitimate means. Conrad Black's fondest wish was that some of those very people would appear in his jury pool, but perhaps ominously for him it was otherwise. For the most part, the approximately 150 members of the Black jury panel were hard-working blue-collar workers who might find it challenging to relate to taking a trip to Bora Bora on the company tab.

I believed that Conrad Black's jury could overcome any prejudices they might harbour about a man amassing obscene amounts of wealth. The larger challenge for the defence would be to withstand the barrage of scorn by the jury for their unsympathetic client. In the forty-five-page questionnaire that was completed by the jury pool, there was significantly no question directed to the ability to remain impartial with a haughty and arrogant defendant.

I happened to be listening in my hotel room this weekend to a recording of a Neil Young concert performed at Massey Hall in Toronto in 1971.

I was struck by a memorable line from one of his songs: "I crossed the ocean for a heart of gold." Conrad Black crossed the ocean for the title of lord. That is the rub in the man. The theme of this trial isn't *Braveheart* but rather *Coldheart*. The enormous challenge for the cross-border dream team of Eddie Greenspan and Edward Genson will be to convince the jurors that although they might dislike their client and view him as an unworthy dinner companion, that doesn't make him guilty of fraud and racketeering.

There is another challenge the defence faced that flowed from the overly indulgent American attitude to free speech. In Canada, the jurors depart from the courthouse as discreetly as they entered. It is a criminal offence for any juror to discuss their deliberations. During jury selection for the Conrad Black trial, Judge St. Eve quickly reminded any potential juror who expressed a concern about the media crush surrounding the case that they didn't have to speak to reporters after the verdict. However, it was implicit that the option was there for them to speak as freely as they wish. They would also have the option to write about the case and seek large book contracts. Which result carries more promise of lucre — bringing down a financial titan and lord or vindicating him?

It is inconceivable that a system of justice should provide any enterprising juror with an incentive to achieve a particular outcome in a criminal case with the consequences to the defendant's liberty so severe. Welcome to America, land of opportunity.

GAGGED

There were seven lawyers congregated around Conrad Black at his counsel table. By my quick calculation, there were more attorneys in the courtroom than at a bar convention. Everyone seemed to be in a cheerful mood. Of course the jury hadn't heard a drop of incriminating evidence yet. I watched Eddie Greenspan sharing a light moment with Barbara Amiel that left both of them smiling.

I noticed that there was little repartee between Greenspan and Genson and the lawyers at the other defendants' tables. I asked Jane Kelly, one of three lawyers from Toronto on Black's defence team, if there was any friction among the various defence camps. I was assured by "Ambassador Jane," as she referred to herself, that a conciliatory accord had been reached and that, in the immortal words of John Lennon, everyone was prepared to give peace a chance. Jane's diplomatic role was to attempt to ensure that no dangerous Scud missiles were launched by Black's co-defendants in his direction. Black had been listed first on the indictment by the prosecution, which left him vulnerable to an ambush.

There was one last matter for Judge St. Eve to consider before the jury was called into court for the commencement of the trial. An emergency motion had been brought by the *Chicago Tribune* seeking the release of the identity of the twelve jurors and six alternates selected for the trial. It might make sense to protect the anonymity of the jurors if this was a terrorism or organized crime case where legitimate security concerns were raised. However, this was a trial where the exhibits would be paper rather than guns and autopsy photos. The defendants in the case were a group of largely paunchy middle-aged men who seemed about as threatening as the servers at the coffee shop on State Street pouring double and triple espressos.

The lawyer for the *Chicago Tribune* highlighted the broad issues at stake in his court filing:

> There is no justification for an anonymous jury. The full names of all prospective jurors have already been read aloud in open court during [the selection process] making the retrospective sealing of the ultimate jury both an ineffective and inappropriate measure. But more importantly, sealing the list of juror names in this public criminal case is an extraordinary measure that is not warranted under the circumstances and violates the public's First Amendment and common law right of access.

I had only been at the trial for a few days and already heady issues of the First Amendment and freedom of expression were being raised. I was probably the only person in court enjoying the constitutional tug of war. I was actually absorbed by the notion of six people sitting as alternates through a trial that could last for months and then simply being told to go home when the jury started its deliberations. In Canada a trial begins with twelve jurors and isn't compromised unless more than two jurors have to be excused during the trial. That is a rare occurrence.

There are profound differences in the American and Canadian approaches to freedom of expression. In the U.S. a man can stand on a street corner preaching genocide.[13] The Canadian approach is more nuanced and sensitive.[14] Although a wide berth is given to unpopular and even untruthful ideas, it is recognized that in order to protect vulnerable communities, there is a point where a democracy can properly limit freedom of speech.

I was astounded to find that the media was free to publish or broadcast the content of the pre-trial hearings in the Black trial. There were no boundaries or restrictions. In America, a newspaper can print the detailed and damning confession of a defendant that later is excluded because the arrested party was denied his right to counsel. By contrast, in a Canadian courtroom, the bail hearing, the preliminary hearing, and all of the pre-trial motions are off limits to the media for reporting until the trial has concluded (or in some cases until the jury is sequestered). There can be criminal sanctions if an order banning publication is deliberately flouted.

THE PROSECUTION

MARCH 20

In his opening statement, prosecutor Jeffrey Cramer tells jurors, "Bank robbers wear masks and use guns. Burglars wear dark clothing and use a crowbar. These four ... dressed in ties and wore a suit."

"He was not stealing from the company," defence lawyer Ed Genson counters. "The company was stolen from him."

THE CUDDLY CURMUDGEON

I applaud the subdued dress look (grey on grey) that Conrad Black has selected for his courtroom wardrobe. His extravagant lifestyle is featured in the prosecution's case, so he doesn't need to become a witness for his adversary by dressing flamboyantly. It would be most unhelpful, for example, for him to arrive at court carrying one of Martha Stewart's Hermès handbags. I am reminded of the lawyer in my office who was defending a *Penthouse* model on a relatively minor drug charge. He took special efforts to warn her about dressing for the solemn occasion of a court proceeding. He was mortified to find her at the courthouse attired in a tight-fitting blouse, short skirt, and black fishnet stockings.

I feel as if I have jumped into a swimming pool only to find that the lifeguard has neglected to inform me that it isn't heated. I watched in baffled dismay as the prosecutor, Jeffrey Cramer, delivered his opening address today with the same fiery rhetoric and flourish that I expect Abraham Lincoln employed for his stirring Gettysburg Address. Cramer's opening was about as distant from the dispassionate and flat opening that a Canadian prosecutor would routinely give as Ontario, Canada, is from Ontario, California. In short order, a Canadian jury would be provided by the prosecutor with the anticipated menu for the trial without the enticing details for the recipe of each course. Regardless of whether the meal consisted of oysters or *foie gras*, the prosecutor's voice would never rise with crackling excitement. Unappetizing introductions such as "I anticipate the evidence will be" or "I expect the witness will testify that" would be sprinkled throughout the curt summary of the case for the Crown.

I chatted with a journalist covering the trial for the *Sydney Morning Herald* and found that we shared a common view that Cramer's opening address was certainly different than anything we had experienced in our respective countries. As he wagged his finger at Conrad Black and his co-defendants, Cramer railed about their looting of the Hollinger International shareholders of $60 million. With faint praise, he referred to the four defendants in the courtroom as some of the most sophisticated men the jury would ever see. Always be wary of the prosecutor who brandishes compliments. Cramer's point to the jury was plain. The ruse of siphoning extravagant sums of money from the shareholders through various non-competition agreements would have been obvious to these astute businessmen. "It's simple, it's simple," Cramer emphasized as he laid out the nefarious scheme of the four men. Cramer was a disciple of the "KISS principle" that all good trial lawyers understand: "Keep It Simple, Stupid."

The prosecution appreciated that there was a gaping hole in its case. Every one of the contentious deals involving the non-compete payments to the defendants was profitable to the shareholders. This was not the financial undertow that resulted from the Enron debacle, where billions of dollars were plundered from the company as thousands of jobs and pensions of Enron employees vanished into thin air.

Jeffrey Cramer's solution was to pull on the jurors' heartstrings using a different approach. With a raised voice, he drew from the bank of wishful thinking. The two groups of victimized shareholders that he identified were elderly people who had bought Hollinger stock for their retirement and parents who had stocked their children's college funds with Hollinger shares.

Cramer's bag of trial tricks in his opening did not rely exclusively on emotional appeal. Plan B depended on frightening them.

"We all know what street crime looks like. A man knocks you down and takes your money. This is what a crime looks like in corporate law ... Bank robbers use masks and carry guns. Burglars wear dark clothing and use a crowbar. These four [defendants] wore a suit and a tie."

Now that it was settled for the jury that Conrad Black had robbed the Hollinger bank in sartorial splendour, it was Edward Genson's opportunity to respond. He began by challenging the idea presented by the prosecution that none of the buyers of Hollinger International assets wanted a non-competition agreement with Black.

"I want you to remember CanWest," Genson told the jury. In the colossal $3.2-billion deal between Hollinger International and CanWest, he explained, it was the purchaser who had asked for a non-competition agreement.

Eddie Greenspan listened apprehensively as his co-counsel continued his opening comments. As a thorough lawyer accustomed to meticulous preparation, Greenspan had repeatedly asked to see Genson's script for the opening. Each of his requests had been rebuffed. Incredibly, he had no more idea of what precise words would be coming out of Genson's mouth than did his adversaries seated at the prosecution table facing the jurors.

Greenspan's worst fears were realized as Genson moved quickly on the offensive by stating that there was no theft from the company by Conrad Black. On the contrary, it was the company, Hollinger International, that had been stolen from him. It was a stinging rebuke to Cramer's opening, but Greenspan worried that Genson had placed an unnecessary and impossible burden on the defence. In the spirit of Conrad Black as victim, the defence was on course to portray the individuals charged with the responsibility for corporate governance at Hollinger International as the true thieves in the night.

Genson touched on a theme in his opening that needed to be addressed directly. "You can't allow the sparkle of wealth to alter the facts of the case," he warned the jurors. A glare of wealth or even a blaring inferno might have been more apt descriptions of Conrad Black's true economic health during the currency of the charges, but Genson's point was sound. It was ironic that a defendant's status among the super-rich had marked him as a displaced person before the jury. Whereas indigence might deprive a defendant of the resources to tussle in a courtroom on an even playing field, the trappings of wealth could translate to a badge of impoverished character.

The best of the four opening statements by the defence was reserved for the last. Ron Safer provided the jury with a stirring imitation of a closing address as he sandblasted the central government theory. The audit committee of Hollinger International, chaired by the former governor of Illinois, James Thompson, not only was aware of the non-competition agreements, but also, Safer noted, "approved them again and again and again."

Safer's opening sealed a unified front presented by all of the co-defendants. There were no early signs of finger-pointing or cracks in the defence. David Radler emerged as a dominant target. "Would you buy a used car from him?" Ron Safer asked. The implication was clear to the jury: a disreputable man like Radler, who tampers with the odometer and hides the rusty spots, can't be trusted as a witness.

The headlines in the newspapers predictably captured the prosecution's sound bite. As a typical example, the *Financial Times* carried the following banner to its Black trial coverage: "Hollinger chiefs 'bank robbers in suits', court told." The buzz around the courtroom, however, was that after the defence openings concluded, the trial was a true contest. "I would acquit Mark Kipnis now," one reporter stated only half-jokingly. The jury was engaged and listening. The jurors were ready to focus their spotlights on the evidence.

I was approached by Genson in the hallway at the break. "Are you the guy who called me a curmudgeon on channel 7?" he asked. I admitted that indeed I had used the description in an interview with the local ABC station. "All my friends are calling me about it. I have never been called a curmudgeon before," he chided me, clearly crestfallen. I could only hope that my unintended slur would be forgotten after the auspicious start to the trial by the defence.

The first witness called to the stand by the prosecution was Gordon Paris. As Mr. Corporate Governance, he had replaced Conrad Black at Hollinger International and played a key role in the Breeden Report that was the precursor to Black's criminal charges. It was Black who had invited Paris, an investment banker with a prestigious business degree from Wharton, to join the Hollinger International audit committee after questions were raised about some dubious management fees.

Eddie Greenspan assumed the task of cross-examining Gord Paris. It was Paris who had negotiated the $60-million settlement with Radler on the eve of the trial. Greenspan and the rest of the defence had expected the prosecution to open with a few minor witnesses, which would have allowed Greenspan time to get a sense of the unique U.S. style of questioning, but now the first witness in the case was awaiting his cross-examination. A famed Canadian barrister and QC was ready for his first foray in a Chicago courtroom. I suspected that the prosecution might regret calling Paris as their first witness. The only question that would linger after his cross-examination would be this: Is Paris burning?

LORD BLOWHARD OF CROSSHARBOUR

The reasons behind the government's decision to call Gordon Paris as the first witness in the trial were initially a complete mystery to me. Chronologically, his evidence related to the final chapter of the case after the alleged fraudulent scheme had been perpetrated. Perhaps the prosecutors assumed that Judge St. Eve would allow them to introduce the damning Breeden Report that cast Conrad Black in such a villainous light. The judge, however, disappointed them by ruling against that action.

Patrick Fitzgerald, the United States attorney closely observing the ebb and flow of the case in the background, was a master of strategy in the courtroom. I began to suspect that he understood that Conrad Black's defence team was so anxious to discredit the case against their client that it would be virtually impossible for them to resist the urge to take the safer course and refrain from asking the first witness a single question. Paris would serve as the perfect foil for this artful strategy.

Stripped of his ability to refer to the incendiary Breeden Report (although he did manage to sneak in a mention in front of the jury), Paris was like a snarling dog straining against its leash to get at its prey. It should have been readily apparent to the defence that Black's successor at the helm of Hollinger International offered little valuable evidence to the prosecutor in his examination.

As Eddie Greenspan quickly learned in cross-examination, Gordon Paris was a dangerous witness. The most memorable features of his evidence came during the re-examination by lead prosecutor Eric Sussman, after the door was inadvertently left wide open by Greenspan. Authorized employee benefits, Paris noted, didn't extend to corporate perks such as birthday parties, New York apartments, or free access to the company aircraft. All three perks were the subject of separate charges in the indictment against Conrad Black.

The acclaimed Canadian lawyer struggled and looked badly out of place in the city where Clarence Darrow tried most of his cases. As the trial judge sustained the steady stream of objections from the prosecutors, Greenspan had the look of a wobbly boxer wincing from a succession of jabs to his abdomen. Greenspan's confusion escalated to the point that on occasion he wasn't certain if he had won or lost an objection. There was a series of long and awkward pauses at the counsel table as Greenspan was educated about some elementary rules of American criminal procedure.

For example, Greenspan attempted to ask Paris about a regulatory SEC filing that he had submitted ten months late. His American co-counsel had written out a sample of acceptable questions he could ask to demonstrate that Paris had lied to the SEC and that the filing was improper. Greenspan instead chose to ask Paris, "You did your best and made an honest mistake?" It was a theme that Greenspan hoped would resonate with the jury in considering Black's conduct. However, the prosecution's ensuing objection was quickly sustained and Greenspan was forced to justify his approach to Judge St. Eve in a voir dire outside the jury's presence. Greenspan thought it was "nuts" that before he could present evidence to show the jury that Paris had made an honest mistake he first had to portray the witness as dishonest to the judge.[1]

At the lunch break, I overheard one of Greenspan's co-counsel remark that he seemed unaccustomed to the American courtroom style. The start of the trial wasn't the time and place, however, for a rudimentary lesson. I wasn't prepared to count Eddie out, though. I doubted that Black's legendary Canadian counsel would permit himself to be publicly shamed a second time with another dismal courtroom performance. And without some noticeable improvement by Greenspan, Conrad Black could begin to furnish his prison cell.

A positive sign for Black was that the jury listened intently to the evidence presented and took notes. Greenspan managed a few smiles in the jury box with his brand of self-deprecating humour, but he clearly had not yet developed any rapport with the jurors. It was still early in the ball game and these were only warm-up pitches. The lineup of star witnesses, including David Radler and members of the audit committee, would mark Greenspan's true test with the jury.

In order to acquire one of the precious few seats in the courtroom reserved for the international media, I was required to line up at seven o'clock in the morning. The journalists covering the trial were generally very approachable and even helpful. There were a few grating comments that I chose not to respond to. One reporter blamed Eddie Greenspan for not pursuing a settlement for his client (generously assuming that Conrad Black would heed anyone's advice).

In one discussion that I overheard in line, a journalist wondered why Black hadn't repaid the questionable compensation he had received for the non-compete agreements. The notion advanced was that Black could possibly have avoided his current legal predicament with that simple gesture. Another journalist nearby scoffed at the suggestion that Black would ever pursue such a sensible course of action. "That would be like asking why Hitler didn't bring back the six million Jews," he said. I was beginning to get the impression that Conrad Black was reviled by a lot of people. His detractors didn't attempt to disguise their hostility, either. But the only opinions that mattered to Black were those of the jurors, and he was indeed fortunate to be perceived by them as a stranger in their midst.

I have resisted the temptation thus far to lapse into the "Montreal bagel syndrome." For the rare reader unacquainted with the malady, allow me to explain. It represents the rigid position that whatever one experiences outside one's own city or town is always inferior to the home product. For example, anyone who has lived in Montreal, Quebec, will invariably inform you in a dismissive tone that the bagels in that cosmopolitan city are much better than the comparable fluffy and inedible bagels in Toronto, Vancouver, or Calgary. I suppose that would include David Radler, whose roots can be traced back to Montreal. With my legal analyst's cap firmly in place, I have been a careful observer of the proceedings in the Black trial and on balance have been favourably impressed. By all accounts, Conrad Black is receiving a fair trial.

There are only four men among the group of jurors and alternates, and so it is remotely possible that Conrad Black's legal destiny will be determined by twelve women. At least two-thirds of the jury will be female. The prosecution should certainly reflect on the wisdom of seeking to introduce several thousand files containing predominantly email exchanges between Lord Black and his wife, Barbara Amiel. Whatever the content of the myriad emails, their presence will create an image of spousal devotion, love, and romance for the jury.

I found the entire issue surrounding the admissibility of the Amiel emails perplexing. In Canada there would never be any question that they would remain sacrosanct and protected by marital privilege. While munching on a Montreal bagel, I raised the matter with a professor at the DePaul University College of Law in Chicago. Apparently, any communication between spouses that is outside the course of the marriage is not the subject of privilege. I never appreciated that marriage could so readily be divided into categories of business and pleasure. For example, what would an American court rule with regards to the following hypothetical example of an email exchange?

Dearest Conrad,

I love you dearly. May I please buy some Cartier earrings with the money you received from your latest non-compete payment? I want to wear them on the plane ride to Bora Bora ~ lol.

Babs

The emails of Conrad Black took centre stage at the end of the first week of trial. "Black's Private E-mails Go Public at Fraud Trial," read the headline in the weekend edition of the *Globe and Mail*. Conrad Black was documented in an April 2003 email delivered to audit committee members Marie-Josée Kravis and Richard Burt reassuring them in his unique bombastic style that he would crush any dissident shareholders: "I will take on the task of hosing down shareholders in need of it as some priority." In another email, responding to questions about non-competition agreements, Black disparaged his challengers as victims of an "epidemic of shareholder idiocy."

Are the jurors being swayed by these graphic emails capturing Conrad Black's descriptive flair? Many of them laughed heartily as Eric Sussman struggled to pronounce the word "calumnies" in one of them. Genson pounced on the opportunity to offer his client's assistance. That suggestion was greeted with more amusement by the jury.

Unfortunately for the prosecution, the emails were neither calumny nor calamity for Conrad Black. I expect that that the jurors will give very little weight to these pompous emails in their deliberations. The caution flag was raised clearly in Genson's opening statement: "That proves nothing except that he has an arrogant attitude when he writes memos in the middle of the night."

Genson's opening was a precursor to a theme that the defence seized upon in the first week of the trial. Using a simple diagram to illustrate his point, Genson had outlined the geographical boundaries that separated Conrad Black and David Radler as they ran the third-largest newspaper empire in the world. It only followed that as the American community newspapers were sold to a variety of purchasers in Radler's backyard, it was therefore Radler who oversaw the negotiations.

The first witness to testify about the purchase of Hollinger International assets was Peter Laino. Laino worked for a media holding company Primedia, that was involved in a $75-million sale that included *American Trucker* magazine. The agreement, which was negotiated exclusively with David Radler, included non-competes with Hollinger International and Hollinger Inc. for $2 million. Laino conceded in cross-examination that in all likelihood the deal was contingent on Hollinger International and its affiliates not being permitted to compete after the sale. There was no apparent ruse, despite what the prosecution had promised in its opening. This was a case in which the buyer really did request a non-competition agreement. The defence was off to a good start.

CANADIAN CURTSY

I have always liked prosecutors. I like them best when they lose my cases. They will, however, at least in a Canadian courtroom, always remain my friends. That is the courtesy title that we attach to our robed adversary. Imagine a particularly contentious moment in a heated trial when the prosecutor has pulled an outlandish stunt in front of the jury. In America, a sidebar is called to avoid any unseemly accusations being hurled in the well of the court. In hushed tones at the far side of the courtroom, the lawyers thrash each other with verbal barbs as the judge attempts to mediate the problem.

Contrast that to a trial north of the border, where the defence counsel politely rises and addresses the judge about the offending conduct: "With respect, your Honour, perhaps my friend should consider his words more carefully," she begins. "His most inappropriate statement in front of this jury bears little resemblance to the evidence this jury has heard."

The prosecutor then has an opportunity to reply in kind to his friend and the judge instantly rules on the matter. The trial then moves forward with almost seamless efficiency.

In the Conrad Black trial, I observed the team of four young prosecutors during the pre-trial motions, and they appeared to be a happy lot. A scowl on a prosecutor's face is a sign of either a prickly disposition or displeasure with the flow of the evidence. A relaxed smile, however, is a troubling sign for the defence. During one of those interminably protracted sidebars that began to infect the trial, the trial judge's remarks drew hearty laughter from the lead prosecutor, Eric Sussman, and his cohort Jeffrey Cramer. It was noticeable that none of the defence lawyers even feigned a laugh. One of them abandoned the sidebar and left the courtroom with his coat and briefcase.

The prosecutors were already gaining the upper hand in the trial. Every advocate must possess the artful skill of feigned laughter for when judges tell jokes during a trial. DVDs of *Seinfeld* episodes are freely handed out at judges' school but to little avail. The finest judges recognize their inherent limitations and mete justice absent of any jocularity.

MARCH 22–27

Hollinger's former manager of corporate finance, Craig Holick, testifies he "funnelled" proceeds from newspaper sales to Hollinger Inc., the Toronto holding company owned by Black and David Radler.

Thomas Henson, a lawyer who represented Community Newspaper Holdings Inc., testifies his company only requested non-competes with Hollinger International and that Kipnis added Hollinger Inc. to the deal. Under cross-examination, he agrees auditors would have reviewed the deal, which Genson contends was negotiated by Radler.

PINOCCHIO

I caught a glance today in court from Barbara Amiel. Our eyes locked momentarily and I immediately convinced myself that she had been drawn to take a peek by my supreme intellect. That idea was quickly rejected, and then I wondered if she had read that I was once chosen as one of Toronto's sexiest men. And then the stark truth dawned on me: I reminded her of one of her gardeners back in London, England. Gardening shears would have been helpful in court today to pare down the incessant habit of prosecutor Edward Siskel of repeating the same question over and over again to emphasize an answer from the witness that he embraced.

The objections slowly began to roll in from the defence side of the courtroom. "Asked and answered," the lawyers would exclaim in unison. The pile-driver method of trial advocacy is transparent to an intelligent jury. This is certainly such a jury. They are studious and undaunted by an assiduous judge who works longer shifts than most hospital residents or articling students.

In his opening statement, Edward Genson had argued that Hollinger was a healthy and successful company worth billions of dollars "until the company was taken away from Conrad Black." In reality, the company that had amassed four hundred community newspapers by 1990 was staggering under the pressure of enormous debt. By 1998, Black and the chief operating officer, David Radler, had begun a mad rush to sell off the media conglomerate's small American community newspapers.

Two such deals worth hundreds of millions of dollars took place with an American company, Community Newspaper Holdings, Inc. (CNHI). A top executive of CNHI, Michael Reed, and the company's counsel, Thomas Henson, were called early in the prosecution's case to bolster its claim that the non-competition agreements in the sales weren't sought out or requested by the buyers.

Both Reed and Henson minimized the importance of purchase and sale agreements that stipulated in plain language that non-competition agreements with Hollinger Inc. were a condition of closing. What is a little lie in a contract if it doesn't hurt anyone or affect the purchase price? Defence counsel pointed out in cross-examination that the agreements would be enforceable and the motion of injunctive relief was a possibility if the non-competition covenant was breached. Reed acknowledged that Conrad Black's prowess in the media world was somewhat known to him and that he was also aware that Black and Radler were partners in a media company, Horizon, that owned community newspapers. But he adamantly denied that he cared about the non-competition agreements that were inserted.

As Jack Boultbee's attorney, Gus Newman, pointed out in cross-examination, "Fiduciarily — if there is such a word," Michael Reed had a credibility problem of his own to overcome. The almost half-a-billion-dollar purchase price paid by CNHI came from a retirees' fund in Alabama. The fact that Reed had entered into a sham non-competition agreement was never disclosed to the lending fund. For a prosecution that rested on a theme of an abuse of shareholders' trust, the duplicity of their own witness tarnished their position. Of course, Reed did profess to have a moral compass. He balked at the suggestion in the final moments before closing the deal that $9 million of the non-competition payments be diverted to Conrad Black and other senior executives of Hollinger International.

I fail to see how a jury could extend a morsel of credibility to Reed's testimony. It was a shaky start for the prosecutors' case. Conrad Black was the invisible man in the CNHI deals. He never attended a single meeting or was involved in any conversation or email related to the deal. The deals were David Radler productions. Mark Kipnis signed the agreements on behalf of the Hollinger senior executives with "his anti-fraud pen," as Ron Safer described it in his opening. If Black was anywhere in the vicinity of the two blockbuster deals with CNHI, his presence would have been unmistakable; Conrad Black never enters a room quietly.

After court concluded, the Black defence called an urgent meeting for that evening. Eddie Greenspan was concerned that the defence was mounting an untenable position regarding the non-competes. The jury would never accept the proposition that the purchasers desired the non-competition agreements. More importantly, it was unnecessary for the defence to travel down that tortuous road. The real battle lay in convincing the jury that Conrad Black and the other defendants were duped by David Radler into believing that the non-competition agreements with Hollinger Inc. were stipulated by the buyers as a condition of closing just as they were with Hollinger International. This was consistent with a plain reading of the language of the agreements and Black couldn't be expected to be a mind reader. If the Hollinger International shareholders were victims of fraud, the culprit was David Radler and not Conrad Black. In any event, the agreements were ultimately approved by the directors of Hollinger International after receiving the blessings of the audit committee. Even if the non-compete payments to Hollinger Inc. were not an economic benefit to the shareholders and for the good of the company, they were properly disclosed and approved.

The notion that the non-competition agreements with Hollinger Inc. were genuinely requested by the buyers was discarded the next day. In two deals completed within a few days of each other, Hollinger had sold off a series of American community newspapers. The first deal was with Forum Communications in Fargo, North Dakota. A couple of Hollinger papers, including the *Jamestown Sun*, were sold for $14 million. In the second deal, about twenty newspapers from Hollinger International's inventory were sold off to the Midwestern company Paxton Media Group. In both deals, the purchasers testified unchallenged that they had no interest in the non-competes with Hollinger Inc. (for $600,000 in total) and didn't care if they were in or out. Lloyd Case, Forum's president, stated that he had barely heard of Conrad Black and didn't view either him or Hollinger International as viable competitive threats.

While his defence was meeting to discuss a dramatic shift in their approach to the buyers' evidence, Conrad Black was in his hotel room at the Ritz-Carlton working through the quiet hours of the night preparing a list of footnotes for his biography of Richard Nixon that was soon due to be released. Black was supremely confident; the cocky air he displayed to the media outside the courtroom was entirely genuine. He was the most composed and self-assured criminal defendant that I have ever encountered in a legal career that has spanned more than twenty years. I became convinced that it wasn't an act. Conrad Black seemingly had ice in his veins and remained unperturbed by the huge stakes that were involved with the trial, including the potential for a sentence that would secure him a place in prison for the rest of his life.

During a break I overheard him in the hallway discussing a recent provincial election in Quebec where the ruling Liberal party was confronted with forming a minority government. Black had a special connection to the province of Quebec. It was in Sherbrooke where he and Radler had bought their first newspaper and ran it successfully.

Perhaps Black's supreme sense of confidence related to a mystery in the case that I believe I have solved. The special committee first reported that Conrad Black had stolen $400 million from the shareholders. From the moment that the indictment against Black was announced by Patrick Fitzgerald, the amount of money that he and his band of cohorts were alleged to have looted from the Hollinger International shareholders was roughly estimated at the far lower figure of $84 million. That figure stuck until Jeffrey Cramer's opening statement, when it was announced that the amount of the fraud was $60 million. The substantial shrinkage of $24 million required an explanation.

Had Cramer simply misspoken? He was already under a surprising attack from the former lead prosecutor against Black, Robert Kent, for presenting "sort of a generic one-size-fits-all, relatively brief opening statement"[2] that left the prosecution open and vulnerable to attack. Eric Sussman was seething about Kent's very public betrayal.

I rejected the contention that the $60-million figure was merely a slip of the tongue. Black's prosecutors were far too diligent and hard-working to make such a grave error. The answer was fairly obvious. It could be traced to the non-competition agreement for approximately $24 million signed between Conrad Black and the CanWest Communications after the sale of a series of Canadian newspapers including the *National Post*. That would account for the difference. CanWest was canned. The prosecution had reluctantly accepted that it would never persuade a jury that the non-competition agreement between CanWest and Conrad Black involved any fraudulent conduct, since CanWest owner Izzy Asper had genuinely insisted that Conrad Black and David Radler be parties to an agreement not to compete because he feared them as competitors. Although Asper has since died, his son Leonard was expected to testify and support that position. An essential pillar of Conrad Black's defence would therefore be established.

The dropping of CanWest from the case against Black marked a concession that non-competes in the Canadian and American markets were treated quite differently. Of course Radler was the catalyst for the agreements in the American media markets. Why wouldn't Black insist on adopting the CanWest model if he was a party to the American agreements? If the jurors begin to ask this question, then the defence has moved one step closer to achieving a not-guilty verdict for Conrad Black.

APRIL 4–5

Fred Creasey, Hollinger's former controller, tells the court that Black's use of a company jet for a Bora Bora vacation raised concerns but was eventually approved by Boultbee and written off as a business expense. The defence attacks him for exaggerating the cost of the flight.

FLY ME TO THE MOON

As I wait patiently each morning in line to get my precious seat in the courtroom, I keep waiting for one of the deputies to pass by with coffee and donuts. Alas, one arrives but only to admonish us that the judge said that there was to be no talking during sidebars, even when the jury was out of the courtroom. I can only pass the time in line chatting with the many colourful journalists assembled to cover the trial. Mark Steyn and I formed an early bond as courtroom companions. We were among the small group of bloggers attending the trial. Steyn was a successful writer and a definite insider in the Conrad Black camp. He was friends with Black and more closely with Barbara Amiel and they regularly dined together in Chicago during the trial.

My first encounter with Steyn occurred in line in the first couple days of the trial. I observed Tom Bower and Steyn engaged in a rousing discussion about the intricacies of the CanWest deal. It was like watching two Trekkies at a *Star Trek* convention debating the merits of a particular episode. At one point I felt the urge to shout, "Who cares?" but I doubted that would be greeted warmly by either man.

Steyn shared with me his first-hand knowledge that David Radler was still involved in the newspaper business. Radler contacted him to inquire about the possibility of carrying Steyn's regular column in his local newspapers. Radler offered him the paltry sum of $3 a column. Steyn refused the insulting offer that would barely cover the cost of a train ride from the airport to the courthouse.

Christie Blatchford, who was covering the trial for the *Globe and Mail*, told me that my codename in her BlackBerry was the name of my hotel in Chicago. I was hereby to be known as InterContinental Steve. I was beginning to feel accepted as a fellow journalist. I even shook Dominick Dunne's hand when he arrived at court. He had been following the beginning of the sensational Phil Spector murder trial in Los Angeles. It was clear to me that Dunne had some catching up to do at the Conrad Black trial. "Who is that?" he asked a reporter. The man he pointed to was Edward Genson, one of Black's lead counsel.

One poignant observation from the press gallery was that we may be the only trial proceeding in the Dirksen courthouse. The frequency of draconian sentences meted out to the lonely defendants who brave the stormy winds of a trial and lose is likely encouraging a host of guilty pleas. The conviction rate has been cited to me at different times as being well over 90 percent. The Supreme Court of Canada once highlighted in a decision that 85 percent of offenders in America either pleaded guilty or pleaded no contest.[3]

The trial heard from a former controller at Hollinger International, Fred Creasey, who worked with Conrad Black and the other senior executives out of the ornate head office at 10 Toronto Street. In the years between 1998 and 2002, Creasey met Black, the CEO of Hollinger International, about four or five times a year. Now, either Conrad Black was extremely anti-social or he wasn't present at the office very often. Surely they would have bumped into each other more than a handful of times in Hollinger's catered lunchroom.

One defence lawyer in poor taste suggested privately that Creasey might have to undress to liven his testimony. However, it was Conrad Black who was being dressed down by the witness. Consider the following sample question posed to Creasey by the prosecutor: "Generally speaking, Mr. Creasey, does a 10-Q contain more or less information than a 10-K?" (These are quarterly and annual filings with the Securities and Exchange Commission, respectively.)

Creasey testified about the delayed and incomplete disclosure to the SEC of various non-compete agreements both in Canada and in the United States. For example, an approximately $12-million non-compete payment to Conrad Black in the $3.2-billion CanWest deal was not disclosed to the SEC in an annual report in a timely fashion. Creasey described a conversation with Black in which he complained that Black hadn't done a very good job of explaining the non-compete payments in the CanWest deal to the public. Creasey professed not to understand the agreements.

I expect that Eddie Greenspan will start his cross-examination by asking Creasey if he understood the balance sheet that disclosed the enormous profits for the Hollinger International shareholders that resulted from the CanWest deal, which was personally engineered by Conrad Black.

There was also some issue as to whether the audit committee of Hollinger International approved all of the non-compete payments in the sales of the American community newspapers. The SEC filings for the year 2000 recorded that Lord Black and three other executives of the company received in total more than $15 million in payments deriving from the sale of newspaper properties in the United States. When related questions were raised by the audit committee a few years later, Black delivered an angry email to Creasey advising him to ignore anything the head of the superfluous committee said, as events were about to supersede them. Black clarified the matter the next day in a calmer email, but his crude outburst will likely linger with the jury. One astute journalist noted that perhaps a collection of Conrad Black's erudite emails should be published. My suggestion for the title was *Lord of the Web*. It has a nice ring to it.

The evidence in Fred Creasey's examination shifted from newspapers to airplanes. Creasey was an exacting man when he set his mind to a task (one worthy quote: "I was aware of what I was aware of"), and he was responsible for allocating costs to the two company airplanes with the exotic names of G-2 and G-4. They were primarily used by David Radler and Conrad Black. Black's plane cost the company about $7 million every year, while Radler's added up to a more conservative $2 to $3 million annually. I estimated that the cost of operating the planes, at $6,000 an hour, was comparable to the cost of Black's seven-member defence team. For some of the disgruntled Hollinger International shareholders that may seem like poetic justice. However, it is the shareholders who are carrying the preponderance of the legal costs for the defence in the trial.

Creasey spotted a one-week trip to Bora Bora that Black took with Barbara in the summer of 2001, using the company jet at a cost of $565,326. "Bora Bora did not fit my allocation and methodology," Creasey declared in the language that accountants use to dazzle friends at parties. When the matter was raised with Black, his swift reply came by email: "Fred, as these are mainly within the U.S. let's charge to Hollinger International. I'm happy to pay, as to half, personally, if this causes difficulties." There were in fact American stopovers on the trip. Following Black's instructions and without any formulated policy, Creasey billed half of the trip to Ravelston and the remainder to Hollinger International.

The defence's position was that Creasey had greatly overestimated the cost of the trip. Creasey agreed that the half share that was billed to Black far exceeded the actual cost to Hollinger International. Greenspan called it "the most expensive flight to Bora Bora in the history of mankind," and suggested that its actual cost was closer to $75,000. How much does a trip to the moon cost? The prosecutors objected to the question, but I suspected that Greenspan didn't care that the judge rescued them on this occasion. The point was established that the real profiteers at his client's jet-setting expense were the shareholders of Hollinger International.

My mind wandered far from the courtroom as I entertained the notion of a half-a-million-dollar trip to a remote island in the Pacific Ocean. Were the serving plates on the plane made of gold? Did the fruit basket greeting the Blacks at their hotel room arrive with a string of pearls? Was Nelly Furtado hired to serenade the couple with "Maneater" in the bedroom? The possibilities were endless.

Greenspan asked Creasey, who had approved the trip's expense, if he had any knowledge of the number of business calls Conrad Black made or emails he forwarded during the trip. In the absence of specific information, Creasey could only agree that Black was a hard worker and that his "life is his job."

Patrick Fitzgerald, another person clearly dedicated to his job, observed some of the court proceedings the morning that Creasey's cross-examination began. I watched as he spent almost the entire time scribbling notes on an unrelated matter and seemed to be a disinterested spectator. During the break, he was chuckling with Eric Sussman. I doubted that they were amused by the testimony in the courtroom. Despite some thirty-five hours and five separate meetings devoted by the prosecutors to preparing their witness, Creasey was evasive and appeared selectively forgetful during his cross-examination. I learned that one defence lawyer began to call him "Queasy." On some of the SEC documents Creasey was described as the "principle accounting officer," but a better title would have been "principle unaccountable officer." For someone who acknowledged that his primary role at Hollinger was the co-ordination of financial reporting, he assumed very little responsibility when he testified.

It was a groundbreaking day at the Conrad Black trial. The jury was exposed to the incontrovertible fact that the non-compete payments to Black and other senior executives were disclosed to lawyers from the leading Canadian law firm of Torys, a team of auditors from the international accounting firm KPMG, and the audit committee at Hollinger International itself. Following a Hollinger Inc. audit committee meeting held on March 2, 2002, a KPMG report noted that "all such [non-compete] payments had been approved by an independent committee of the Board of Hollinger International and the Auditors had reviewed the relevant Minutes of the independent committee and were satisfied."

The non-compete payments that were plainly disclosed in various public filings and financial statements included $80 million advanced in the CanWest sale and more than $15 million in connection with the sales of American community newspapers in 2000. When Pat Tuite suggested that the chair of the audit committee, James Thompson, was a very tall individual (and therefore less easily intimidated), Judge St. Eve interrupted and jokingly said, "Don't start talking about height." It was one moment in the trial when everyone in the courtroom erupted in laughter.

Conrad Black appreciated that the defence was scoring points with the jury. At one point, he glanced back and smiled at his daughter, Alana, who grinned broadly. Document after document was shown to the jury with the same eleven magic words: "The company's independent directors have approved the terms of these payments." This represented the heart of the defence of Conrad Black. The next phase of the trial would continue with a parade of outside professionals, including a couple of lawyers from Torys and the New York law firm of Cravath. The two law firms apparently had provided conflicting advice about the need to disclose the non-compete agreements with various individuals in the CanWest deal.

Ed Genson was finally beginning to warm up to me. We had a timely discussion during a break about matzo pancakes and Chicago delis. "If it wasn't for the publicity and big money in the case," he stated, "Conrad Black would never have been charged." I asked him to clarify what he meant by "publicity." "Publicity for the prosecutors," he answered. Tuite later added that the prosecutors hadn't laid a glove against the defendants in the case.

While Black was winning the trial, the task for the defence was far from finished. The prosecution would mount more Bora Bora lifestyle evidence that would not rest well with jurors who were currently earning $40 a day for jury duty. David Radler was set to draw Conrad Black into a sinister conspiracy to defraud the Hollinger International shareholders.

My day ended with a dinner with the charming Dominick Dunne and a few locals at Gibsons, a well-known steakhouse in Chicago. (As a true contrarian, I ordered salmon.) Dunne complained that whenever he met Eddie Greenspan in the men's washroom at the courthouse, Greenspan didn't bother to say anything to Dunne or shake his hand. The two men had had a prior public spat that spilled onto the pages of *Vanity Fair* magazine.

I enjoyed listening to Dunne's endearing stories about his celebrity crowd, although his meal was cut short when he nearly choked on a piece of steak. He was saved by our server, Mohammed, who spent about fifteen minutes alone with Dunne and then paid for a cab to return him to his hotel. It was a touching display of kindness by a server who had earlier been scolded by Dunne for not recalling the precise way that his steak should be cooked.[4]

I was interested to learn from Dunne that Nancy Kissinger was livid with Conrad Black for entangling her husband in his trial. Henry Kissinger was one of the cast of luminaries whom Black had enlisted for the Hollinger board. Nancy worried that poor Henry's reputation might now be sullied. At the very least he would merit a mention in Black's biography of Richard Nixon.

SENSES AND SENSIBILITIES

While I profess to have no particular interest in profanity, it has its proper place and time. One of those approved places is the courtroom. Witnesses are sworn to tell the truth (in America a promise suffices) as they recount the vulgar details of overheated and angry exchanges that they participated

87

in. On countless occasions, I have been in a Canadian courtroom where a judge prevails upon a hedging witness to repeat the precise slurs that were spoken. "We have all heard it before," the judge adds with a benign smile.

Not, evidently, in Chicago. The truth in a Chicago courtroom is an edited version of events. In a critical moment of the trial, Gus Newman began to cross-examine Thomas Henson about a negotiating session at the *Chicago Sun-Times* building conducted with David Radler over the CNHI deal. Henson portrayed Radler as a rude and abusive man who was prepared to feign anger if it assisted in closing a deal. Prior to storming indignantly out of the meeting, Radler had stood inches from Henson, the witness recalled, and raised his voice: "You're wasting my fill-in-the-blank time, and you wasted your fill-in-the-blank time." Ouch, that really hurts.

Are the jurors at the Conrad Black trial so delicate that we dare not risk offending them? I wonder if the same standard is applied to the criminal defendant who has hurled obscenities at his arresting officer. Put the middle finger of each hand firmly in the air if you accept that the officer's statement in court would be recited in the following fashion: "He said, 'You cops are nothing but fill-in-the-blank pigs and you can all go to fill-in-the-blank.'"

As a further matter, consider the dilemma of defence attorneys confronting the task of cross-examining David Radler. The cross-examination about his *Sun-Times* tirade would proceed as follows:

> Q: Now Mr. Radler, did you tell Tom Henson that "You're wasting my fill-in-the-blank time"?
> A: No.
> Q: You didn't say that?
> A: No, I never said anything about filling in the blanks.
> Q: You didn't?
> A: No, I told him that he was wasting my time and his time.
> Q: Before you used the word "time," did you mention "fill-in-the-blank"?
> A: How many times do I have to repeat to you, counsellor, that I never told Henson to fill in the blank?

It has therefore been established that it is permissible to describe a protagonist as a slut in the elevator but not to declare someone to be vermin in the courtroom. The Black trial has been a real lesson in courtroom etiquette for even a veteran trial lawyer like me. I am a particular favourite of Kevin, the rather stern but efficient court deputy, because I bow my head and face Judge St. Eve each time I enter or leave the courtroom. I advise Kevin that it is a sign of respect for the court. "You English guys can really show the rest of them some manners," Kevin whispered to me one morning. I resisted informing Kevin that Canadians are distinct from their Commonwealth brethren across the ocean. We have no Old Bailey and our version of European football is called soccer. And, as Conrad Black has discovered to his chagrin, the two countries, Canada and England, have separate passports.

In the Chicago courtroom it seems decorum is a requirement only for those seated in the public gallery. The media has been admonished that talking during a sidebar may result in banishment from the courtroom, as will the cardinal transgression of possessing a ringing cellphone. Two chastened members of the press (one from the local ABC station) were forced to depart for cellphone violations. They have not been seen at the Dirksen courthouse since.

A different standard of civility applies to counsel in the courtroom. I have watched as lawyers routinely make intemperate objections while seated. There are more objections in one day of the Black trial than you might expect to see in a two- or three-week jury trial in Canada. The rapid-fire objections are generally made by title and without explanation. "Objection, asked and answered, Judge," would be a typical example. The rulings of the judge generally follow with the dispatch of a sushi chef with a chopping knife.

As I watched the flurry of objections one morning from the courtroom gallery, I was reminded of a scene from the film *A Civil Action*. John Travolta portrays a plaintiff's counsel bringing a lawsuit on behalf of eight families in Woburn, Massachusetts, who claimed that their children contracted leukemia from drinking water polluted by two nearby corporations, Beatrice and W.R. Grace. The attorney for the defendant corporations, played by Robert Duvall, shared his bevy of courtroom secrets with a class of law students. One favourite tactic dealt with objections. Objections were always an effective tool to break the rhythm of the opponent's cross-examination.

"The fewer objections he gets, the better his case will get," Duvall warned the students. "If you should fall asleep at the counsel table, the first thing you should say when you wake up is 'I object.'" (As a word of caution, this should not be attempted in bed with your partner.)

The attorneys never make their submissions respectfully. Indeed they are never fearful of advising the judge what they think or believe the correct ruling should be. "I don't care a whit what you think, Mr. Skurka," any Canadian judge would gruffly interpose if I dared to emulate my American counterparts. While Eddie Greenspan has bravely attempted to import some of the Canadian customs to the courtroom (including his accent, which Genson told the jury was funny but only because he's from Canada), I have yet to hear him refer to any of the prosecutors as "my friend." There is a frosty relationship between Greenspan and the four "kids," as they have been sometimes referred to, at the prosecutors' table. There is never a word exchanged or even a simple greeting in the morning. The antipathy hasn't spilled over to the trial, but the credit for that rests largely on the watchful eye of a vigilant trial judge. Any hint of discord in the courtroom results in a sidebar being called for a private huddle with the parties. However, like any lemon-scented air freshener, the sweet odour lingers only temporarily.

Eddie Greenspan assured me that the defence team has not yet decided whether Conrad Black would testify in his own defence. I accepted his word on the subject. He was unhappy that one prominent criminal lawyer in Toronto questioned why he didn't pursue a plea bargain for his client. Black's instructions were clear and unequivocal. He had insisted on a trial and a fight to the finish. Even his wife's brooding pessimism about his prospects at an American trial couldn't dissuade him from mounting a vigorous challenge. A guilty plea was entirely out of the question.

The defence team understood that a realistic assessment of Black's need to testify could occur only after David Radler testified. Radler was the only witness at the trial who could directly implicate Conrad Black. Months had been devoted to preparing for his cross-examination. Greenspan viewed the cross-examination of Radler as the most important of his legendary career.

Radler's golden deal with the prosecutors was already secure. After Black's trial was completed, he would be able to take advantage of his front-of-the-line ticket and begin serving his abbreviated sentence in a British

Columbia penitentiary near his home and family. Radler was reported to have taken half a sleeping pill the night before his guilty plea, confirming that he was only somewhat restless about his predicament. He had already emerged as the final contestant in an ultimate game of *Survivor* with his former cohorts at Hollinger International. When he eventually entered the courtroom as the prosecution's star witness in the case, he could gaze calmly at the desperate faces of the castoffs from their shared adventure. It was a race of the swiftest for self-preservation and he was the clear winner. Membership in the prosecutors' camp does have its privileges.

The question remained whether Conrad Black would heed his own lawyers' sage advice about testifying. Ultimately, the decision would be his to make. Black, a historian who had written about the lives of two American presidents, Franklin D. Roosevelt and Richard Nixon, would need to study the illuminating lesson of another president, Bill Clinton, for guidance in his current situation.

The threat to Clinton's presidency and possibly his legacy can be traced to a single decision he made about a legal case. In his book *The Survivor*,[5] former *Washington Post* reporter John Harris chronicled Clinton's time in the White House. The failure to settle the Paula Jones civil case began a chain of events that eventually required the president to testify about his relationship with Monica Lewinsky. It was his allegedly untruthful answers on that subject that served as the catalyst to the subsequent impeachment hearings.

John Podesta, Clinton's deputy chief of staff, was in the Oval Office when the crucial meeting took place with Robert Bennett, the president's attorney, to decide how to proceed with the Paula Jones lawsuit. A presentation was made by Bennett outlining the various arguments for settlement. He made it abundantly clear to Clinton that he supported a settlement as long as the terms weren't so severe as to depict Paula Jones as being truthful about her supposed tryst with the president. The settlement could be convincingly portrayed to the American people as removing a political albatross to free Clinton to carry on with running the country.

Bennett then laid out the chances of winning the case if it went to trial. By the end of the meeting, Bennett had made no firm recommendation and left President Clinton to make the decision in the absence of any strong advice. "Podesta, who was himself a lawyer, would later cite the case as an object lesson in how lawyers can let their clients down by being too respectful," Harris wrote. "There are times, and this was one, where somebody needed to grab the client by the lapel, shake him, and scream: 'Are you out of your goddamn mind?' No one said this to the president of the United States."[6]

The parallel lesson for Conrad Black was striking. Would his boundless arrogance cause him to treat his legal team as potted plants or would he genuinely listen to his highly skilled counsel's advice? This question remained one of the great mysteries of the trial.

CHICAGO JUSTICE

Eddie Greenspan has decided that he will go on the lecture circuit after the trial to speak about the astonishing differences between the American and Canadian systems of justice. Everything in America is designed to get the defendant convicted, he explained to me. "Moldaver is dead wrong. This is what the result would be if we let it happen." In a speech to the Criminal Lawyers' Association, Justice Michael Moldaver of the Ontario Court of Appeal (and a former law partner of Greenspan's) had warned that criminal trials were spinning out of control and that "long criminal trials are a cancer in our criminal justice system and they pose a threat to its very existence."[7]

Greenspan's premonition about a tumultuous ride at trial was realized before he ever appeared in Chicago for the case. He received a call from Edward Genson, who told him that he had some bad news. The U.S. Attorney's Office prosecuting their client was considering charging Greenspan with obstructing justice for refusing to turn over the boxes taken from 10 Toronto Street. Greenspan felt he was simply protecting his client's legal rights by forcing the American prosecutors to use the Mutual Legal Assistance Treaty (MLAT) to seize the boxes. He couldn't believe that he was now being threatened with the same serious criminal offence his client faced. "I went ballistic," he told me. "These prosecutors didn't care about other people's legal systems." He was reminded of the people who were killed in Panama City during Manuel Noriega's abduction to be tried in the United States.

While the issue soon faded, Greenspan had experienced first-hand the feeling of being caught in the same choking grip that ensnared his client.

Greenspan had strong views about the trial judge as well. He woke up one morning in the final few days leading up to the trial to find her picture on the front page of the *Toronto Star*. She was a diminutive woman, but the picture was distorted to make her look seven feet tall.[8] However, it was the content of the article that followed that provoked Greenspan's ire. In it, the judge's father provocatively declared that his daughter would keep Black in line during the trial.

Greenspan immediately contacted Genson at his home. Genson was unmoved by his co-counsel's disconcerting attitude. He knew the judge and had conducted cases in her courtroom. Greenspan wanted her removed from the case. A Canadian judge wouldn't dare engage in a similar stunt. "You don't understand — she's better than 75 percent of the judges we have," Genson admonished him. He also refused to believe that the judge had authorized her father's strident comment. Amy St. Eve, a youthful George Bush appointee and former Whitewater prosecutor, was, according to Ed Genson, a trial judge that the defence could ill afford to lose.

It was still too early in the trial for me to form my own independent assessment of the judge. Greenspan's comments remained with me as a cautionary flag, especially when he told me that he even missed O'Driscoll. We both laughed after he made the stunning comment. Justice John O'Driscoll (fondly known as "OD") had been widely known in Toronto before his retirement to be the absolute worst draw for any lawyer to get as a trial judge. As a lawyer, O'Driscoll had defended Jimi Hendrix nine months before his untimely death in a London, England, hotel room. Barristers were known to sob openly when they learned that OD would take carriage of their client's case. If there was a top ten list for the judge with the most murder convictions reversed on appeal because of grievous trial errors, O'Driscoll would surely be near the top of the list. One lawyer in Windsor was found guilty of contempt for impudently stating during the trial that O'Driscoll was "the captain of the Crown's ship."

Whenever I was asked by the judicial selection committee to offer my opinion on prospective appointments to the Ontario judiciary I assumed the task seriously. If I were to choose one quality that a judge must possess, it would be the ability not to prejudge the evidence. One judge confessed to me over a beer in his backyard that he continued to struggle through every trial fighting the irresistible urge to leap to conclusions about the defendant's guilt. If he was inclined to convict at the end of the case, he would insist on reserving his decision until the following morning to allow himself time to reflect on the evidence presented at trial.

Allow me to demonstrate the inherent flaw that is common in many of us to jump to the worst conclusions rather than consider that there may be an innocent explanation. The example is drawn from an actual Powerball lottery. Twenty-nine American states participate in this particular lottery in which the jackpot is paid individually to each winner. Each contestant is required to pick a combination of five or six numbers. The odds of choosing the five numbers that would be drawn are one in 3 million. In this Powerball lottery, 110 players chose the same five winning numbers — 22, 28, 32, 33, and 39. Statistically, there should have been only four or five such winners, and the lottery was compelled to pay almost $19 million in unexpected payouts that stretched its reserve fund to its limit. The Powerball officials were quick to suspect fraud, and the executive director of the lottery suspected that a devious scheme was in place to cheat the system.

The mystery of the Powerball fraud was solved when the gleeful winners began to claim their prizes. Each of them reported that their numbers were gathered from fortune cookies that were handed out in various Chinese restaurants. The trail was followed to a Long Island factory owned by Wonton Food that produced 4 million fortune cookies every day. The investigation revealed that there were in fact 4 million cookies that contained the winning combination of numbers.[9]

The story vividly captures the perils of prejudging a situation before all of the relevant facts are gathered. A second lesson is to eat in as many Chinese food restaurants as possible and to pay attention to your fortune cookies.

AL CAPONE, JOHN GOTTI, AND CONRAD BLACK

I was standing outside the courtroom ready to dial my law office at the break when I noticed him approaching. His hand was outstretched and I began to panic. Do I call him Lord Black or Mr. Black? There were just seconds to make the decision. "Mr. Skurka, I have seen you on television," he remarked. Lord or Mr., which would it be? My heart was racing. "Thank you, Mr. Black," I replied as we shook hands. He smiled politely and walked away. At the last moment I had recalled that Eddie Greenspan had earlier brought a motion seeking to forbid the prosecutors from referring to his client as His Lordship.

It reminded me of a murder case in West Chester, Pennsylvania, where the defence attorney for a defendant, Demetrio Fiorentino, had objected to any prosecution witness referring to his client's nickname, "Scuz." It is fortunate for Conrad Noir (a.k.a. Lord Tubby) that none of his colourfully wicked nicknames can be used in court.

While court was in recess last Friday, Judge Amy St. Eve released her ruling denying the *Chicago Tribune*'s motion to disclose the names of the jurors in the case. The reason was summarized in one terse sentence: "In a case like this that has garnered intense national and international media attention, releasing juror names during the pendency of trial threatens the integrity of jurors' ability to absorb the evidence and later render a verdict based only on that evidence."

It is interesting to note that on the jurors' questionnaire, there was a question devoted to the profile of the case and the ensuing media coverage. A few members of the jury panel voiced their concern that their privacy might be disrupted by an intrusive media. The judge allayed any such concerns by emphasizing the grave impropriety of such conduct. The likely reason for her decision to ban publication of the jurors' identities rests with the debacle that occurred at the end of the fraud trial of former Illinois governor George Ryan. Two jurors were dismissed during deliberations after the *Tribune* uncovered their failure to reveal previous run-ins with the law. The reconstituted jury convicted Ryan and the interrupted deliberations are now the subject of an appeal. Judge St. Eve explicitly referred to the Ryan case in her ruling. It seems to this simple Canadian lawyer that the *Chicago Tribune* should indeed be applauded for its efforts to expose possible malfeasance and deceit by jurors in a criminal case. It highlights the very reason that the identity of jurors should be part of the public record. The honest juror has nothing to fear.

I simply refuse to abide by any decision to maintain a nameless jury. I have therefore assumed the task of henceforth identifying the seventeen jurors and alternates with Lewis Carroll characters. From this point forward, the jurors shall be named as follows: Alice, the White Knight, the Caterpillar, the Dormouse, the Knave of Hearts, the King of Hearts,

Humpty Dumpty, the Mad Hatter, the Cheshire Cat, the Duchess, Bill the Lizard, Tweedledum, Tweedledee, the Mock Turtle, the March Hare, the White Rabbit, and the Queen of Hearts. I predict that Humpty Dumpty will be selected as the foreman and will be ably assisted by all the king's horses and all the king's men.

APRIL 10

Prosecutors introduce correspondence between Hollinger executives about Black's use of the jet. "I gather there is a move afoot to make me pay $600,000 for the cost of our flight to Bora Bora," Black wrote to Atkinson. "Needless to say, no such outcome is acceptable." Defence attorneys contend the audit committee insisted Black use the plane because of security concerns.

BORING BORING

You can tell that the trial is getting dull when court watchers begin to look forward to the lawyers' testimony. Where is Roxy Hart with her "razzle dazzle" when you need her? The highlight of the day for me was meeting a United States attorney from Patrick Fitzgerald's team who maintained that he had no idea what the case was about. The prosecutor spoke effusively about Judge St. Eve. Words like *intelligent*, *hard-working*, and *efficient* came effortlessly from his mouth. The word *fair* was noticeably absent. (I always worry when prosecutors praise a judge.)

I can certainly attest to the judge's admirable work ethic. I had to get up at four o'clock this morning in Toronto to make it to court in time for the 9:15 start to the court day. The day continued with Fred Creasey, the "hear no evil, see no evil, speak no evil" controller and financial overseer at the Hollinger companies. "What is a hippie?" Ron Safer asked him in cross-examination. Although temporarily jolted from my sleep-sitting state, I was disappointed to learn that *HIPI* is the acronym for Hollinger International Publishing Inc.

Matters seemed to pick up when Safer questioned the witness about his knowledge of The Gap. Did Conrad Black's vast empire extend beyond the *Chicago Sun-Times* to include jeans and T-shirts, I wondered. Sadly, it was the other gap. Generally Accepted Accounting Principles (GAAP) was the governing standard for auditors. As Safer cross-examined Creasey about the plain reading of various corporate documents and filings, he made it clear that "I'm only asking you from a GAAP perspective." The questionable handwritten wiring instructions in the second CNHI deal directing that $9.5 million be wired to Black, Radler, Boultbee, and Atkinson were now lauded for their open disclosure to the accountant reviewing the closing book. "There is an audit trail," Safer noted, which allowed accountants and auditors to scrutinize the transactions and determine where the money was going and coming from.

The importance of GAAP is that it was used to plug the remaining leak in the defence theory. While the non-compete payments to the individual executives were included in various quarterly and annual reports filed with the SEC and distributed to Hollinger International shareholders, the non-compete payments made to the holding company, Hollinger Inc., were not disclosed. In 1999 the total of these non-competes was about $21 million. This represented a prominent roadblock to success with the jury for Black and his co-defendants. As Safer effectively adduced from Creasey in cross-examination, no one in the Hollinger accounting field offices, such as Roland McBride, flagged these non-competes and suggested that they be added to financial disclosure transactions under GAAP. The same was true for KPMG, Creasey, and any member of his staff. The board of directors at Hollinger Inc. was also aware of the payments.

The position of the defence ultimately will be that while there may have been delayed filings of complete information or even gaps in disclosure of all the various non-compete payments, there was no attempt to conceal anything from the Hollinger International shareholders. Mistakes were made that were not even detected by the very professionals and gatekeepers charged with the responsibility to monitor the complex financial transactions. Even the re-examination of Creasey by prosecutor Julie Ruder seemed better suited to a grievance filed with the SEC rather than a weighty criminal fraud trial.

There was one ominous cloud for the defence today. Peter Atkinson's junior attorney, Michael Schachter, appeared to stake the unique position in cross-examination that his client perceived the moneys received from the Hollinger International newspaper sales as management fees or bonuses rather than non-competition payments. The jury will never accept the dual premise that the payments were bonuses for Atkinson but non-compete payments for Black and Boultbee. It is a formula that spells disaster for all of the defendants. I describe it as the "Maxwell Smart defence." As KAOS's Mr. Big is set to destroy him, Smart begins the following exchange with his adversary:

> Maxwell Smart: At the moment, seven Coast Guard cutters are converging on us. Would you believe that?
> Mr. Big: I find that hard to believe.
> Maxwell Smart: Hmmm ... would you believe six?
> Mr. Big: I don't think so.
> Maxwell Smart: How about two cops in a rowboat?

The Maxwell Smart defence reminds me of a great advocacy lecture I once heard given by the late Irving Younger. Younger told the story of a farmer's goat that broke into a neighbour's gated fence and ate the cabbage that had been planted. In the ensuing lawsuit, the owner of the goat's defence was presented as follows:

1. I don't own a goat.
2. If I do own a goat, it didn't break into the defendant's yard.
3. If my goat did enter the yard, it didn't eat the cabbage.
4. If it did eat the cabbage, my goat mistakenly believed the cabbage belonged to me.
5. If my goat wasn't mistaken, it was insane

This story makes a telling point. The spray-gun method of presenting conflicting theories to a jury spells destruction to the defence.

Barbara Amiel grasped the point from her seat in the courtroom gatherings. She passed a note to Conrad Black that read, "Whose side is Atkinson on?" Her husband's response reflected his eternal sense of optimism about the trial. "Don't worry, it will all work out in the end." Barbara Amiel showed the notes to Mark Steyn in the cafeteria on the second floor. She told him that she wasn't so sure.

THE SLEEPING GIANT

"I object on the basis of relevancy, speculation, foundation." Those words were actually uttered today in court by prosecutor Julie Ruder in response to a question posed in re-cross-examination by Eddie Greenspan. "Sustained," ruled Judge St. Eve. We have witnessed more foundation at this trial than can be found at an Estée Lauder factory. Now, I have been a jury lawyer for more than twenty years and an adjunct law professor at Osgoode Hall Law School for over a decade. I must admit that I have absolutely no clue what an objection based on "foundation" means.

There is also the objection of last resort used by the prosecutors at this trial, namely, "argumentative," which from my vantage point in the courtroom translates to a body blow being inflicted to the witness's credibility. If cross-examination is described as the greatest engine to search for truth, then the objection in an American courtroom is the emergency brake. Greenspan was also having some difficulty with the objections being made in the courtroom. He was afraid that if he objected, he would breach yet another rule and would be cited for contempt with the result that he might spend three months in jail. He had a contentious discussion with his fellow defence counsel about objecting. He had been teaching evidence for some thirty years at law school and he still didn't know what "argumentative" means.

There was a moment in the trial today when Eddie Greenspan roused himself from his lethargy. There is no doubt that the maze of rules, procedures, and customs of a Chicago courtroom had reduced Greenspan to a shadow of the courtroom maestro that he was reputed to be. Today marked the first time that Greenspan rose and openly took issue with a prosecutor's tactics. "The door just can't open every time someone says something," an animated Greenspan declared after the prosecution sought to expand their redirect examination of Fred Creasey. The momentum continued with Greenspan's questions of the witness. "Is there a book that lists where accountants can round up or down?" Greenspan asked, eliciting laughter from some of the jurors. Creasey agreed that in 2003, the audit committee of Hollinger adopted a policy that Conrad Black was permitted to use the corporate jet for all of his travels (even to Bora Bora) because of lingering security and terrorism concerns. Bora Bora had been carefully chosen by the prosecution as the cornerstone of its lifestyle fraud allegation against Black, and by the end of Eddie Greenspan's probing questions it had been eviscerated.

APRIL 11–12

Lawyer Darren Sukonick, of Toronto firm Torys LLP, admits in videotaped testimony that he suggested to Hollinger executives that non-compete payments could be used to avoid paying taxes on corporate bonuses.

Lawyers delve into the $3.2-billion deal that saw most of Hollinger's Canadian newspapers sold to CanWest Global in 2000. CanWest asked for non-compete agreements with Black and Radler, but not Atkinson and Boultbee. Prosecutors allege the latter inserted themselves improperly into the deal.

TORY SPELLING

Even the jurors were chuckling when Conrad Black's emails detailing his disastrous trip to Bora Bora were introduced by the prosecution. Prosecutors always get discouraged when jurors laugh at the evidence during a trial. The jurors in this case are well aware of the sentences that are measured by quarters of a century for the white-collar defendants in the Enron, Tyco, and WorldCom cases. There can therefore be nothing amusing to a jury that sees its final port of call at a guilty verdict in a similar corporate looting scheme.

There is another reason introducing the emails was a blunder on the part of the prosecution. There are aspects of them that are very helpful to the defence. For example, Conrad Black wrote in one exchange that "David [Radler] has always put out of mind the implications of being a public company. As I have said before, a degree of accommodation with contemporary norms is what we need." In another email to Peter Atkinson, he agreed that David Radler had been stirring things up and that a policy that governed personal use of the Hollinger planes should be established that took into account that all personal perks were not corrupt. Black emphasized that a policy regarding the planes must distinguish "business, quasi business and non-business expenses." The absence of any pre-existing policy was the Hollinger International board's fault. Was the Bora Bora trip hidden from the company's controller, their auditors, or their lawyers? The answer is a resounding no. The shareholders hardly deserve to cry foul if they now take issue with the expenditure. It is undoubtedly a huge mistake that the trip was included by the prosecutors in the indictment and it will splash to their detriment on the rest of their case. In the parlance of the justice system, this tactical error is described as prosecutorial overreaching.

The Seventh Circuit Bar Association considered a weighty issue at one of its regular meetings for the attorneys in the region. A vote was called for the members to determine the best opening statement made in lawyer movie history. The clear winner was a surprise. It was the statement made by the character played by Joe Pesci in the film *My Cousin Vinny*, which goes like this: "Uh, everything that guy just said is bullshit. Thank you."

Lawyers aren't known for their economy of language, and today the jury was treated to the start of some twelve hours of videotaped testimony from two lawyers from the law firm of Torys who were involved in structuring much of Hollinger International's sale of the *National Post* and the Southam newspaper chain to CanWest for $3.2 billion. The videotape is shown on three television monitors in the courtroom. The jurors understand that the refusal of the Torys witnesses to step into the Dirksen courthouse in Chicago is significant. If Conrad Black had duped them, what possible reason would they have to play hide and seek? It will be clear to the jury that Torys is a prominent law firm in Canada. Black didn't retain his cousin Vinny to work on a deal of this magnitude.

The first lawyer from Torys to begin his testimony, Darren Sukonick, believed that the non-compete agreement with CanWest was legitimate. It doesn't matter that Sukonick testified that a portion of the payments were added quite close to the time that the deal closed. It doesn't matter that he testified that Atkinson asked that both he and

Boultbee be inserted into the agreement to receive money from the non-compete agreements. It isn't determinative that Atkinson wanted the non-compete payments referred to as bonuses. Atkinson may have panicked and mischaracterized the non-compete payments in a more palatable fashion. That attempted ruse doesn't inextricably lead to a conclusion that he was a party to a fraud.

If this was a massive conspiracy, why aren't all the actors reading from the same script? Why would inconsistent positions be advanced to skilled lawyers by the different defendants in the case? Would the lawyers at Torys have included the non-compete agreements to Atkinson and Boultbee if they had any concerns that they were improper? Why did Conrad Black and his wife choose to attend a Wagner opera in Seattle if they knew that he was Hitler's favourite composer? Ignore the last question. I don't want to distract you with a question about perks. That would be prosecutorial overreaching.

The Torys law firm had its genesis in the law firm Tory, Tory, DesLauriers and Binnington. When the firm merged with a New York office, its name changed to Tory, Haythe. The 330-member law firm settled on its present identity after a senior partner was forcibly pushed out for some questionable behaviour. The firm has been beset by some further Hollinger mudslinging that it failed to act in the company's best interests during a series of deals that led to transfers of staggering sums of money to Conrad Black and others. A $30-million settlement with Hollinger followed, leaving the pundits to decipher the reasons for Torys' unlikely misfortune.[10] I have a theory that I am certain is correct. It all relates to the rule of threes.

I was introduced to this rule several years ago at a criminal law conference that I attended in Buckhead, Georgia, just outside of Atlanta. The first speaker was an attorney from New Mexico who shared one of her courtroom secrets with her attentive audience. "Always speak to the jury in sets of threes," she advised. She went on to explain that sprinkling her language with three consecutive words or expressions created a uniquely soothing pitch that struck a memorable chord with jurors. She provided some examples and I began to reflect on some of my own: "Edgar Allen Poe," "Abraham, Isaac, and Jacob," "Blood, sweat, and tears," "Free at last; free at last; thank God almighty we are free at last."

I arrived back in Canada eager to put my new courtroom arsenal to the test. When I presented my passport at Canadian customs, the official politely asked me where I was coming from. "Buckhead," I replied. "Pardon me?" I was startled by the custom officer's terse voice and detected a scowl on his face. "Buckhead," I repeated. There was silence as I was now greeted with a cold stare. Then it dawned on me. The irate customs officer had confused the letter *b* in *Buckhead* with the sixth letter of the alphabet. I quickly turned to the rule of threes to rescue me from my predicament: "Buckhead, Georgia, America," I amended. The scowl was replaced with a smile and I was ushered through customs without any further difficulty.

Torys partner Darren Sukonick (if only it had been Tory, Tory, Tory) continued his uncomfortable videotaped testimony today. In a heated cross-examination, he admitted that it was his idea that Hollinger International pay non-compete fees to company executives as a means of withholding tax on corporate bonuses. As the author of the payment plan, he added in his best *Seinfeld* imitation that he did not think there was anything wrong with that. He further conceded that he had advised Hollinger's lawyer, Mark Kipnis, that the company wasn't required to publicly identify the non-compete fees received.

There are a series of benefits that result to Conrad Black's defence from Sukonick's explosive testimony. The first is that Sukonick is clearly not a partisan of or advocate for the defence and therefore his important concession will ring truer for the jury. Secondly, it severely undermines the upcoming testimony of the prosecution's central witness, David Radler, who is anticipated to tell the jury that he and Conrad Black hatched a bogus scheme to pay themselves bonuses cloaked as non-compete payments. Thirdly, it provides the beginning of a safety net for Conrad Black in the event he chooses not to testify. It leaves the door ajar for Greenspan and Genson to argue to the jury at the end of the trial that there was simply no case for their client to answer. And finally, it develops a credible claim that if the non-compete payments were not always spelled out in various corporate filings and reports, it was the result of Torys' failure either to advise the company executives to disclose them or indeed to urge them against it.

Putting it more succinctly, today was "*Tora, Tora, Tora,*" for the defence.

TILTED

RADLER'S ROTTEN DEAL

Last week I travelled from Chicago society to the Law Society. The trip was far less exotic than it might sound. The Law Society of Upper Canada governs the legal profession in Ontario, and when an invitation was extended to me to speak at a conference, I dutifully agreed as a loyal subject. The topic of the program dealt with communicating with the media and I was joined by such illustrious panellists as John Rosen, a formidable Canadian barrister, and the former chief justice of the province, the Honourable Patrick LeSage. I am always pleased to share a stage with Pat LeSage. He represented the finest qualities in a trial judge.

In his view, trials were not to be determined by polls, demonstrations in the street, or the public whim but rather by the cold, antiseptic light of the courtroom. The individual's right to a fair trial was never to be compromised. In over two decades on the bench, he prided himself on never citing a lawyer for contempt and cautioned his fellow judges about invoking the dreaded c-word in court. His preferred course was to invite the lawyer to appear before him for an informal chat where a velvet hammer was used to warn the wayward lawyer to smarten up. It worked every time.

John Rosen was an early mentor in my career. I worked on my first murder case with him as a student in a case that highlights the stark differences in sentencing in Canada and the United States. The client had been convicted of first-degree murder and after a successful appeal was awaiting his retrial. As with any murder case, the facts were sordid and violent. The deceased man was a drug dealer who trafficked in methamphetamine, better known as speed. His body had been discovered lying face down with his hands cuffed behind his back on a farm west of Lindsay, Ontario. The pathologist's report indicated six gunshot wounds, including a fatal shot that penetrated the brain. Two different guns were used in the shooting.

It was a challenging first trial for our client. He testified in his defence that he was informed of the murder by a friend, who was the dead man's supplier, and as a favour went searching for the body, intending to move it elsewhere. Unable to locate the gravesite, he was headed back to Toronto, along with two other men, when his car was stopped at a gas station. It was about 4:30 in the morning. The officer noticed blood stains in the back seat of the car, along with a new garden spade that had soil attached to it. The connection was eventually made to the homicide.

The new trial had been ordered by the Ontario Court of Appeal on a legal principle that now applies in every criminal case in the country. During the first trial, one of the jurors received anonymous phone calls on a couple of occasions. The caller related to the juror that one of the accused men had killed twice before. The juror discussed the alarming calls with a second juror. Eventually the calls were brought to the attention of the trial judge and he decided to embark on a private inquiry of the two jurors in his chambers with only counsel present. The trial was allowed to resume after assurances were given by the two jurors that they could still decide the case impartially. This secretive process was firmly rejected by the appellate court, which held that every material aspect of a defendant's trial must take place in his presence with a full opportunity to observe the fairness of the proceedings.

Eventually our client's case was resolved after the Crown attorney agreed that he could plead guilty to a charge of second-degree murder for the minimum eligibility of parole after ten years. John Rosen asked me to handle the plea. I can actually say that I spent my very first day as a lawyer in court with freshly pressed robes representing a man who had been sentenced to life imprisonment. It could only go uphill from there.

Both John Rosen and Chief Justice LeSage had also been involved the most notorious case in Canada's history — the Paul Bernardo murder trial. Bernardo was accused of the brutal kidnapping, rape, and murder of two teenage girls, Kristen French and Leslie Mahaffy, in St. Catharines, Ontario. The path to arrest Bernardo began with an unrelated discovery that he could be the suspected serial rapist in an eastern suburb of Toronto. Bernardo's wife, Karla Homolka, was viewed by the police as a potential co-conspirator in the unsolved rapes and they attempted to interview her. Homolka told them nothing and instead retained a local criminal lawyer, George Walker, to assist her. Walker presented the police with a shocking hypothetical question: what consideration would his client receive if she provided solid information backed up by her testimony that Paul Bernardo had murdered Kristen French and Leslie Mahaffy? The police were asked to assume that his vulnerable client had only been complicit in the crimes because she was traumatized and feared for her life. Walker secured opinions from a respected psychiatrist and a psychologist that Homolka's conduct could reasonably be attributed to battered wife syndrome.

The matter was thoroughly reviewed at the highest level of the Attorney General's Office and the prosecution agreed to a ten-year prison sentence for Homolka in exchange for her truthful co-operation. The matter was revisited when Homolka suddenly recalled her role in the death of her sister Tammy, and two years were added to her eventual sentence. The guilty plea and sentencing hearing were completed in advance of Bernardo's trial.

By the time the murder trial began, there was one further significant development in the case. Bernardo's previous counsel had held onto a series of videotapes for over a year that depicted his client torturing and molesting two captive teenagers. Far from the hapless victim that Homolka had portrayed herself as, the videos implicated her as a willing participant. The plea negotiation with Karla Homolka was denounced as a "deal with the devil." There was a collective sense of public outrage that Bernardo's wife had quite literally gotten away with murder.

Chief Justice LeSage presided over the case and John Rosen was Paul Bernardo's counsel. As his client's trial approached, a lingering question troubled Rosen. He wondered, "How can I kill Homolka on the stand? She is smart and has probably studied every transcript associated with the case." Rosen had ably defended hundreds of murder cases and understood that he had no choice but to go for the jugular and expose Homolka as a killer. She wasn't the victim at all but the real perpetrator of the girls' murders. The Crown had made a huge mistake buying into the victimization theory, and Rosen intended to exploit it. He was convinced that a conviction for second-degree murder or even manslaughter was possible for Paul Bernardo.

The planning of a critical cross-examination is an arduous and draining process. Rosen decided that his questioning of Homolka needed to be inspired from within rather than a structured attack on her credibility. He worried that talking about it with anyone, including his law office staff or his wife, would inhibit his spontaneity. The media contingent following the sensational trial were placing bets as to how Rosen would begin his cross-examination. Not a single reporter predicted it correctly.

John Rosen watched intently as Homolka answered the prosecutor's questions over the course of six full days. He studied the jury and observed them shifting in their seats. He felt that the jurors were showing visible discomfort and even anger with Homolka's contrived portrayal of herself as an abject victim.

Chief Justice LeSage called on Rosen to begin his questioning, and he strode purposefully to the witness stand. His plan was to have the jury snap to attention as he demonstrated to Homolka who the true victims in the case were. "Who's that?" Rosen demanded in a booming voice that could be heard at the back of the courtroom. Rosen was still pointing at the photograph in his hand while Homolka replied in a subdued voice that it was her sister. "That was your sister when she was alive, right?" Rosen shot back immediately. Homolka could only agree. Rosen then marched to the registrar's desk and pulled out a second photo that had been entered as an exhibit. It was placed in front of the witness's face and she was asked to identify it. On this occasion, Rosen didn't wait for a response. "That's a picture of your dead sister after having her drugged and sexually assaulted. Correct?" Homolka agreed. Rosen then played out the same dramatic scenario with the photos of Leslie Mahaffy and Kristen French. In a matter of minutes, Rosen had shattered the fragile illusion that Homolka was a victim worthy of the jury's compassion.

Ultimately, Paul Bernardo would be convicted of first-degree murder. The seized videotapes were as devastating to him as they were to Karla Homolka. John Rosen had a transcript of her guilty plea and sentencing hearing. Homolka eventually served every last day of her twelve-year sentence — more time than some murderers serve in prison.

Unlike Karla Homolka's situation, David Radler's sentencing did not take place prior to Conrad Black's trial. It is anticipated that he will receive a twenty-nine-month penitentiary sentence that can be served in Canada along with a fine. I am not aware of a single criminal case in Canada in which a co-operative accomplice or informant's sentencing has been adjourned until he has finished testifying. It is foreign to a sense of fairness.

In fact, when an inquiry was called to examine Karla Homolka's deal (and concluded that it was supportable), the uniquely American approach of delayed sentencing for an accomplice who has made a plea bargain was examined. It was fine to leave the threat of dire consequences hanging over the witness's head if his performance in court didn't meet the prosecution's expectation.

The American approach has been "roundly condemned" in many Canadian courts and held to be a "distasteful procedure" and one that "should not be tolerated."[11]

Jurors are denied information to assist them in assessing credibility; in fact, they may be unable to properly evaluate what influence the benefits or expected benefits of a good performance for the prosecution may have on the witness's testimony. Equally problematic, deferral of sentencing may motivate informants to give "the most 'helpful' (as opposed to the most truthful) testimony, to enhance their position."[12]

By postponing David Radler's sentencing, the prosecutors in the Conrad Black case may have induced Radler to seek their favour rather than to seek the truth. There is a striking imbalance between a twenty-nine-month prison sentence for a co-operative principal in a sophisticated $60-million fraud scheme and the twenty-five years in prison that likely awaits Conrad Black if he is convicted of all charges. Does Black's defence have full disclosure of the precise parameters of the prosecutors' agreement with Radler about his upcoming testimony? Is it dependant in any manner on the prosecution's assessment of its veracity? Have early parole considerations been canvassed? Has seizure of Radler's considerable assets been contemplated? Eddie Greenspan must know the answers to all of these questions before he embarks on Radler's cross-examination. The alternative is a recipe for a miscarriage of justice.

APRIL 16

William Rogers, a senior lawyer at Cravath, Swaine & Moore retained by Hollinger in a separate matter, testifies he was shocked to discover non-compete payments had not been fully disclosed to shareholders. He says he immediately notified Kipnis that the payments needed to be reported, contrary to the advice from Torys.

THIS BUD'S FOR YOU

I knew that court today would be different. It began with a prisoner telling Judge St. Eve at an early morning adjournment that he watched her on television and that she looked wonderful. Then we heard some parting words from Darren Sukonick, who in his best patriotic voice told the jury that he would not to travel to Chicago to testify because he was asserting his rights as a Canadian citizen.

However, there was no lingering concern that he would be charged if he crossed the border. Perhaps that explains Conrad Black's fervent desire to regain his Canadian passport. He could pull a Sukonick and vanish from the case back to his home and native land. The best question in cross-examination came from one of the myriad defence attorneys (you need a scorecard to get their names right) who, after getting Sukonick to agree that Hollinger shareholders, the SEC, and anyone with a computer could access the various non-compete payments to the senior executives, then asked, "Aside from all these it was a secret?" The jury's laughter drowned out the judge's voice as she sustained the prosecutor's objection.

Sukonick acknowledged that the chair of the audit committee, James Thompson, was aware that senior executives of Hollinger International were receiving millions of dollars in non-compete payments from companies purchasing newspapers from Hollinger. Sukonick was an unmitigated disaster for the prosecution. The jury has heard much about due diligence investigations by lawyers in the case, but the most glaring example of a failure to exercise good judgment and due diligence rests with the team of assistant United States attorneys who are charged with the prosecution of Conrad Black. Fairly soon Eddie Greenspan will be able to use one of his best punch lines from a previous case: "I wish I was as thin as the evidence in this case."

The only reasonable doubt that has so far been established in this case is whether the prosecutors are scrambling because the evidence in their case is sagging or their trial skills are lacking. We are three weeks into a $60-million fraud case and all the jury has heard about the impact on the Hollinger shareholders is that they stood to make over $3 billion from the CanWest sale. There are now whispers that the prosecution's proposed witness list of some forty witnesses will be pared down considerably. It is a bit late for that decision. The lawyers from Torys and the accountants from KPMG should never have been called because they have drilled a gaping hole in the prosecution's case.

After today we can add the attorneys from the prestigious New York and London law firm of Cravath, Swaine & Moore to the laundry list of botched prosecution witnesses. The law firm's New York office is located at Worldwide Plaza, a fitting address for a law firm with some five hundred attorneys and international stature. In other words, it is the perfect law firm for Conrad Black and his co-defendants to retain while they are perpetrating a fraud right before their legally trained eyes. The first Cravath witness attorney to be called was William "Bud" Rogers, to be followed by Paul Saunders, Henry Kissinger's personal attorney.

Bud Rogers was served up on a platter for the defence as he described his shock and dismay at the shoddy legal opinion provided by Torys that the executives' non-compete payments didn't have to be disclosed under the U.S. securities laws. Rogers noted that it wasn't even a close call, but it was close enough to spend time with some of his partners "reflecting and analyzing" to determine if they were missing something. It wasn't simply a matter of a disagreement among lawyers but, more ominously, an attempted cover-up by Sukonick, who pretended in an email to Peter Atkinson that Torys and Cravath were on the same page on the disclosure issue. I wonder what the jury will do with Rogers's assertion that it was patently false that Cravath agreed. At one point the trial judge admonished Rogers to try to answer the question he was being asked. "I know you're a lawyer and it's hard for lawyers sometimes," she gently scolded him. It may indeed be difficult for the lawyers, but what of the poor clients beset by conflicting advice? Somehow in these thickets of mendacity and mediocrity Conrad Black was defying his legal advisors and committing a giant fraud.

The decibel level in the courtroom rose considerably as the lawyers began some verbal jousting. In the boxing ring the referee calls a ten count when an opponent is winded. In an American courtroom the judge declares that a sidebar is in order.[13] Michael Schachter raised a heated objection that prosecutor Jeffrey Cramer was intentionally asking his witness an inappropriate question. The lead prosecutor, Eric Sussman, leaped to his feet and sought to have the disparaging comment stricken from the record. A ten-minute sidebar ensued, with several of the lawyers returning to the counsel table laughing. It was a fitting ending for a bizarre day. One chap in the gallery nearly had heart palpitations when his cellphone went off. He set a world record for a fifteen-yard dash to the exit door. As Judge St. Eve noted, the man was "going out one way or the other."

The prosecution highlighted today that the non-competition agreement in the CanWest deal with the individual executives was noted on the face of the agreement to be a "critical condition" of the agreement. The words aptly describe the state of the prosecution's case at this moment. It is in critical condition.

Calling Dr. Radler to the stand.

Today marked a busy day for lawyers in court. It began with Pat Tuite trying three times to turn off his cellphone, which played the theme from *The Exorcist* as his ring tone. Bud Rogers returned to court with his own attorney in tow. It is an American phenomenon that witnesses facing no legal jeopardy demand legal representation. Once court started, lawyers were examined by a series of attorneys representing other lawyers. If it all seems too confusing, imagine how the jury must have felt.

I spent the twenty-fifth anniversary of the enactment of the Canadian Charter of Rights and Freedoms in an American courtroom. Conrad Black complimented Eddie Greenspan and me for importing the Canadian custom of bowing our heads in respect to the judge each time we enter or leave the courtroom. When I reminded Mr. Black of the Charter's anniversary, he told me that constitutional law was his best subject. There is a major scoop for you.

Patrick Fitzgerald returned to court this morning after a hiatus from the proceedings and sat about fifteen feet away from his nemesis, Conrad Black. The two protagonists never exchanged more than a glance. Fitzgerald and Greenspan met in the hallway during a break. In a polite conversation, Fitzgerald told the story about a case he was involved with in which he had devoted years to extraditing a defendant residing in England.

Fitzgerald had the opportunity to watch Bud Rogers feign modesty as he agreed with the suggestion in cross-examination that his law firm, Cravath, Swaine & Moore, is one of the best corporate and tax law firms in the world. It was the firm's publicist's fault, he claimed, if the Cravath website promoted the firm as "unmatched" in legal talent. Cravath won't bend its ethics for any client, Rogers explained. If issues of conflict arose in particular financial transactions, he agreed that "these weren't wink and nod issues." That is important in this case because fraudsters generally rely on surrounding themselves with "wink and nod" professionals to protect their devious crimes from exposure. Over the course of the next two weeks, the jury will be treated to teams of lawyers from Torys and Cravath, Swaine & Moore and accountants from KPMG.

Shock and raw disbelief was the major theme of the day in court as Rogers continued to distance himself from the flawed advice that Torys gave about disclosure of the individual non-competes in the CanWest deal. After a memo written by Beth DeMerchant, the lead Torys counsel on the transaction, was displayed in which she outlined her reasons for supporting the non-disclosure, Rogers could be seen nodding his head in apparent disgust. The sharp conflict between the star law firms bodes well for Conrad Black and his co-defendants.

In most fraud cases, the paper trail left behind by the defendants is the smoking gun. In May 2001, after Peter Atkinson was advised by Bud Rogers during a phone call that the Hollinger annual report was incomplete, Atkinson's handwritten notes reflect that he contacted Beth DeMerchant at

Torys and ensured that the error was corrected in the impending quarterly report. The quarterly report was in fact amended in less than a week at Atkinson's direction. DeMerchant sent an email to Atkinson and Boultbee indicating that she had no difficulty with the revisions suggested by Cravath.

DeMerchant's video testimony began at the end of the day. The most significant part of her testimony was her description of the lawyers at Torys who worked on the CanWest file. She named seven separate lawyers and then noted that there were "many others." What is the expression? "Too many cooks spoil the broth."

Conrad Black's name barely received a mention today. He has almost disappeared from the case. He is the principal defendant in a $60-million fraud and racketeering trial. Even DeMerchant hesitated when asked if she was familiar with Conrad Black's business acumen. She had only limited dealings with Black, and her comments were limited to general observations. Perhaps the prosecution should consider calling Margaret Thatcher as a witness. At least she has the advantage of knowing Mr. Black.

APRIL 18

Torys lawyer Beth DeMerchant testifies via videotape that she gave
the same advice as Sukonick, but realized her mistake after Cravath's
protests and advised Hollinger to disclose the non-competes.

DEMERCHANT OF PENANCE

The CanWest deal took place on Beth DeMerchant's watch. As the partner in charge of the deal for Hollinger International, she supervised
and had overall responsibility for the classroom of Torys lawyers working
on the multi-billion-dollar transaction. And she dropped the ball. The proxy
circular filed with the Securities and Exchange Commission and released
to the company's shareholders contained glaring errors that included the
missing disclosure of the non-compete payments to individual executives.

DeMerchant described a meeting with Peter Atkinson in which she
told him that "unfortunately there is a problem here" and apologized for
the mistakes of her law firm. When prosecutor Eric Sussman asked if there
was some further discussion, she curtly replied that she "didn't think Peter
would appreciate a mealy-mouthed mea culpa." The use of an alliteration
seemed appropriate given the Shakespearean elements of both pathos and
courage that marked DeMerchant's dramatic testimony. The jury watched
this former senior partner of a pre-eminent Canadian law firm admitting
to grovelling before her client, acknowledging that she didn't know tax
law and shouldn't have ventured into that area, and being bested by her
American legal counterpart. DeMerchant never wavered from accepting
the blame, although it was clearly not hers alone to properly bear.

There were moments during her testimony today when DeMerchant closed her eyes and sighed. Her body language poignantly told the story of her angst and sense of pain far more than anything she said. DeMerchant claimed that it wasn't her role to devote "laser attention" to the details of the CanWest deal. She delegated much of the detail work such as the non-competition agreements to the number two lawyer on the deal for Torys, Darren Sukonick. "If I was run over by a bus, he would be able to step in and fill my shoes," she said. Sukonick is presently keeping busy with the firm's office renovations, which I am told he is performing splendidly.

Ultimately, no harm to the Hollinger International shareholders ensued and the disclosure was corrected in a later filing. Peter Atkinson and Jack Boultbee would have been within their rights to fire Torys on the spot and react angrily when the problems were reported. However, they instead demonstrated grace and understanding, and the jury surely took notice. In a message left with DeMerchant on April 24, 2001, Atkinson set out the desired course of action: "Beth, I had another round with Bud [Rogers] that he initiated today on this disclosure issue and then Conrad and Jack and I had a discussion about it. We decided that we'd better receive a written opinion from your firm with respect to it. We don't want to run any unnecessary risks here although we're not going to get excessively jumpy either. So if you could take that on board...."

The prosecution's theory about CanWest was that Atkinson and Boultbee inserted themselves into the non-competition agreements with CanWest. DeMerchant didn't support this position. On the contrary, she couldn't recall if CanWest pressed for them to be included or if Hollinger suggested they be added. The special committee had tried to cajole her to agree that Atkinson and Boultbee had inserted themselves into the agreement, but she resisted. That piece of evidence is a dark cloud that will hover over the remainder of the prosecution's case. The jury will now wonder about the pressure brought to bear on any other witness in the case by the Hollinger International special committee to falsely implicate the co-defendants. Point for the defence.

Even the notion that the non-competes to the individual executives in the American community newspaper sales were not disclosed suffered a blow today. DeMerchant recalled a meeting with the prosecutors in March 2006 in which she advised them that she had earlier been aware of non-compete payments made to Atkinson and Boultbee in the first CNHI transaction. The prosecution's case is in tatters and there is no coherent theory being presented to the jury. Conrad Black is not even charged with fraud in relation to the CanWest deal (although it originally formed part of the indictment). His lawyers have been relegated to passive spectators in the courtroom as Atkinson's and Boultbee's counsel take centre stage.

Not to be outdone, Conrad Black has grabbed some headlines by recklessly comparing the prosecutors to Nazis in a discussion with a *Toronto Star* reporter. If he maintains that foolish standard, he may yet be convicted. To paraphrase *Hamlet*, "To be haughty or not to be haughty, that is the question."

PREDICTION: CONRAD BLACK WILL NOT TESTIFY

Richard Breeden, the former SEC head charged with investigating the misdeeds at Hollinger International, was apparently so furious with Beth DeMerchant's testimony that she was pressured to change her story that he was consulting with his lawyers to determine if he could vacate the $30-million settlement with Torys.

The great mystery in court today had little to do with Conrad Black or his co-defendants. Only the detective skills of Hercule Poirot or Inspector Banks could unearth the answer to the rather large question that loomed over the trial. What was the hourly rate of Paul Saunders, the noted litigation attorney from Cravath, Swaine & Moore? Saunders wasn't keen on providing any helpful clues in his exchange with Peter Atkinson's attorney, Michael Schachter.

"Well, how much do you charge an hour?"

"I actually don't know."

"Don't most lawyers bill by the hour?"

"No, that's not necessarily my understanding. Time spent is only one of many factors in billing."

The jury received a brief tutorial today on legal fees. If they were in law school yearning for the lucre of Bay Street or Wall Street, the information may have been useful; however, there was a stunning lack of relevance to the issues that the jury has to decide in this case. Does it matter a whit that DeMerchant's income during the CanWest transaction was between $600,000 and $900,000? Is the prosecution or the defence case advanced by the jury learning that Bud Rogers's hourly rate was in the range of $400 to $600 years earlier? It made for salacious testimony that will grab headlines (and increase applications to the two law firms), but it was also one more day that an ebullient Conrad Black skated through without the slightest misstep.

The jurors do not have to be erudite legal scholars to understand the one basic principle that Paul Saunders was called to clarify. Hollinger International was at dire risk of being riddled with shareholder law-suits for not disclosing the fees paid to executives of the company in the CanWest deal. Excuse me for inquiring, but hasn't Torys already owned up to that mistake and accepted a public flogging? It is the same law firm that also negotiated a deal worth more than $3 billion for the benefit of the Hollinger International shareholders.

Another mystery at the Conrad Black trial is the disappearance of the British press. There is one lonely reporter from the *Daily Telegraph* whose articles have been rejected by the paper's editor consistently since the Bora Bora trip was introduced into evidence. This same *Daily Telegraph* had noted prior to the trial that the locals in Chicago viewed the possibility of Black being acquitted as "marginally less likely than Elvis turning up as a court-room usher." I can verify that there have been no Elvis sightings at the trial.

I'm sorry that author and journalist Tom Bower won't be around the courthouse to quiz me about my latest prediction. For the record, I have not been privy to any special insight by any of the parties to the case. I have also not shared breakfast with any of the jurors, had a latte at Starbucks with the judge, or consulted any of the various psychics monitoring the trial.

Here it is then: Conrad Black will not be called to testify at his trial. My thinking has changed on this subject. Early in the trial, I felt that Black needed to testify to win. But after Jeffrey Cramer's stirring opening, which had me convinced that Black was a bank robber, the case for the prosecution has progressively disintegrated. The prosecutors will be hugely disap-pointed, because they must now realize that Black's testifying is their only hope to salvage their sinking case. Patrick Fitzgerald would be accorded a front-row seat for the spectacle of watching his bombastic arch-enemy inevitably collapse under the weight of his own angry rhetoric. It won't happen. The more likely scenario is that one or more of the co-defendants will be called to testify. Mark Kipnis was the insider who primarily dealt with the Hollinger board and with David Radler. It is his signature that routinely appeared on the various transactions and non-compete agreements and he can verify his understanding of their authenticity. His lawyer, Ron Safer, told the jury in his opening that Kipnis had only limited contact with Conrad Black. It will be a daunting task for the prosecutors to connect Kipnis with any nefarious plan along with his co-defendants. He never received any funds from any of the non-competition agreements involved in the multi-billion-dollar sales of Hollinger International's media assets in Canada and the United States.

There is only one variable that can upset my prediction. David Radler could perform spectacularly on the witness stand. To do so he will have to withstand days of withering cross-examination from Eddie Greenspan and an admirable supporting cast of attorneys.

BLACK AND WHITE

"Conrad Black deserved every dollar he made." My father was quite animated when he called me early Saturday morning. It isn't a good sign for the prosecution when my astute dad is siding with Black's defence team. He had just read the *Globe and Mail* article describing the skilful negotiations that led to Black "outfoxing" the Asper family on the CanWest deal. The sale came at a time when Black was persuaded that the newspaper business in North America had peaked and Hollinger International was shedding many of the community newspapers it owned in the United States.

In a shining example of textbook negotiation, Black exploited Izzy Asper's fervent desire to add newspapers to his Canadian media empire. When Asper contacted Black with an offer, Torys was instructed to close the deal before Asper realized that CanWest was the only viable purchaser and could therefore dictate the market price. "The concern was to complete the agreement with CanWest as quickly as possible before CanWest realized there were perhaps no other attractive offers in the wings," Beth DeMerchant testified. When the deal was completed, CanWest became Canada's largest media company, and Asper was predicting that the Hollinger sale would be a "model for similar convergence activities throughout the Western world." It was also enormously profitable to the shareholders of Hollinger International.

The warm and fuzzy exchange between Izzy and Conrad (as the two Palm Beach, Florida, neighbours signed off to each other) included an acknowledgement by Black that "we're willing to be flexible" on the management fee that would be charged. He subsequently offered to reduce the annual fee to manage the Canadian papers from $19 million to $6 million in exchange for increasing the purchase price. That significant concession placed an additional $13 million in the coffers of the Hollinger International shareholders.

The *Chicago Tribune* noted on the weekend that Black's Toronto-based lawyer, Edward Greenspan, declined to say whether he would call Izzy Asper's son Leonard, the chief executive of CanWest, as a witness. The reporters must believe that Canadian lawyers are dumber than doorposts. The defence has already scored a touchdown on the CanWest evidence. Shouldn't the question properly be directed to the prosecutors if they hope to prove that Boultbee and Atkinson inserted themselves into the CanWest non-compete agreements?

The Chicago papers seem to have forgotten that Conrad Black is no longer charged with fraud in relation to the CanWest deal. In the Sunday edition of the *Chicago Sun-Times*, the paper noted, "The government alleges that Black and other former executives stole about $84 million from Hollinger International, now called Sun-Times Media Group." Note to the *Sun-Times*: $84 million was the correct figure before the prosecutors were forced to scramble and modify the quantity of the fraud after the videotaped testimony of Sukonick and DeMerchant, completed weeks before the trial, determined that Black's and Radler's non-compete fees in the CanWest deal were certifiably kosher.

As Conrad Black continues to offer courtside colour commentary of the trial and add fodder for prosecutors, it becomes clearer that he will never testify in his own defence. Before I take issue with His Lordship's propensity for out-of-court utterances, I must first state my obvious conflict. He has become my main competition as the legal analyst at the trial. This must be stopped.

I fail to understand why the prosecutors continue to allow Black to speak freely to the media on the record as he puffs up his defence and denigrates his accusers. Trials should be won on the merits of the case and the evidence called in the courtroom. Sanguine protestations of innocence should only come after the jury's verdict. Comments made in the hallway to reporters are free shots. There is no risk of cross-examination or adverse findings of a trial judge (such as the Delaware commercial court judge who said of Conrad Black that it "became almost impossible for me to credit his word"). My vocabulary has expanded and my Scrabble play has vastly improved by listening to Black's articulate hallway harangues. However, my respect for the trial process has been diminished.

It was understandable that Black stridently and vocally asserted his innocence before his trial began. After all, when Patrick Fitzgerald of the U.S. Attorney's Office announced his indictment in November 2005, he described Conrad Black as someone who lived large for years on millions of shareholder dollars and further stated, "Insiders of Hollinger — all the way to the top of the corporate ladder — whose job it was to safeguard the shareholders, made it their job to steal and conceal."

I once had a client who was pilloried in the media at the time of his arrest. It was not a typical shoplifting or impaired driving case. It involved international intrigue, chemical weapons, Saddam Hussein, and the United Nations. In 1996 an oil-for-food program was created to allow Iraq, a country that had been under the dictates of U.N. sanctions since the invasion of Kuwait more than five years earlier, to sell oil in order to purchase medicine, food, and other humanitarian goods and to pay war reparations. Hussein's corrupt government undermined the program by collecting more than $2 billion in kickbacks from various companies.

My client, Ron, was charged near the inception of the oil-for-food program. He was an auctioneer with the auction company retained by the Canadian government to sell forty-five Canadian military helicopters. The allegations against Ron were that he was part of a sophisticated conspiracy to send the helicopters through the Philippines to Iraq and the nefarious Hussein regime where they would be fitted for chemical warfare to attack the Kurds. Most of the helicopters were seized at a warehouse outside of Picton, Ontario, but eleven had been flown to the United States before they were intercepted. These were extraordinarily serious charges that Ron faced. He was the last person I would believe to be an international arms salesman. He genuinely accepted that the helicopters were to be used in medical emergencies or for spraying in areas of Iraq that were dangerously mosquito-infested.

Ron's preliminary hearing took place in the same courtroom in Picton where Canada's first prime minister, Sir John A. Macdonald, had once tried his criminal cases. At the conclusion of Ron's hearing, the judge summarily discharged him from all of the counts he was facing, dismissively pointing out that "the penny never dropped in the case."

It was a resounding victory, but one aspect of bitterness lingered for my client. At the time of his arrest, a police officer had speculated in the media that Ron must have known about the chemical weapons conspiracy and received a payoff. The statement was patently false but there was no way for Ron to remove the stain that tarnished his reputation. Publicly fighting back would only serve to reinforce the fabrication about his role in the case.

Prosecutors in Canada never hold press conferences. It is not a feature of the common law tradition. We have even ascribed a rule for it — the *sub judice* rule. I will share a secret with you about lawyers and the use of Latin. We constantly sprinkle our language with Latin terms to sound ever so majestic and eloquent. Buffoonish would be a more apt description. Barristers may wear black gowns (and wigs in the United Kingdom) and speak incessantly of *stare decisis* and *actus reus*, but it is all for show.

I was taught my first Latin term at Osgoode Hall Law School. My law professor, Louise Arbour, was petite in stature and a giant in the legal world. She would later become a member of the Supreme Court of Canada, a war crimes prosecutor, and a United Nations high commissioner for human rights. This was all accomplished before she was thirty. (The last sentence was a *non sequitor*.) Professor Arbour taught my class the meaning of the overarching principal in criminal law of *mens rea*. She used the case study method, and the case chosen to illuminate this Latin mystery was decided by the Yukon Territory Court of Appeal. Mr. Ladue, the subject of the appeal, had been convicted of copulating with a woman who was dead. He had unsuccessfully raised the improbable defence that he thought that the victim was alive but unconscious. Mr. Ladue's conviction was sustained because he had the requisite *mens rea*, or criminal intent, to commit a rape.

The court allowed for "the most exceptional case" where a defence of *mens rea* could be raised if the defendant could show that he did not know the body was dead and believed that he was acting lawfully and innocently. In other words, only an admission by the defendant of the most wretched and passive sex life imaginable could raise the spectre of a defence. It is an admission that I predict with some degree of confidence will never be made in a courtroom, but the legal principle illustrated by the case endures.

APRIL 23

Marilyn Stitt, a KPMG accountant who audited Hollinger International, testifies she pressed executives to disclose the CanWest non-competes and was surprised to learn later the company had not disclosed other similar payments.

SILENCE IS GOLDEN

It is never a good sign for the prosecution when it has to mount a defensive position to soften the blow from a glaring weakness in its case. That is precisely what happened in court today as Marilyn Stitt, a partner at the international accounting firm of KPMG, testified at the Conrad Black trial. It was KPMG's auditors who had access to the books and records of Hollinger International. If a $60-million fraud occurred, it happened on their watch.

The theory of the prosecution is that Stitt, a chartered accountant, and her team of auditors at KPMG were duped. Black and his co-defendants created an audit trail, a false paper trail that was designed to deceive a group of accounting aficionados. Stitt's role as an auditor, she testified, was generally not to be searching for a fraud when she conducted an audit. Excuse me for asking, but isn't that exactly one of the roles that an auditor performs? Would the shareholders of Hollinger International be reasonably content with the company's accountants generally accepting the bona fides and good faith of the officers and directors of the company and not checking for any possible fudging of the company's financial records?

Indeed, Stitt did take an active role to ensure that the non-compete payments to Black, Radler, and the other senior executives were authorized. A meeting with two members of the Hollinger International audit committee, James Thompson and Richard Burt, took place on February 25, 2002. Stitt, who called for the meeting, was present with three of her partners. The non-compete deals for both CanWest and the American community newspapers were raised. Not a single objection was voiced.

A song from *The Graduate* comes to mind — "The Sound of Silence." As Stitt noted, "We were looking for confirmation and clarification that they had in fact been previously approved. Nobody objected at the meeting." Significantly, Stitt stated that she viewed the members' silence to be a tacit confirmation of prior approvals by the audit committee. Point for the defence.

The relief from dry accounting evidence was found several blocks away at the Cook County courthouse. DNA testing led to the exoneration of a Chicago man, Jerry Miller, from rape and kidnapping charges. Miller had spent twenty-five years in prison before being granted his freedom today to the sound of loud cheers in the courtroom. Miller's wrongful conviction was the two hundredth in the United States that was established through DNA testing. DNA has become the criminal justice system's greatest ally to cure injustice.[14]

It is important to remember, however, that DNA is not a panacea and plays a part in only a small number of criminal cases. Many miscarriages of justice remain undetected.[15] Many of the wrongfully convicted languish in prison cells with little hope of relief. That was almost the tragic tale of Sherry Sherrett, a woman in Trenton, Ontario, who was charged with the murder of her four-year-old son and committed for trial in 1998.

I appeared on *Canada AM* early this morning to talk about Sherrett's case. She had eventually pleaded guilty to infanticide on the basis that she agreed that she may have smothered her baby while suffering postpartum depression. She was sentenced to a year in jail and her eldest child was taken from her and put up for adoption.

The reason *Canada AM* was devoting a prominent segment to Sherrett's case was soon apparent: after the chief coroner in Ontario ordered the exhumation of her baby's body it became clear that no crime had occurred. There was no evidence of injuries or a fracture to the baby's skull that had been reported in the original pathology report. The author of that report, Dr. Charles Smith, had been the subject of an extensive critical review conducted by the Office of the Chief Coroner in Ontario. Sherrett's was one of thirteen cases where criminal convictions based on Dr. Smith's findings were placed in serious jeopardy. It represented a scandal of epic proportions, and the premier of Ontario today ordered a full public inquiry into all thirteen wrongful dispositions. The victims in these miscarriages of justice have been falsely branded as child killers, have had their liberty needlessly stripped from them, and have witnessed their families torn apart. How could the system fail them so miserably?

I had my own experiences with Dr. Charles Smith in a child homicide case. It is a case that I will never forget. It was the Atikian case. Sonia Atikian suffered from a painful knee problem in the spring of 1979. Her doctor informed her that it was a chronic problem that she was unable to treat. As the pain worsened, a friend suggested that she visit a herbalist, Gerhard Hansville, who claimed to possess healing powers derived from the natural remedies sold from his store in Markham, the House of Herbs. Mrs. Atikian's knee improved under his care and she began to attend a number of Hansville's classes and lectures.

When Sonia Atikian gave birth to her third child, Lori, Hansville persuaded her to delegate the baby's diet and medical care to him. When the baby became ill and her husband, Khajdour, urged her to take Lori to the doctor, Hansville's curt reply was that it would "be like putting a gun to her head." Both parents became terrified of harming their child if Hansville's edicts were ignored. Lori's condition deteriorated rapidly and her mother rushed her to Hansville's store. He placed the baby first in a machine that produced electromagnetic waves and then wrapped her in cabbage leaves to draw the poisons from her body. Lori Atikian died the following day. She was extremely malnourished.

Sonia and Khajdour Atikian were charged with failing to provide the necessaries of life to their daughter. The pathologist who performed the autopsy was Dr. Charles Smith. I was retained to represent Khajdour, Lori's father. I recall cross-examining Dr. Smith at the trial. He turned away from the lawyers and the judge and faced the jury. "Let me walk you through it," he told the jury. Emotively, he compared Lori to children dying of starvation in African countries like Ethiopia. Like a conductor twirling his baton, he instructed them about the intricate causes of her death. Smith was the most formidable expert witness I ever faced in a criminal case. I am not surprised that other juries were swayed by his evidence. He left a powerful impact on the jury in the Atikian case. They convicted both parents in the span of a few hours. The trial judge had previously charged the jury that the baby perished in the city of Toronto and not "upon some frozen tundra in the Arctic, nor was it in the remote dunes of the Sahara Desert." The judge had signalled to the jury that excellent medical care was available to both parents and they chose to ignore it. It seems ironic now that Dr. Charles Smith represented conventional medicine in that courtroom.

The Atikian case proceeded before two further retrials before it concluded. A wonderful group of lawyers dedicated themselves to work on the case. Two of them would eventually become judges on the Superior Court of Ontario.[16] The case was won after a piece of critical disclosure that shattered the prosecution theory that the Atikians waited and plotted their response before calling 911 was accidentally uncovered. Through the Crown's negligence, it had never been disclosed to the defence. Given that it was five years after the Atikians had been first charged, the trial judge, Ed Then, found that it would be "an affront to fair play and decency" to allow the case to continue. In staying the charges, he made the following comment: "Nothing worse can happen to them after this ... I don't even have enough adjectives to describe how bad it is for them."

I was reminded of that comment this morning when I spoke on television of Sherry Sherrett's ordeal. It placed everything else in perspective for me. The system works only when all the parties in a trial operate fairly and by the rules. The alternative is a skewed result and an inevitable injustice. It is a lesson worth remembering in every criminal case.

APRIL 24–26

Richard Burt, a former U.S. diplomat and one-time member of Hollinger's board of directors and audit committee, testifies board members relied on Black and Radler in making important decisions. "I always found they were a very close team," he says. He says he knew nothing about non-compete payments. Genson produces documents, bearing Burt's signature, in which the payments are disclosed.

Black's lawyers try to distance their client from Radler, contending Black ran the *National Post* and *Daily Telegraph* while Radler looked after the *Jerusalem Post*, *Chicago Sun-Times*, and smaller community newspapers in the U.S.

PREDICTION: RADLER NEXT WEEK

When I arrived in court this morning, I was quite certain that there had been a full moon the night before. It was a day full of surprises. It began with the lead prosecutor, Eric Sussman, approaching me and a CBC radio reporter at a morning break in a friendly exchange.

"You guys are here for the good stuff," he exclaimed. We chatted about wrongful convictions, problem pathologists, and Marilyn Stitt's testimony.

"Do you understand what's going on?" he asked. Comprehending the evidence was not my failing. Rather, it was being able to hear the questions being asked in cross-examination. The young associate from Jack Boultbee's defence team assigned the questioning of Stitt apparently thought it was best to whisper lest he wake up the court deputy, who was napping at the back of the courtroom. Canadian courtesy is becoming infectious.

The prosecutor was talking freely while a repentant Conrad Black was at his best behaviour and maintaining perfect decorum outside the courtroom. Inside the court, Patrick Fitzgerald was back as an observer and the irrepressible Tom Bower had returned from London to offer his caustic commentary about the trial. Bower had once told *Slate* magazine that the Canadian press was divided into "The Black Team" vs. "The Vermin and Sluts." Today Bower sat cozily during the proceedings next to one of his protagonists, the prolific Mark Steyn, who was busy sending regular updates of the trial on his BlackBerry. I strained to listen as the two men discussed Bower's prospects for a lawsuit with Conrad Black. In the days leading up to the start of the case, Black had emailed Bower and promised him "a spectacular trial." A spectacular yawner would have been more accurate.

I would endorse a summary judgment for Bower's lawsuit. The trial had lapsed into the lethargic pace of the dull and mundane. I became convinced that the sudden drop in the courtroom temperature (Christie Blatchford was forced to wear her coat) was simply the judge's attempt to keep the jury awake. Ed Genson had another plan. He brought out the confidential working document for employees of KPMG that was designed as a character Rolodex for the executives at Hollinger. Conrad Black was devoted to making efforts to raise the market price of Hollinger shares. David Radler, on the other hand, "had little use for professionals." The jury burst into laughter. Another point for the defence.

An actual quote from Marilyn Stitt today: "We didn't review it. We read it." Pearls of wisdom are to be expected from a chartered accountant associated with one of the top four accounting firms in the world, replete with clients from Fortune 500 companies like Apple, Citigroup, and General Electric. Parsing Stitt's evidence made it abundantly clear that whether it was to KPMG Chicago, the auditors for Hollinger International, or to KPMG Canada, the auditors for the parent holding company, Hollinger Inc., all of the non-competition payments for the U.S. community newspaper transactions as well as the CanWest deal were disclosed. For example, all of the non-compete payments to Hollinger Inc. and the individual executives of Hollinger were disclosed in the working papers for the audit of Hollinger Inc.

While guided by a compass of "professional skepticism," somehow Stitt didn't recall these payments "catching my attention." Never mind that there was a *Globe and Mail* article or a press release with the salient details about the non-compete payments. Stitt's blissful ignorance about the non-competes was entirely beside the point. It was the fact of disclosure that vitiated any suggestion of fraudulent concealment of the payments by the defendants. As the classic song goes, "Where is the fraud?"

Julie Ruder asked no questions in redirect (it really was a strange day) and the prosecution ushered in their next witness, Richard Burt. Never one to lose an advantage, Jeffrey Cramer drew from Burt that he had been working as an advisor to Henry Kissinger's firm for the past month and that three of his prior government postings (including assistant secretary of state for Europe) were approved by the American Senate. The jury may recall that Clarence Thomas's questionable nomination to the U.S. Supreme Court was also approved by the same Senate.

Burt was invited to join the Hollinger International board of directors by Conrad Black for an annual retainer. Eventually he became a member of the board's audit committee. His role was to represent the shareholders and investors of the company. The working conditions could be harsh. When travelling abroad at the time of a board meeting, great effort would be expended to obtain the relevant material being considered at the meeting and review it. When attending the meetings in person and providing management advice, precautions were taken not to fall asleep. Conrad Black and David Radler persistently interrupted each other, which must have helped. A puppet show of Bert and Ernie (memories of *Sesame Street*) would have livened the agenda.

It was an audit committee that by Burt's candid admission lacked any component of auditing. Management would be relied on a great deal to provide full and accurate information. Good faith was assumed to be in place. The auditors of KPMG were relied on to some extent. The prosecution ended with some momentum. Burt noted that he was not aware in some instances that non-competition payments were advanced to Hollinger Inc. in related-party transactions. He also acknowledged that he never asked for the minutes book. Stay tuned for vigorous cross-examination to follow tomorrow.

Richard Burt came and left the courtroom with an attorney, continuing a trend that began with Darren Sukonick. Every single witness that has followed has come to court with his or her own counsel. The lawyers smile quite a bit and shake the prosecutors' hands at appropriate times during the evidence. Of course there is absolutely nothing else for them to do. Actually, to be fair, that isn't quite true. I once rode the elevator with Bud Rogers and his ebullient attorney. It was suggested that they stop at the second floor and enjoy the delicacies of the cafeteria. Rogers had an amiable lunch companion.

Burt will be followed to the witness stand by Marie-Josée Kravis, another former member of the Hollinger International audit committee. My bold prediction du jour is that they will be followed by David Radler next week. That will leave a series of prosecution witnesses to testify about the remaining perks (the Park Avenue apartment and the Manhattan birthday party) as well as the discovery and contents of the boxes taken from 10 Toronto Street. The final witness will be star witness James Thompson. The prosecution's case will then presumably end (in one more month) with a bang rather than a whimper.

A SQUARE IS A CIRCLE

Tom Bower approached me today with a proposal for a bet. "Five dollars that Black takes the stand and testifies," he said assuredly. I smiled and the ante was raised to ten dollars. I told Bower that I didn't feel that a monetary bet was in order, but our disagreement was on record. He told me that his Conrad Black book has sold more than twenty thousand copies in Canada. I'm quite certain that Black's libel lawsuit against Bower was a boost to sales. The problem with any libel case is that it invariably publicizes the very material that the offended party is seeking to suppress. It is a lose-lose proposition. As one astute judge once shared with me, "You can't win a pissing war with a skunk."

The distinguished English barrister Geoffrey Robertson was set to embark on a trial in 1995 with a daunting task. The plaintiff was the Princess of Wales. Robertson's client was the manager of a health club who had arranged for a hidden camera to take photographs of Princess Diana exercising on a piece of gym equipment called an adductor. The ensuing photographs of the princess's inner thighs were sold to a sleazy tabloid. A seven-page spread appeared in the Sunday edition titled, "DI Spy SENSATION." The Princess of Wales launched a lawsuit seeking hefty damages for the flagrant invasion of her privacy.

The case, however, never made its way to the Old Bailey. Robertson described the reasons for the turn of events:

> A few days before "the case of the century" was due to be tried, there was a deal done between the parties to avoid any embarrassment my cross-examination might cause to the Princess of Wales. This was disappointing, if only because I would probably have caused more embarrassment to the newspaper. It is always deflating for a counsel when a "big case" settles at the door of the court (a condition which my wife calls *courtus interruptus*), and this was a lost opportunity to make some good law.[17]

Conrad Black will never have to be concerned about being sued for libel. His language is incomprehensible to ordinary folk like you and me. More of his uniquely erudite emails were introduced into evidence today by the prosecution. The jury was treated to beastly descriptions such as "corporate governance faddishness" and "belligerent robot" (I didn't know that robots had feelings). I haven't quite deciphered the importance of highlighting Black's silly diatribes with references to "Pearl Harbor," "nest featherers," and a "reservation," but I know that they will be fodder for the racy headline seekers tomorrow. It didn't loom as the major story inside the courtroom today.

There are critical moments in a lengthy trial when the defence has to step up to the plate and understand that the entire game is on the line. Today marked such a day of high stakes and I am here to report from the courtroom that there is both good news and bad news for the defence. The good news is that the cross-examination of Richard Burt has not yet been completed. The bad news is that their report card is marked with a prominent "0" for their cross-examination today. Three of the jurors were struggling not to fall asleep, and perhaps more alarming to the defence, one of their own colleagues actually dozed off for a few minutes.

During the pre-trial hearings, the attorneys on both sides were openly attacking each other. Judge St. Eve made it crystal clear that the sniping had to stop. There was now a relaxed atmosphere in the courtroom, punctuated by casual banter among the lawyers. There is far too much frivolity every day in this case. One of the journalists told me that the trial reminded her of a frat party. The prosecutors were observed rolling their eyes today during cross-examination. I trust the jury to see through this type of transparent pandering for the abject conduct that it is. I miss the formality and civility that is featured in a Canadian courtroom. I even miss my robes.

I once attended a lecture given by Pamela Mackey, Kobe Bryant's excellent lawyer. She spoke with conviction and passion about her underlying philosophy in every case: if the prosecution wants to get to her client, they will have to get through her first. That is truly a standard for an advocate to aspire to.

Richard Burt seemed to be enjoying himself immensely on the stand. In the midst of his cross-examination by Benito Romano, Atkinson's lead counsel, Burt advised him that he was "doing a great job." At the conclusion of Romano's questioning, Burt actually thanked him. I was not surprised. The cross-examination was disjointed, uninspiring, and open-ended. Romano actually began a question with the words, "Can you think of any reason…?" Any experienced trial lawyer will understand that if a hostile witness is provided with an opportunity to offer an explanation, it will arrive laden with silk and adorned with precious jewels as a gift to the prosecution.

Burt, with his rich baritone voice, grey pinstripe suit, and perfectly coiffed grey hair was in complete control of the interview that largely substituted for a vigorous cross-examination. A typical exchange would involve Romano demurely inquiring if Burt had seen the disclosure of the controversial non-compete payment in Hollinger International's 10-K, the annual report for SEC. A firm denial was a signal to move on to another area.

Richard Burt was a member of the audit committee. He signed his name in that capacity to reports that were distributed to Hollinger International shareholders that contained the following statement: "The company's independent directors have approved the terms of these payments."

The payments at issue were the non-compete payments that are the foundation for the $60-million fraud alleged against the shareholders. Burt convincingly portrayed himself as an innocent dupe and distanced himself from a trail of complete complicity in authorizing these non-compete payments. He effectively managed to put the proverbial square peg in a round hole. Answers in cross-examination such as "I really didn't focus on this"; "I signed because I missed the paragraph"; "I relied on information and briefing by management"; "I'm not a lawyer"; and "I certainly didn't approve them" were allowed to pass unchallenged.

The defence completes the cross-examination of Richard Burt tomorrow. His credibility has to be crushed or indeed a crashing point in the case has been reached. There is still time for the defence to regroup and end the momentum that now rests on the prosecution side of the courtroom.

Conrad Black couldn't conceal his apprehension today. He is relying on Ed Genson, one of his formidable counsel, to mount a blistering cross-examination of a witness who is a former diplomat schooled in the art of the ruse. I have no doubt that Genson will attempt to portray Burt as a self-serving liar who has contrived a fiction for the jury that misrepresents his true role in the audit committee of Hollinger International. It will be a pivotal moment in the trial of Conrad Black.

SLIPPERY WHEN WET

> *"You were being paid $5,000 a meeting and you didn't read [the financial statements], did you sir?"* Genson asked.
> Assistant U.S. Attorney Jeffrey Cramer leapt to his feet in objection.
> — The National Post, April 26, 2007

Allow me to place the prosecutor's objection in some perspective. In Canada, Eddie Genson's question would be about as objectionable as a prosecutor asking a murder defendant whether it occurred to him to stab his wife when he picked up the knife from the kitchen sink. It really does feel like *Alice in Wonderland* in that Chicago courtroom. The process is getting "curiouser and curiouser." Cross-examination, by its very nature, is heated and contentious. It is not meant to resemble courtly teatime in an English manor. It is the paprika and hot sauce in a trial. If I hear the prosecutors utter the insipid objections "argumentative" or "asked and answered" one more time during cross-examination, I shall feel compelled to take the matter up in a sidebar.

I have made a bold decision about my life today that I will share with you: I am planning a career switch. Please don't become alarmed, because it makes eminent sense. I shall offer my services as a member of company boards. I will not be too selective about my choices. The only criteria is that my pay scale match the swelling stipend paid to Richard Burt: $170,000 over three years is a promising beginning on the gold brick road. (I wonder how that will play to a blue-collar jury.) Let's see now. If I strive to duplicate Burt's three boards, I will be over the half-million mark.

I watched Burt's testimony carefully and I believe that I understand my responsibilities perfectly. I shall be paid $5,000 for every board meeting that I attend. I usually won't have the agenda prior to the meeting, let alone any documentation to review. I will also receive some stock options in the company to keep me interested in the welfare of the shareholders.

I will join the compensation committee with one other board member, where I will take special concern of rapid increases to the annual directors' fees. There of course will be corresponding increases in annual stock options for outside directors. As a precautionary measure, I will include a former U.S. attorney as my companion on this committee as a buffer against any unwarranted criticism. I will also join the audit committee of the various boards. Although I have no accounting expertise, that is not an impediment because I won't be performing any audit functions whatsoever. I will retain a respected accounting firm to meet with our committee privately for a few minutes to determine if there are any substantial disagreements with management. They are extravagantly paid as well and therefore few issues should arise. I can wholly rely on the assurances of management to fulfill my elementary auditing responsibilities. I don't need to be concerned about any of the intricate details such as figures or minutes in my cursory review of any financial transactions. Most of it is repetitive and boilerplate. As a shield against any probing of my fulfillment of duties, my response will be, "Remember, I'm bad on dates."

Travel to board meetings is optional. I have the luxury of joining in from my office by telephone. Thankfully, these aren't videoconferences and I can accomplish other tasks during the meetings. Perhaps a catered meal from an Oliver & Bonacini restaurant will soothe the tedium of management's presentations.

Finally, if I am ever held to account for a suspected breach of my fiduciary duties to the shareholders, I have an escape hatch — I was the innocent dupe and hapless victim of management ogres. If a former chief arms control negotiator who made recommendations about nuclear warfare can get away with such a claim, it should be a snap for a criminal defence lawyer.

The defence didn't fare well with poking holes in the credibility of Richard Burt today, and he left the witness stand relatively unscathed. Marie-Josée Kravis is on the stand tomorrow. The time has arrived at this trial for Eddie Greenspan to demonstrate why he is regarded as one of Canada's foremost criminal lawyers. It isn't his legacy at stake. It is his client's freedom.

APRIL 27–30

Marie-Josée Kravis, a prominent economist and audit committee member, testifies she didn't approve any non-compete payments. A combative Eddie Greenspan, representing Black, takes issue with almost every aspect of Kravis's testimony. He produces eleven documents with information about the non-competes bearing her signature. Judge St. Eve warns Greenspan for being too aggressive in his cross-examination.

THE TRIPPING POINT

He felt as though he was wandering in the forests of the sea bottom, lost in a monstrous world where he himself was the monster. He was alone. The past was dead, the future was unimaginable. What certainty had he that a single human creature now living was on his side? And what way of knowing that the dominion of the Party would not endure for ever? Like an answer, the three slogans on the white face of the Ministry of Truth came back at him:

WAR IS PEACE

FREEDOM IS SLAVERY

IGNORANCE IS STRENGTH

— George Orwell, *Nineteen Eighty-Four*, 1949

The equivalent inscription outside of the Hollinger International audit committee boardroom would be as follows:

READING IS NOT SEEING

SIGNING IS NOT ACKNOWLEDGING

AUDITING IS NOT REVIEWING

Perhaps when Julie Ruder asked Marie-Josée Kravis if she observed the Hollinger logo at Barbara Amiel's birthday party, this was the logo that she was referring to.

When I was growing up in Toronto, there was a successful game show called *Concentration* where the contestants were required to locate two matching squares. Consider, for example, the evidence of Ms. Kravis and Mr. Burt. Both of them just "missed" the disclosure of the various non-competition payments in memos, filings, and documents sent to the audit committee members. Both of them failed to notice any division of geographic responsibilities between Conrad Black and David Radler. If the non-competes were known to them, they certainly would have triggered an alarm bell as related-party transactions. The lavish birthday party in the Manhattan restaurant wasn't a business expense. Match, match, match, and match.

The tripping point for the prosecution is that even if the mirroring tales of woe are believed by the jury, the stark reality is that the items now in question were repeatedly disclosed to the audit committee of Hollinger International in the same manner that they were disclosed to the outside auditors from KPMG who were charged with the responsibility of advising the committee. Open disclosure is not a usual feature of fraud cases.

While on the subject of prosecution tripping points, permit me to add another. There seems to be no prospect looming of a single victim of this alleged massive fraud being called to testify. By contrast, in the Enron case, the prosecution could have enlisted enough witnesses to fill Enron Stadium in Houston. (The stadium has since been renamed.)

It was related to me on good authority that in the midst of the cross-examination of Richard Burt, Barbara Amiel was observed at a break in court in an animated discussion with her husband. She was apparently voicing her displeasure with the unsettling manner that Burt was being questioned by the defence. Conrad Black was doing his best to assuage her concerns. Black later approached me in the hallway. "We're taking your advice," he shared with me. "We're bringing in the big hitters. Genson is okay. Newman is getting too old." I may have been entitled to savour the accolades if indeed I had uttered a word of the advice that Black attributed to me. In fact he was hallucinating.

I had an early lesson in client appreciation for my work. It happened in a case that I handled with my former law partner, Leslie Pringle (now Justice Pringle). It was an exotic case that involved ski slopes, drugs, and the lovely Georgian Bay in central Ontario. The word *exotic* might be slightly misplaced. Two skiers were discovered smoking a joint after a run down a hill at a busy Collingwood ski resort and were both charged with possession of marijuana. Our erstwhile clients were in the television business and travelled to the United States for some of their work.

Unfortunately for our clients, a policy of zero tolerance for drug offences had been instituted under President Reagan's direction. The effect of this policy was to bar the entry of any visitor to the U.S. with a drug offence on his record. A relatively minor case suddenly took on profound importance for our clients. Leslie was well versed in drug prosecutions with her experience at the Department of Justice. In preparing for trial, she discovered that the police had failed to serve our clients with notice that the two cigarettes seized had tested positive for traces of marijuana. It could be our lucky break in the case.

On the day set for trial, we instructed our two clients to arrive at a very early hour and locate a seat inside the courtroom the moment it opened to the public. There were no washroom breaks permitted either. Leslie and I realized that the courtroom was a safe haven for our clients. If they set even one foot outside, the police could correct their error and effect service of the notice. That was all that the law required.

When the judge entered the courtroom, the local federal prosecutor began to call a long list of cases. We waited patiently for our turn. At some point, I caught a glimpse of a court officer motioning our clients to step outside of the courtroom. I simply smiled at the officer and firmly directed the two men to remain motionless. Shortly afterwards, a despondent prosecutor announced that the charges were withdrawn.

Leslie and I were elated and waited to be greeted by our clients. The two men rushed hurriedly past us without even speaking a word of gratitude. The perceived slight was later allayed when I learned that they were racing to the men's washroom.

Well, it's back to the Radler watch at the Conrad Black trial on Monday. I can keep the case in its proper perspective.

MAY 1–2

Former Illinois governor and Hollinger audit committee member James "Big Jim" Thompson tells the court he only "skimmed" the company's filings with the SEC, believing they had been approved by legal counsel and senior management. He concurs with Kravis and Burt that the committee was unaware of non-competes to individual executives and disputes defence claims that Hollinger's affairs were "divided" between Black and Radler. Greenspan attacks Thompson for skimming the documents, contending the payments were disclosed in the documents he approved.

HOT POTATO

My worst fears materialized in court today. I was sitting in the gallery listening to prosecutor Julie Ruder's damaging redirect examination of Marie-Josée Kravis. "Leading," I whispered loud enough for Ed Genson to hear. "Leading," he shot back to the judge. "Sustained." I won a ruling without even being counsel in the case. Genson and I chatted about my faux pas after court. "You couldn't help yourself," he contended as he attempted to provide me some cover. I informed him that he had just given me a leading compliment.

There was a great deal of buzz inside the courtroom today. The local media awaited the grand entrance of Jim Thompson, the former governor of Illinois, to testify. According to a FOX television reporter, Thompson still carries a great deal of clout in the Dirksen courthouse. After former governor George Ryan, whom Thompson was assisting in defending, was convicted of racketeering and fraud, Thompson managed to orchestrate a clandestine getaway without Ryan having to face an anxious media pack angling for the lucrative "governor in handcuffs" shot. Now it will be Thompson's turn to stage his own vanishing act. How will a former United States attorney and chair of the audit committee of Hollinger International explain to a jury of his former constituents that he missed repeated references in filings and proxies of the non-competition payments to Conrad Black and other senior executives that he approved?

The prominent height of Marie-Josée Kravis's heels drew some gasps from the gallery as she strode into court this morning. Other than a pair of striking diamond earrings that were partly obscured from view, there were few clues for the jury that she was the wife of a New York billionaire. There will be no Martha Stewart courtroom chic comparisons in the gossip column of the *New York Post* on Tuesday.

The Kravises clearly have a busy social calendar. They lasted only fifteen minutes at Barbara Amiel's birthday party in that fashionable Manhattan restaurant. Perhaps their limousine was parked illegally. It was just enough time to see Donald Trump seated next to the birthday girl. "We didn't stay for dinner," Kravis told Eddie Greenspan in cross-examination. I now understand why she is so magnificently thin. She doesn't eat. Her social stature was only challenged once during questioning. When Patrick Tuite pointed out that Leslie Wexner was on the Hollinger board, he tried to impress her with his knowledge of Wexner's ownership of The Gap. "It's The Limited," she replied. Kravis knows the store chain well, as she acquired her memory there.

The attorneys in the case continued their audition for the Comedy Club without noticing that yet another witness was shuffling off her own responsibility in a classic blame game. In a matter of minutes she had ascribed blame to Conrad Black and management, Mark Kipnis, the passage of time, her limited financial acumen, and KPMG for any shortcomings in her less than stellar work on the audit committee. "*J'accuse*" was the password of the day as the gatekeeper on behalf of the Hollinger International shareholders attempted in vain to explain why she allowed the gate to swing freely open.

Kravis might have been wondering why she needed to join a fashionable trend in the case and bring a lawyer today to court. Tuite seemed more intent on inquiring whether she had enjoyed the city of Chicago's beautiful weekend weather than asking her a single probing question in cross-examination. I could have advised him that Kravis was more likely to be enjoying the elaborate spa inside the Peninsula Hotel than strolling through the crowded stores on Michigan Avenue.

When Kravis mentioned that Hasbro was one of the boards that she served on, Tuite responded, "I won't toy with that." The judge asked him if he was put up to that statement by his co-counsel, Gus Newman. Everyone shared a good chuckle, but the judge's inquiry was well placed. Newman's jocular and self-deprecating cross-examination style has a certain Rodney Dangerfield quality to it. If only the man could get some respect. Tuite made it clear to the witness that she had the court's respect: "You come here," he told her, "you get exhibits named after you."

Then it was Ron Safer's turn. He actually made an effusive reference to "Ambassador Burt" in one of his questions. "I bet you didn't spend a lot of time reading *American Trucker*," he asked Kravis. She assured him that she didn't. Safer later made amends for his rather feeble attempt at humour with a serious reference to Kipnis exhibit GMS 2 depicting the identification of related-party standards. It is a subject of some conjecture as to what fascinating concept GMS 3 will lead to. Three people with gas, perhaps? I was pleased to see that Eddie Greenspan didn't try to drive a truck through the holes in Kravis's testimony. However, he did try to tell one joke. Without the CanWest non-compete signed by Conrad Black, Izzy Asper "could have been burned to a crisp by the *Sun*." Kravis was the only person in the courtroom who didn't appreciate that the reference was to the *Vancouver Sun*, which CanWest was purchasing in the deal.

Greenspan was concerned that the prosecution was getting the upper hand. "I was mad as hell about Burt. She's lying. Tuite didn't touch her. I'm mad at her." Greenspan signalled from the start of his questioning that the time for lobbing sponge softballs at the witness was over. There would be no "good morning" or pretentious greeting from him. The stereotype of the courteous Canadian was shattered by the lawyer from Toronto who became engaged in a rather heated exchange with the witness. There were times when Greenspan was admonished by the judge. "Don't talk at the same time and don't argue with the witness," she scolded him. I thought there should have been bells chiming in the courtroom to celebrate the occasion. We were actually observing the kind of vigorous, credibility-stripping cross-examination that has been such a rare visitor to this trial.

Greenspan pointed to a Hollinger International SEC filing (one of eleven similar examples) that highlighted the non-competition payments to Black, Boultbee, and Atkinson.

"Did you read this paragraph?" Greenspan demanded.

"At the time I didn't," Kravis replied.

"You didn't?"

"I've testified a few times that I missed it."

The cross-examination was not vintage Eddie Greenspan, although he did get Kravis to agree that she was financially literate and not merely a rubber stamp. There are still a few cobwebs from his receding supporting cast role on Black's defence team. The jurors did not spring forward in anticipation as he began his questions in the manner that a Canadian jury surely would. The judge did not accord him the polite deference that he would receive from a Superior Court justice. The rules and procedures are still foreign to him and it showed at times. Yet, with all of these apparent setbacks, it was still one of the more effective cross-examinations at the trial. To borrow the expression of one respected journalist covering the trial, the rubber stamp got quite a workout.

GOVERNOR AND GENERAL

The British are back. They have returned and descended on the courtroom with their usual anti-Black fervour. Today, however, they were passing around their BlackBerrys and their discussion turned to the travails of another lord in trouble. Lord John Browne of Madingley, the man responsible for developing BP into a global success in the oil industry, was forced to resign his exalted position today. Apparently he had lost a court battle to the tabloids and his lies in court about meeting his gay companion were exposed. Our trial across the pond seemed tame by comparison.

The British journalists were treated to the American version of royalty today. Former governor James Thompson, chair of the Hollinger International audit committee, was called to testify. A crowded courtroom, including four sketch artists, awaited him. Although sixteen years had passed since he held political office, his title remained. Even the judge called him "governor." Ed Genson once stated that he had never defended a lord before. I am confident that Eddie Greenspan has never cross-examined a governor before.

The *Chicago Tribune* described the former governor as being "very relaxed and affable" as he took the witness stand in the very same courthouse where he once served as the chief prosecutor. It was old home week for him. He happened to be one of the first people from Chicago to be introduced to the jury. The lawyers are mainly from Toronto and New York, and the witnesses who have testified have come from three separate countries, but few have been locally based. Eric Sussman began by asking Governor Thompson to provide the jury with his background. Thompson made a point of noting that his elementary school, high school, university, and even law school (Northwestern) were all based in Chicago.

"I'm one of you," he was telegraphing to the jury.

There were three highly paid lawyers ensconced in the first row who accompanied the governor at all times outside the courtroom. He is not in any legal jeopardy. The threat of an SEC enforcement action has abated as it has for his fellow members of the audit committee. I wondered about the usefulness of legal counsel until Thompson reminded Sussman that his lawyer had provided him with a list of the boards that he served on. There is taxing legal work for you. There were twelve or thirteen boards of public companies on one piece of paper. It is simply not possible for one man, even a former law professor and United States attorney, to remember names like Maximus and Passione. Maximus Passione. That is the closest that we will get to anything sexual in this trial.

Sussman attempted to anticipate the defence questioning that would follow. Filings were shown to the governor where his signature appeared on documents disclosing non-compete payments to individual executives in the United States community newspaper sales. The conclusion in the documents that the company's independent directors had approved the terms of the payments was patently false, he steadfastly maintained. Thompson's explanation for missing the disclosure was far from defensive. He looked askance at Sussman in a way that suggested that he thought that the question was a rather silly one.

"I skimmed the draft," he told the prosecutor, describing documents the company would file with the U.S. Securities and Exchange Commission. He wasn't looking for the non-compete payments and didn't detect them in various other filings. Thompson faces a unique problem with his credibility.

Unlike Richard Burt and Marie-Josée Kravis, he is an experienced lawyer. Burt and Kravis went to great pains to minimize their legal background. Kravis told Greenspan, "I'm not a lawyer. We established that this morning."

Thompson can play the perennial blame game and pass off responsibility to management as much as he desires, but the reality is that an audit committee is set up as a part of an important system of checks and balances. It isn't sufficient to claim, as Thompson did, that he would "expect they [management] would inform the non-committee, I mean audit committee…" Thompson got it right the first time. Either this was a non-existent committee that recklessly abandoned its fiduciary duty to shareholders and was slumbering during its watch or it was, as the defence suggests, a concoction of lies invented to appease their potential pursuers. Like a good general, Governor Thompson is leading the charge to the innocent dupe explanation. It may be just a bit too contrived and neatly packaged for this jury to swallow.

The jury is difficult to read at this relatively advanced stage of the trial. The jurors are far more selective about taking notes than they were at the beginning of the trial. There is no single lawyer who has established any special rapport with the jury. It is partly a function of there being far too many lawyers involved in the case. The pace of the trial is gruelling, with the day generally lasting from just after 9:00 a.m. until 5:00 p.m. It appears to be taking its toll on the health of some of the defence lawyers and journalists. The only person with a spring in her step is the trial judge.

Governor Thompson continues with his cross-examination by Greenspan tomorrow, followed by lawyers for the other three defendants. That will be followed by redirect, further cross-examination on the redirect, and then possibly redirect on the last round of cross-examination. I get dizzy thinking about it. I hope that the governor is getting a good night's rest. He can be assured that Eddie Greenspan won't get a wink of sleep tonight as he prepares for the final curtain in the case. It will be a huge day.

THE BANALITY OF DRIVEL

I have decided on a title for the prosecution's case. From this point forward it shall be named "Clearasil" after the effective blemish-cleansing solution. The pristine case presented by the team of prodigious assistant U.S.

attorneys cannot be tarnished by any imperfections. It is soft, smooth, and silky. Blemishes in their witnesses' evidence are simply not to be tolerated.

A case in point are the three luminaries from the audit committee of Hollinger International. Richard Burt, Marie-Josée Kravis, and James Thompson all testified independently that they faithfully performed all of their fiduciary duties on behalf of the shareholders. By their account, they were gatekeepers extraordinaire. The mere fact that collectively on thirty-three occasions they missed any reference to non-compete payments to individual executives in relation to the U.S. community newspaper sales surely doesn't detract from the exemplary standard that these audit committee members set for audit committees of other public companies. In fifteen instances, Burt, Kravis, and Thompson signed their names on public disclosures that were filed with the SEC providing comfort to financially illiterate shareholders of the company.

Governor Thompson explained that he had merely skimmed all of the documents that contained the non-compete references along with the customary conclusion that the company's independent directors had approved the terms of these payments. I learned a great deal today about the skill of skimming from the testimony of Governor Thompson. Eddie Greenspan lapsed into calling him Mr. Thompson near the end of his cross-examination, but I will continue to accord him the title of "Governor." I cannot say that I share Pat Tuite's experience of knowing the man socially and professionally for forty years. Tuite began his cross-examination by advising the witness that in honour of his great service to the state, he would call him "Governor." It was followed incredibly by an attempt to impeach his credibility.

Since I possess the apparently unusual habit of reading every word on a page that I choose to review, skimming is a skill that is fresh and novel to me. It must first be understood that there are no skimming schools and that the practicalities of skimming can be refined only with practice. The first rule is that when skimming a document you don't necessarily see every paragraph. Skimming is particularly appropriate when the document is lengthy, but even in a document as brief as seventeen pages, skimming is still the preferable course. There is no requirement that skimming be requested by another party.

It is highly recommended that when skimming a document, it be skimmed from the beginning. This will maximize the amount of time saved poring over the body of the document. It is forbidden to exhibit preference for one part of a document over another when skimming. While it is true that skimming opens the possibility that the reader won't see any inaccuracies, the excuse that the contents were assumed to be true can be relied upon to displace any criticism. It works like a charm every time. For instance, skimming may provide an acceptable excuse to answer any issues raised by a possible SEC enforcement action. It conveniently shifts the blame to the offending party, such as management or the outside auditors. If anything is amiss, it was their responsibility to point it out or raise a question.

Skimming should only be relied upon selectively. It may be one thing to skim filings with the SEC, but it would not be appropriate, for example, for a governor to skim a death warrant ordering the execution of a prisoner.

The optimal time to resort to skimming occurs when one is attempting to distance oneself from some damaging part of a document. It provides excellent cover from being exposed to embarrassment from multiple inconsistencies or other difficulties. If an incriminating statement is highlighted, the correct response is, "I skimmed that page and missed it."

What can even the best advocate do with that in cross-examination? Eddie Greenspan was left to wonder aloud if it was a remarkable coincidence that the governor missed reading all eleven passages that mentioned the U.S. non-competes. In this situation, rather than conducting a blistering cross-examination, even an accomplished attorney could only muster some bluster.

I will provide you with my objective and legally literate opinion about the Conrad Black trial. The defence is winning. Mark that down. The prosecution is still struggling to develop a coherent theory seven weeks into the trial. The prosecution's case is the *Titanic* searching for an iceberg. Perhaps they grew unduly confident that the wilted attack by the defence on Richard Burt's credibility portended an uneventful journey for the other two committee members. It is true that Burt skated through his cross-examination with all the ease of a featured performer at the Ice Capades. His sharp blade inflicted some damaging blows. It was a huge mistake for Black's defence not to enlist the same lawyer to conduct the cross-examination for all three audit amigos. Instead Ed Genson carried the ball for Burt while Greenspan cross-examined both Kravis and Thompson.

Today was Eddie Greenspan's moment to shine in the courtroom. The trial has been demoralizing for him and I am quite certain that there have been times when he has regretted taking the case. But from the moment that he stood at the lectern today and indicated that he was "absolutely" ready to proceed, he put on a clinic of masterful cross-examination. With Barbara Amiel sitting in front of the governor's wife and watching from the gallery, Thompson was left staggering in the witness box, with each successive answer making it clearer to the jury that he was confabulating his evidence. "These words are the words," answered a confused Thompson at one point. Greenspan was unrelenting. "Hollinger didn't pay you $60,000 to skim documents? They never asked you, 'Please skim these'?" Thompson's answer was irrelevant. Some of the jurors stopped looking at him.

The cross-examination was punctuated by the petulant objections of the lead prosecutor, Eric Sussman, whose face grew redder as the day progressed. The objections largely fell flat and only made Greenspan more defiant. "I'm not moving from that question," he advised the judge. It is ironic that in a trial marked by a vast sea of objections by the prosecutors, they allowed by far the most objectionable question posed at the trial to go unchallenged. It was a harmful question as well because it tarred all three members of the audit committee with the same soiled brush. After asking the witness if it was a remarkable coincidence that he missed reading the critical passage eleven times, Greenspan noted that Kravis and Burt had said the same thing. The following exchange then took place:

> Q: I'm going to suggest to you, Governor Thompson, that you read all these things; you thought they were right; and when there was some criticism, all of the three of you conveniently forgot.
>
> A: That is false.

The proper objection that would surely have been sustained by Judge St. Eve was that the question called for Thompson to speculate about the motives of Kravis and Burt. Unfortunately, it was skimmed over by the prosecutors. This is not the momentum that the prosecution hoped for when they determined that David Radler would testify at the beginning of next week. Eddie Greenspan is set to conduct the cross-examination, and it will be harder to acquire a seat for that courtroom battle than a ticket to a Rolling Stones concert. Radler, Greenspan, and the case ending with a whimper. The prosecution can't get no satisfaction from that prospect.

ON THE FLY

Ed Genson turned to me before court started in the morning. "Tell me Eddie didn't kick ass with these last two witnesses," he challenged.

The trial reached a surreal stage for me today. I had befriended a couple of assistant United States attorneys who regularly attend the Conrad Black trial to observe the proceedings. One of them is well known for his role in assisting with the establishment of a new legal system in Afghanistan.

At our morning break, Black approached us in the hallway and introduced himself. He proudly indicated that he and Patrick Fitzgerald had recently enjoyed a very civil encounter. The two men had nearly bumped into each other in their rush to leave court and then exchanged a quick apology. The thought of Conrad Black saying the word *sorry* to his archenemy and nemesis brings me hope that anything is possible. For a brief moment I lapsed into a dream of the Toronto Maple Leafs winning the Stanley Cup. I really am spending too much time in Chicago. Did I mention that Pamela Anderson sat next to me on my plane ride home?

The State of Illinois must have set some kind of world record for indicting leaders of government. I was advised today that four of the state's governors have been convicted in corruption scandals in the state's history. One of them, George Ryan, was found guilty of taking graft, including gifts and vacations, in return for steering state contracts and licences to a few selected friends. The prosecutors at Ryan's trial cried foul when his lawyers sought to introduce a question on the jury questionnaire about the death penalty. Specifically, it related to Governor Ryan's popular role in clearing death row in his state and commuting more than 160 death sentences. Thirteen of the men sentenced in these cases were ultimately exonerated and freed.[18] Ryan became a folklore hero in the wrongful conviction movement and was the keynote speaker at a conference at Harvard Law School at which I was invited to attend to speak on a panel on jailhouse snitches and informants. I hope that Ryan attended my session. It may have some practical implications for him now.

Jim Thompson prosecuted one of the four governors in his role as a United States attorney in the 1970s. This is the same man who professed not to understand the meaning of corporate litigation or to have reviewed a financial statement in any of his criminal cases. Thompson returned to court today with his coterie of lawyers in tow. One of them was carrying a rather large litigation brief. I can't imagine what could possibly be inside it. Truth serum, perhaps.

Thompson impressed me as one of the most unsavoury and untruthful witnesses that I have ever observed in a courtroom. He was smug, defiant, and arrogant in his answers in cross-examination. Years of political campaigning brings out the best in people. Thompson's basic story that he adamantly adhered to was patently absurd. He had met with the team of prosecutors on three separate occasions since the trial started but had refused a request to meet with Ron Safer, Mark Kipnis's lawyer. Thompson is still a consummate politician and knows which side of the courtroom to ally himself with. His insipid loyalty to Conrad Black was discarded when it conflicted with protecting the lucrative flank of his board positions.

At one point this morning, Safer asked Thompson to peruse a document. He observed that he had promised not to "pile on" on the recurring theme of skimming but later relented and asked Thomson if he had skimmed it. That brought an indignant objection from Eric Sussman, who asked that the egregious comment be stricken from the record. The ruling was swift. "Ladies and gentlemen," Judge St. Eve told the jury, "you will disregard that last question." That meets the definition of a hollow victory for the prosecution.

Safer was, for once at this trial, less than deferential in his questioning and effectively focused on testimony that the governor gave the previous day. Thompson had told Sussman that in relation to changes made in filings for the CanWest deal, he didn't think that anything was said to the audit committee about outside counsel. Safer pressed forward and ultimately Thompson conceded that the committee may indeed have been told that outside counsel was used. The clear contradiction may not have registered with a seemingly impatient Thompson, but it surely did with the jury.

Safer previously had demonstrated that Thompson had approved management fees, compensation fees, and stock options for the extravagant amount of almost $300 million while he chaired the audit committee at Hollinger International. Thompson maintained that he never asked for a single piece of supporting documentation to authorize these payments. This was an audit committee predicated on blind faith.

Thompson was also paid $18,000 for one day of gruelling work during which he attended a series of meetings and claimed to have only skimmed the related documents. As Greenspan pointed out in his re-cross-examination, it was Thompson who by his own account was culpable for breaching the trust that the shareholders had placed in him. Thompson denied this, of course.

When Thompson's languid evidence concluded and the jury was gone, he strode to the prosecutors' table and shook their hands. He gave them a thumbs-up sign. My first thought was that it wasn't his thumb. It is difficult to say whether Thompson's dramatic exit was only a pretentious cover on his part to preserve his legacy or whether he is sufficiently delusional to bask in some sense of false optimism about the state of his testimony. He was an unmitigated disaster for the prosecution.

There was still talk around the courthouse about Eddie Greenspan's masterful dismantling of Governor Thompson's credibility. Cross-examination requires prodigious planning and a bit of good fortune. I experienced the benefit of luck in a case that I handled several years ago. I was defending a police officer charged with sexually assaulting a teenage girl who had just escaped from the group home where she was residing. The girl claimed that my client's assault occurred in his squad car, and she was able to pinpoint the precise street location of her attack.

My client gave a dramatically different view of what transpired. He said he had discovered the complainant wandering the streets at four in the morning and ensured that she was returned safely to her group home. My defence theory in the case was that she had conveniently manufactured the assault to deflect attention from her escape from her group home. She happened to hate the police, and my client served as a convenient target.

A couple of months before trial, I asked Mitch, a law student who was articling with me, what his plans were for that evening.

"Working at the office," he said matter-of-factly.

"Where will you be at four in the morning?" I inquired.

"I was planning to be asleep."

Mitch forgot that for a lowly articling student, sleep was a luxury. I informed him that I would pick him up at a pre-arranged time in the middle of the night to visit the alleged scene of the assault at the time it supposedly took place. Visiting the scene of the crime, or supposed crime, is a routine practice of mine. In one instance my car almost got stuck on a snowy bank on a desolate road north of Toronto, in the precise location where my client had supposedly arranged for the ambush and murder of her husband.

I picked up my weary student and we headed through the empty streets of Toronto's east end and then parked my car in the spot of the "crime." We just sat there in total silence.

"Do you smell something, Mitch?" I asked him.

We both agreed that an overpowering smell of bread had instantly filled the car when we parked. About a block northwest of our location, we discovered a huge Wonder Bread factory where bread was being baked for the day's shipments. Trucks waited in the driveway of the factory, ready to deliver the fresh bread that was baking in the ovens.

The teenaged complainant had never mentioned anything about the smell of bread in her statement to the police. In a careful cross-examination I established that she couldn't remember anything unusual about the location of her assault. The jury returned with a not-guilty verdict within a couple of hours.

While cross-examination may appear effortless in court, every question is generally structured in advance, tightly woven to afford the witness a minimal amount of wiggle room. If you give the witness the rope to hang your client, it is a given that it will be used generously.

Ed Genson passed by to say hello at a break in the proceedings. He was bemoaning the fact that he wasn't going to be cross-examining David Radler on Monday. "He's my kind of witness," he said. It is abundantly clear that Eddie Greenspan is ready for Radler. The curtain for the trial's main act will finally be opened on Monday. I no longer hear complaints about the case being exceedingly dull. Radler has injected some much-needed excitement.

WAL-MART JUSTICE CHOPPER

The life of a trial lawyer is not one to envy. Disparaged at parties (unless someone is seeking free advice on a speeding ticket), trial lawyers tend to gravitate to mates who possess similar litigious instincts. Long hours at the office are fuelled by repeated shots of caffeine. In court they must battle the occasional ornery judge, skeptical juries, and adversaries dedicated to obstreperous interruptions of their witness examinations with strident objections.

Nights are filled with depressing visits to clients draped in bright orange jumpsuits in jails, where there is a lingering odour of ammonia wafting through the corridors. The final part of the day is spent researching arcane principles of law in dusty books authored by knighted law professors who have limited practical experience. For some of them, the notion of a class action lawsuit is a class project.

Fragile egos and rampant insecurity are the trial lawyer's hallmarks. Indeed, articling students and law clerks were created by compassionate law societies to provide a supportive environment for courtroom forays. "That was a brilliant cross-examination" and "You had me weeping with your closing" are the automatic responses of the dutiful sycophant. The slightest hesitation of fulsome praise is grounds for immediate dismissal.

Trial work is conducted in an open and public courtroom where quiet sneering in the gallery area is permitted. Unlike the surgeon, whose patient is suitably sedated, the trial lawyer must be scrutinized by his client, whose TiVo feeds him a steady diet of *Law & Order* and *Boston Legal* episodes. The staid performance rarely meets the client's exceedingly high expectations.

Occasionally, there are very appreciative clients. I once had a client, Melissa, who was a most unaccomplished thief and would regularly call on me to represent her after she got caught. One day she called and told me that she had an urgent matter to discuss with me. She told me that she was in love with me. After I picked myself up off the floor, I explained to her gently that it was only natural that she feel some sense of attachment to the person constantly throwing her the life preserver. She appeared to understand.

Antacid tablets and Tylenol No. 3s are best stored in a safe and secure location in the lawyer's briefcase. Witnesses for the opposing party have been trained like circus seals to inflict severe pain whenever they are asked open-ended questions starting with the dreaded word "why." In a day filled with hundreds of questions, it is inevitable that even the best advocate lapses into a few "why" questions. The indelible memory of those crushing moments endures through the few hours budgeted for the trial lawyer's foreign state of sleep. And then the next day begins the process anew.

There are occasionally magical moments during the course of a trial when the trial lawyer's efforts are rewarded. Take for instance Eddie Greenspan's cross-examination of Jim Thompson. Christie Blatchford aptly described Greenspan in the weekend edition of the *Globe and Mail* as "the epitome of the brash Canadian." She further praised his excellent work by noting that Greenspan was "brusque and argumentative" and gave no quarter to anyone.

Lest the bloated ego of the barrister be duly inflated, there are always naysayers and detractors to splash cold water in his face. The local Chicagoans have not been as generous in their views of Eddie Greenspan's courtroom finesse. *Underwhelming* is the word that one veteran lawyer used to describe it.

Others have been equally critical. One of the most respected media gurus in the windy city, Mike Miner, openly questioned the wisdom of Greenspan's role as Thompson's courtroom duellist.

"Plus he's Jim Thompson — the first witness some of the jurors in this Canada-centric trial will have ever heard of, the guy the state office building a couple of blocks up Dearborn is named after. Jurors are so likely to want our guy to do well that I wonder if it was a mistake for Greenspan, a Canadian, to have cross-examined him. The jury might have warmed more to Greenspan's co-counsel, Ed Genson, an old-time Chicagoan."[19]

Trial lawyers must also be resourceful. This may require them to juggle a number of cases at the same time. For example, apparently Jim Thompson's Chicago-based attorney will return on behalf of David Radler when he begins his testimony on Monday. He will first have to await Judge St. Eve's decision as to whether his client's testimony was "based on speculation and surmise," as defence lawyers have argued in a motion to limit the scope of his slings and arrows.

The motion is a significant one for the government. The alleged speculation is conceded in the motion to possibly be a determinative issue in the case. It quotes from a prepared statement Radler read to the grand jury a couple of months prior to his guilty plea: "It was obvious that our plan to insert ourselves as recipients of non-compete fees — was a plan to engage in a series of related-party transactions. It was obvious that we would not honour our [fiduciary] obligations regarding these related-party transactions because we would not disclose the truth."

It is unprecedented in my experience to have a viable issue in a trial that an accomplice is speculating that his co-participants knew about the crime being committed (in this case a $60-million fraud). The starting line for David Radler's key evidence is that "I suppose that Conrad Black and his co-defendants knew about my devious plot with the non-competes." Huh? Will it be Radler's evidence that he never had a single conversation or exchanged a single email or fax with Black or the other men that outlined a plan to defraud the shareholders? Is this a case based on a "wink and nod" theory?

There is great anticipation building about Radler's forthcoming testimony. It is the last gasp for the prosecution's case, but Radler has the ability to revive it. His rotten deal looms in the future. The puppet strings will be invisible as he enters the courtroom, but he is the marionette of the prosecution. His prize for exemplary courtroom co-operation will be the twenty-nine-month sentence and quarter-million-dollar fine that awaits him. This shocking American practice of delayed sentencing is a breeding ground for miscarriage of justice.

I have become a keen observer of the American system of justice during this trial and my report card presents a rather bleak picture. Many features of it are tilted in favour of the prosecution. Attempts are being made to erode the system's fairness even further. The *New York Times* reported on Saturday that the U.S. Justice Department has asked a federal appeals court in a recent court filing with respect to detainees at Guantanamo Bay, Cuba, "to limit the number of times lawyers challenging detention could visit detainees and to allow officials to read lawyers' mail to detainees."[20]

It is difficult to imagine that a country steeped in a democratic tradition could seek to limit the access a lawyer has to a client under any circumstances. The competing principle is full answer and defence. I suppose that every system of justice must decide on its priorities.

MAY 7–8

Radler takes the stand for the prosecution, having pleaded guilty to one count of fraud in exchange for a twenty-nine-month sentence (to be served in Canada) and $250,000 fine. He testifies Black concocted a plan to reroute millions of dollars of shareholders' money to senior Hollinger executives. He also claims the non-compete agreements were never brought to the board's attention.

AT THE SNACKING ELF

I was introduced to a new coffee shop near the courthouse called Intelligentsia. The jury was asked to suspend its "intelligentsia" today as it heard about Conrad Black's planned surprise birthday party for his wife, Barbara Amiel. It must have been inspired by Truman Capote's masquerade ball at the Plaza Hotel. Or perhaps Marie Antoinette's pre–Bastille Day bash.

Three menus were inscribed in the finest calligraphy for the party and filled with delightful amuse-bouches and succulent entrees. The meals were to be doused with an endless supply of $320 bottles of Dom Pérignon. A mezzo-soprano commissioned from the Metropolitan Opera Company was accompanied by a pianist performing on an upright piano with a matching bench. Songs from *Samson and Delilah* and *Carmen* were featured on the program.

La Grenouille, described as a highly respected French restaurant in New York, was the scene of the splendid event. The total cost of $54,000 surely surpassed the average annual income of the jurors.

Ed Genson successfully made the point that the party was hosted by Conrad Black and Hollinger International Inc. His client had personally paid for $20,000 of the total bill, including the $569 calligraphy expense. As for the matching piano bench, that was Hollinger's cost to bear. There are limits that must be respected.

Genson also highlighted that the guest list of luminaries, including people with the last names of Bloomberg, Wintour, Trump, and Walters, had substantial connections to the media. Perhaps Barbara was there to invite Conrad and Donald to appear on *The View* with Rosie O'Donnell. Marie-Josée Kravis abruptly left the party when she discovered that the devil doesn't wear Prada.

David Radler was present, of course. My first question in cross-examination would determine whom he dined with. If he wore the shiny pink tie that he wore to court today, he dined alone. Even the party planner for the surprise party came with a lawyer, and Radler, not to be outdone, came with two. As he strode nervously into court today and described the first seeds of his friendship and partnership with Conrad Black, the classic old song "Those Were the Days" should have been serenading the courtroom. The jurors seemed energized as Radler was announced as the next witness. It was plain to see that they have been anxiously anticipating this "Et tu, Brute" moment at the trial.

Eric Sussman demonstrated signs that he had also recently frequented the Intelligentsia. These are a couple of examples of actual questions asked by Sussman of Radler today: "Are there French-speaking and English-speaking areas in Canada?" "Did you know anything about tractors?"

The first venture for Radler and Black was the *Sherbrooke Record*. Radler seemed perfectly unqualified for the newspaper business. One of his prior ventures was the business of Inuit settlements.

Their first deal was consummated in another French restaurant, Au lutin qui bouffe. That translates to "At the snacking elf." I am prepared to bet that there was no Caviar Beluga sur Gaufrettes served at the dinner. That is more suited to Conrad Black's exotic tastes.

The two men built a media empire together. In his understated manner, Radler wrote in a memo that "it wasn't CBS, but it is a living." It was the threat of separatism that propelled them to search for other markets beyond La Belle Province. One of their early media gems was the *Chicago Sun-Times*, which was the eighth-largest newspaper in North America.

Now there are droves of readers from their former paper reading about their present predicament.

David Radler did appear to be a puppet in court — not for the prosecution but for Conrad Black. Radler testified that he did not make any major financial decisions without consulting Black. Black was totally informed of the sale or acquisition of any newspaper. The unspoken message for the jury was that Radler's fraudulent non-competes received Black's blessing.

Radler gave his evidence today in an apparently unscripted and unrehearsed manner. However, this may be the most prepared and rehearsed witness in the history of civilization. Have I missed anyone? It will be the daunting task of Eddie Greenspan to shatter the transparent veneer and expose Radler's bellicose character. He will have to undo thousands of hours of preparation in the process. My suggestion to Greenspan is to rest without asking a single question. Radler has said that his plea agreement is contingent on telling the truth. I accept that if Radler claimed that he had sudden pangs of conscience and insisted that he had acted solo in defrauding the Hollinger shareholders, the government would shrug and proceed with the promised deal. Can there be any question that they would urge Judge Amy St. Eve to carry the deal forward after Black walked away as a free man? What a cynical lot all of you are.

The next couple of days at the trial will largely dictate the outcome for Conrad Black. If Radler excels on the witness stand, Black will be forced to testify. Think about George Bush coming before a grand jury to explain his proof of weapons of mass destruction in Iraq and you will have a taste of the impending disaster.

The pace of the trial has really picked up. There were some dry patches today that provided some weary jurors with moments of rest. That will not be the case tomorrow. I am so excited that I am thinking of renewing my subscription to *American Trucker* magazine. I plan to dine at La Grenouille the next time that I visit New York. And I have scheduled a trip to the Nicholas Hoare bookstore in Toronto, where I will purchase a long list of books that I have postponed reading. I plan to skim them all. Life is grand.

THE BLAME GAME

"Why do they need two hundred pictures?" By chance I happened to be standing beside David Radler at the lunch break as he tried to escape the paparazzi and their flashbulbs. Radler should have been far more concerned about incurring the wrath of the prosecutors. They weren't a happy bunch today. Radler was summoned back to meet with them after court with his lawyer in tow. There is trouble in Dodge City. David Radler is trying to dodge a lengthy prison sentence.

After basking for a day in the glow of credibility, the first cracks in Radler's suntanned shell finally began to be exposed. It started with the $2-million non-compete fee paid to Hollinger Inc. in the *American Trucker* deal: Radler claimed not to know whose idea it was. About a million dollars fell into his lap illicitly and he was feigning ignorance about its origins.

Radler then testified about a phone call with Black in January of 1999, in which Black told him that the parent company, Hollinger Inc., deserved a portion of the non-compete fee allocated in the first deal with Community Newspaper Holdings, Inc. (CNHI). The figure suggested was $12 million, which represented 25 percent of the total non-compete fee. That percentage became the template for the series of future non-compete payments. Radler testified that Black planned to use the money Hollinger Inc. received from the non-competes to erase some of its mounting debt.

Did Radler endorse Black's plan? He told the jury that he listened and he certainly didn't say no. The incredible Mr. Radler. He didn't like the transaction but remained unsure if it was legal. According to Radler, his participation in a sophisticated $60-million fraud scheme began with passive acquiescence. It is now clear why Radler was summoned urgently to meet with the prosecutors late this afternoon. They have realized that he is the victim of a wrongful conviction.

Radler refused to concede that he acted criminally. When asked why he didn't share his bogus non-compete scheme with the Hollinger board, Radler noted that "I could have but I don't think they would have agreed." The directors, he commented, would likely have asked some tough questions. Such an astute observation from a man who once acted as the chief operating officer of one of the largest media empires in the world. There would in reality have only been one question from the board: "When can we get back the money that you stole?"

The prosecution announced to the judge today that there is a smoking gun in the case. They later apologized when they realized that a colleague had been discovered placing a lit cigarette in an FBI agent's gun. That will be the closest the prosecution gets to finding some corroboration for their star witness.

Remember those infamous boxes that Conrad Black secretly removed from the Hollinger head office. It was all captured on videotape and formed the basis for an obstruction of justice charge against Black. I now believe that Conrad Black was setting the prosecution up by creating a piece of what seemed to be hard evidence that would ultimately be proven worthless and would be the symbol of a failed case. You might compare it to Johnnie Cochran's challenge to O.J. Simpson's prosecutors to get his client to try on the glove: "If the box doesn't fit, Conrad walks."

We learned today in a session held in the jury's absence that the most incriminating documents in the boxes are rambling musings that Conrad Black sent to David Radler. "Springtime contemplation of musing," set in March 1999, evoked memories of Gus Newman of the song "Springtime for Hitler" in *The Producers*. That touched a chord with me. I ruminated about the idea of watching the prosecution of a case that is doomed to fail and instead becomes a popular success. Any worthy candidates?

Back to the contents of the boxes. There were Christmas musings, summer musings, and the finest collection of musings ever retained and stored for posterity. The prosecutors may now regret dedicating months to retrieving the stack of boxes. Black's attorney surprisingly suggested that his client was pining for a book contract when the musings were penned. One of his co-counsel, Michael Schachter, was even less diplomatic, dismissing them as pointless and a waste of time. Black has already removed Schachter's name from the list of recipients of autographed copies of his future book.

The judge was confronted with the unusual task of breaking up a heated exchange this morning between Eric Sussman and Conrad Black's attorneys. Laughter and gaiety are the usual hallmarks of this courtroom. Anything contentious must quickly be shuffled to "the well" for a sidebar.

"Just don't get me to referee," she told the defendants' lawyers. Sorry, Judge, but that is precisely your role. During the skirmish, Gus Newman stated, "I'm not placing blame on anyone." Black's lawyers, Greenspan and Genson, were far less circumspect in their assessment of their client's team of prosecutors. The gloves were off today and it was great theatre. Genson noted that the prosecutors were turning him falsely into their straw man and piñata by misrepresenting his opening address.

Greenspan was equally livid. He told the court in answer to Sussman's complaint about the intractable delay in securing the boxes that just because the defence hadn't gone down on their knees to the prosecutors' request didn't mean they had obstructed justice. Conrad Black was properly exercising his constitutional rights. I resisted the temptation to stand up and sing the Canadian national anthem.

At one point during the to and fro, Sussman made a passing comment that if he got in trouble in Canada Greenspan could represent him. "No, I won't," Greenspan replied with a deadpan expression.

He was entirely serious. The stereotype of the courteous Canadian has been forever shattered. Blame it all on Eddie Greenspan.

MAY 9

Pointing to Radler's past lies to internal Hollinger committees, prosecutors, and FBI agents, Greenspan attempts to paint Radler as a serial liar motivated by his plea bargain to give testimony favourable to the prosecution. Greenspan refers to Radler's arranged transfer to a minimum-security prison near his Vancouver home, and Canada's more lenient parole regulations, as a "sweetheart deal."

Greenspan also notes Radler negotiated non-compete agreements long before Black purportedly suggested their use, and the lawyer attacks Radler's claims to having had a close business and personal relationship with Black.

FOUL BALL

The musings of Conrad Black were introduced into evidence today and I was not the least bit amused. In fact, I felt a certain kinship with the character played by Peter Finch in the movie *Network*: "I'm mad as hell and I'm not going to take this anymore." The musings surely provided some comic relief to the trial. But as Ed Genson correctly noted in a motion for a mistrial, their introduction was inappropriate and "appeals to class prejudice." The prosecution is playing the class card to full effect. For example, the jury is now aware that Black justified in a note to company executives his decision to have the shareholders pick up half of the cost of a chef and other hospitality expenses at his London home. The home, he noted, was used for corporate entertainment that was quite productive at times.

This epitomizes bad character evidence and nothing more. The grave danger is that it will distract the jury from focusing on the charges in the indictment by poisoning their view of Conrad Black. If the facts were altered and Black had used his home in London as a hospice for cancer patients, would that fact be admissible in court? Of course not, the prosecution would vehemently argue. What possible relevance does it have to these proceedings? Well, what is good for the goose is good for the humbug.

The insidious plea agreement of David Radler was explored today in cross-examination by Eddie Greenspan. Greenspan pounded away at the theme that Radler's impending sentence would be dictated by lead prosecutor Eric Sussman's evaluation of his testimony. "If you come off your script," Greenspan goaded him, "you know the government will tell the judge you're a liar, don't you?" Radler rejected the notion that he knew that Sussman was the key to his future. He claimed that he was gaining a greater appreciation of the prosecutor's role from Greenspan's questions and further accused Greenspan of putting words in his mouth as he disagreed that he was tied to a script.

Radler's professed ignorance of Sussman's role is patently false and silly. He is represented by one of Chicago's finest criminal defence lawyers and it would be inconceivable that Radler's deal wouldn't be spelled out in bold print. It would be plainly explained to him that the bargain was contingent on his co-operation at the trial to the satisfaction of the prosecutors. At one point in his testimony, Radler complained to Greenspan that "it's a game." That is an apt description for his false presentation to the jury about his sweetheart deal. It was about as transparent as saran wrap.

There was a moment during Radler's examination that provided a window into his true mindset about his deal. He advised Sussman that when he met with prosecutors and FBI agents in 2004, he was admittedly less than candid. "I was trying to rationalize some of the transactions," he explained. "I was fighting back."

Radler added the following words: "The fact was I was offered ..." It takes little imagination to contemplate how Radler would have finished the sentence if he hadn't caught his mistake. The deal that he was offered was the recipe for the dramatic shift in his story to appease the prosecutors.

As he glances at Conrad Black at the defendants' table facing the prospect of a lifetime in prison, Radler is constantly reminded of the sage course he has followed. I happened to ride down the elevator in a small group with him from our twelfth-floor courtroom. The man standing next to me was calm and smiling. Radler even attempted to shake Gus Newman's hand after exchanging polite greetings. Here was a man who had been called a liar more times than Bill Clinton and he was perfectly relaxed minutes after leaving court.

The odd couple in the courtroom is not Radler and Black. It is Greenspan and Sussman. I can confidently predict that the two men will never be seen at Wrigley Field enjoying a beer together at a Chicago Cubs game. There is an obvious antipathy between them that surfaces frequently in court. At one point Sussman tried to summarize the answer he expected Radler to give. Ed Genson interjected, "I thought the witness was supposed to testify." Greenspan quickly added, "I'll cross-examine, Mr. Sussman." It was clear that he meant it.

The facade of collegiality in the case is quickly being eroded. In one of his musings in September 2002, Conrad Black concluded that "it has been an implacable struggle." That is a fitting description for the manner in which the prosecution is disclosing its case to the defence. Everything, from the order of witnesses to the documents relied upon, is apparently being turned over to the defence reluctantly and in a dilatory fashion. Greenspan and Genson are becoming increasingly vocal with their concerns about Conrad Black's fair trial rights.

I learned today that it is best not to dart out of the courtroom a few minutes early. Invariably something totally unexpected occurs that is very newsworthy. At the end of court today, Radler's attorney addressed Judge St. Eve to complain that Greenspan had journeyed into the forbidden land. His alleged faux pas was to ask a couple of questions that were protected by attorney-client privilege. Greenspan had only established that Radler had lied to his own counsel. This was part of a pattern of deceit that was forcefully established. Radler had lied to investigators from the FBI and the Postal Service. He had lied to prosecutors, including Eric Sussman. And he had lied to the special committee. David Radler was a serial liar.

Greenspan's ultimate point was that the jury shouldn't trust him. This theme will be further developed tomorrow as the cross-examination by Greenspan continues. His client's fate largely hinges on the next few days of the trial. He is in a foreign courtroom with the entire world watching. This case will define his legacy as a courtroom master. I therefore approached him gingerly late today with an important question that has perplexed me since the first day of trial. "Eddie," I asked, "do you happen to know where you can get a good bagel in Chicago?"

The answer will have to wait for another day. Apparently Eddie Greenspan had other serious matters to consider.

THE BUZZ

Ron Safer, Mark Kipnis's attorney, made a deliberate choice at the beginning of the trial to ensconce himself with the rest of his defence team at the far side of the courtroom. There are times when his team is barely visible to the jury, which is precisely Safer's objective. He wants his client to maintain a low profile and to lie outside the prosecution's radar gun.

While keeping the veneer of a joint defence, Safer fully appreciates that his client rests in a very different position than Conrad Black and his other co-defendants. The unique line that Safer will repeat over and over to the jury in his closing address is the following: "Why would Mark involve himself in a $60-million fraud involving non-competition payments and not receive a single payment of his own?"

There was a dramatic development in the trial today, and it involved Safer. Eddie Greenspan was engaged in the continuation of his combative cross-examination of David Radler. There were repeated objections by Eric Sussman that at times devolved into acrimonious exchanges. At one point Greenspan asked to publish an exhibit. Safer advised the judge that he required some time to review it and a recess was granted.

When court resumed, Greenspan launched into a fairly innocuous question about the non-competes. Safer stood and objected, although the question had no direct bearing on his client: "That was certainly asked and answered," he stated in a tart voice. Greenspan seemed startled and stared at him for a couple of seconds in disbelief. The objection was sustained and Greenspan moved on to his next question.

After almost two months of the trial, this represented the first objection by one co-defendant against another. Its significance could not be lost on the jury. Safer was attempting to create a safe distance between his client's fate and that of Conrad Black. He was telegraphing to the jury that this was not a defence parade in which the charged men were moving in synchronized step.

Why did Kipnis's counsel choose the very moment that Greenspan was cross-examining the star witness in the case to symbolically create a possible chasm with Black? There can only be one reasonable answer for the strange timing. Safer was deeply concerned that Radler, the pivotal witness in the case, was withstanding Greenspan's withering questioning and bouncing back intact. In other words, Conrad Black was possibly losing the trial.

The ominous sense that the momentum had shifted sharply in favour of the prosecution was shared by many of the journalists I spoke to during the course of today's abbreviated proceeding. A fair number of them have witnessed the entire trial and share a fairly sophisticated understanding of the evidence. The buzz among them was that Greenspan was losing the major battle and that Radler was frustrating him.

Radler was a disquieting witness who was deliberately forestalling Greenspan from developing any rhythm or cadence in his questioning. He repeatedly answered Greenspan's questions with accusations that he was "manoeuvring all over the place" and "taking things out of context." He personified the difficult and evasive witness. Radler's countless hours of preparation, including a mock cross-examination, were reaping dividends. He had been shaped and moulded to be faster and quicker than "Fast Eddie." His habit of ranting rather than responding should have been curtailed by the judge but it rarely was.

I watched David Radler intently today along with the jury. There was a solemn mood among the jurors as they scrutinized Radler's answers and demeanour during cross-examination. They are a difficult bunch to read, although it is clear that Ed Genson is their favourite lawyer in the courtroom. He manages to connect with a Chicago jury in a manner that none of the other attorneys can emulate. His rapid-fire style of cross-examination can be disarming to witnesses. A novel approach for the defence on Monday would be to allow Genson to cross-examine for a limited period of time. Radler hasn't been prepared for this particular Eddie, so the tactic might prove to be effective. Eddie Greenspan could then change the pace and ask the concluding questions.

Every trial has its peaks and valleys. Patrick Fitzgerald was seen yesterday at a break huddling with the Black prosecutors. The prosecution knows that if they can weather the Radler storm, their port of destination of multiple convictions looms closer. The defence also realizes that Radler may be the perfect storm that will send all of the defendants to prison. The stakes are indeed high, and the next few days of the trial will likely settle the outcome. We will see Eddie Greenspan's skill as a polished advocate put to the test. It is the most important cross-examination of his stellar career. I wouldn't bet against him. Not just yet.

D-DAY

An attorney from Chicago who has attended select parts of the Conrad Black trial is quoted in the weekend edition of the *National Post* with an interesting comment about the jury: "These people are tired. They've heard from the star witness and now they want to move on."

The jury has heard from a star witness who has seen more rigorous training than an Olympic discus thrower and who has emerged bright and shiny from his mock trial and elaborate preparation. He has everything to gain by clinging to his script with all of the tenacity of a man holding for dear life to a life preserver thrown to him at sea. The prosecutors are holding the rope and are waiting to haul him ashore. But his salvation is delayed until his co-operation can be assessed. A guilty verdict for Conrad Black guarantees a perfect score for Radler. The prosecutors sit at a table only a few feet from him watching intently as he helps to put the hook into the Big Kahuna.

Radler is not going to succumb easily even to the best cross-examiner. His resilience has been surprising but it should have been expected. The notion that Greenspan should hold up the white flag and resist questioning further because the jury may be weary and ready to move on is absolute nonsense. (And I say this with great respect, of course.)

Greenspan's cross-examination thus far has been a relatively hit-and-miss encounter with the elusive Mr. Radler. When a respected journalist like Theresa Tedesco from the *National Post* describes the cross-examination as "messy," it must be cause for concern in the Black camp. Currently, Radler appears to be winning the high-stakes battle in the courtroom in the eyes of the jury. However, a top-gun advocate like Eddie Greenspan has the ability to bounce back, overcome adversity, and regain the advantage with the witness. He should not be underestimated. Monday is D-Day at the Conrad Black trial. This will be Greenspan's opportunity to shift the drift winds away from a guilty verdict for his client. It represents his last-gasp attempt. If he fails, Conrad Black may have to testify in his own defence. The Watergate burglars had a better chance of appearing credible to a jury.

I sense among the Conrad Black detractors a disturbing air of pleasure and delight at Black's sudden misfortune in the courtroom and the public pillorying of his famous Canadian counsel. I overheard one of them actually say, "I'm smiling now." Tom Bower reported in the *Sunday Times* that Eric Sussman left the court smiling after the last day's session and that Radler laughed as he passed Black on his way to the doorway. I will give Mr. Sussman the benefit of the doubt. Perhaps he was smiling as he realized that he may not have to ask a single question of Radler in redirect examination.

I suspect that for members of the glee club, the presumption of innocence was only a barrier to overcome rather than a meaningful legal principle to ensure that due process and a scrupulously fair trial were accorded to Conrad Black. A criminal trial is not a game or sporting match. I will say this much with certainty: innocent or guilty, I would never relish my prospects as a defendant in an American courtroom. To borrow a tennis expression, it is always ad-in for the prosecution. I would even be prepared to settle for deuce.

LET ME CALL YOU SWEETHEART

Well, the real F.D.R. finally revealed himself in court today. Not the subject of Conrad Black's biography, of course. Frank David Radler walked into the courtroom as the David who fought bravely against a Goliath for several days. By the end of the court session, he emerged as an emperor with no clothes. Radler's shining credibility was tarnished by Eddie Greenspan today, and the damage to the prosecution's case may be irreversible.

Greenspan will be the focal point of blame if Black loses this trial. He assumed that risk when he agreed to handle the case in an American courtroom. The trial judge is extremely tolerant of Greenspan's misadventures with the local rules of evidence and procedure two months into the trial. The jury may be less forgiving.

Greenspan took a different approach today after a restless weekend and it reaped immediate dividends. The most critical point that Greenspan established was the absence of a single fax, email, or memo that supported Radler's contention that Black initiated the bogus non-compete scheme. This distinguishes the Black case from the other high-profile American corporate fraud cases in which documentary corroboration abounded. The judge will be required at the trial's conclusion to offer a cautionary charge to the jury about accepting Radler's evidence absent any supporting evidence. While more diluted than the equivalent Vetrovec warning in Canada[21] (named after the Supreme Court of Canada decision that created the legal principle), it nonetheless will likely have a critical bearing on the jury's decision in the case.

Greenspan crystallized for the jury, for the first time in the trial, the theory of the defence. This was a major failing in the defence's opening addresses. After accusing Radler of making the best deal of his life with the prosecution, Greenspan continued: "For that deal — that incredible sweetheart deal — you had to give the U.S. government what they wanted, when no crime was committed by anyone but you."

According to the defence theory, the rogue and scoundrel in the dishonest non-competition scheme for the U.S. community newspaper deals is David Radler. He arguably conned his co-defendants, the Hollinger International shareholders, and the prosecutors who made his artificially sweet deal, and, most significantly, is now attempting to dupe the jury in the case.

Radler made a serious misstep today. Rather than admit that his relaxed sentence was potentially abbreviated, he attempted instead to portray the lustrous shine on his deal with the prosecutors as a bit rusty. He seriously maintained in answer to a question put by Greenspan that he was uninformed that his twenty-nine-month prison sentence, to be served in Canada, could be shortened with parole considerations by almost two years.

He feigned ignorance that the sentence could be reduced to six months served in a Canadian prison. Greenspan immediately shot back, "Until this moment you didn't know that? I think I'm going to send you a bill."

The notion that Radler wasn't tuned in to the precise sentence he is facing is complete balderdash. It is implausible that he wouldn't be overly curious about his own parole eligibility, and it would be highly unprofessional for his acknowledged stellar Vancouver lawyers not to have spelled it out in detail. It is a mystery why it is not explicitly set out in Rader's written plea agreement with the prosecutors. It is also an immutable assumption that every prison inmate knows two facts as he is about to commence a prison sentence: his visiting privileges and his earliest release date.

The comfortable and defiant Radler vanished from the courtroom today, replaced by an irritated, nervous man who realized that he was beginning to look foolish with some of his answers. When Greenspan snapped at him that it was easy for him to lie, Radler responded, "I don't believe I have to answer that." Judge Amy St. Eve dropped the ball by not insisting that Radler answer the question. A few of her rulings were also questionable. When Gus Newman received a damaging and non-responsive answer from Radler, he swung around and pointed at the prosecution's table: "Do you feel that this gratuitous remark," he asked Radler, "strengthens your position with the people at this table?"

Eric Sussman made an objection with no name that was sustained. The question posed was perfectly appropriate and the ruling forestalled a full inquiry of Radler's fishy deal. However, today marked the best day for Judge St. Eve in the trial. Her decisions were otherwise even-handed and she firmly chastised Sussman outside the jury's presence for leaving an improper impression with the jury that Greenspan was not operating in good faith. She was visibly angry at the lead prosecutor for allowing matters in the courtroom to descend into the personal arena. She wasn't prepared to deal with it in a secretive sidebar, either. It was about time that she interceded in this fashion. Every mocking objection by Sussman to a Greenspan question has been made with his voice raised and his head nodding in apparent disbelief.

Greenspan is not without fault, as he occasionally baits his adversary in a boisterous tone. It has become an unfortunate and nasty sideshow to the trial. It was, however, a red-faced Sussman who stormed out of the courtroom moments after the judge's admonition.

Radler has one final day on the stand and the prosecution will then move to its final phase. The case is marching to its conclusion. In a few weeks it will be clear if Conrad Black will be ushered out of court in handcuffs or leave with his freedom intact. There will undoubtedly be a few more twists and turns before the final chapter is written. It will be a dramatic conclusion to a fascinating case.

SLIP SLIDING AWAY

I find myself continuing to struggle with a number of differences in proce-dure between the Canadian and American justice systems. For example, it is fairly common for an attorney at this trial to begin a question and then suddenly change his mind in mid-sentence and declare it to be "withdrawn." The air is sprinkled with some magical potion and the question is asked again as if nothing else had ever been spoken.

A more jarring difference is the use of objections made by opposing counsel during statements to the jury. In Canada that would occur about as frequently as a winter without a raging snowstorm. However, in the Black trial, both defence and prosecution objected with impunity. In one instance, Ed Genson successfully objected to the prosecutor's opening as "personalizing the jury." I wondered how an objection would be framed for misleading the jury. The following passage was included in the open-ing statement of Jeffrey Cramer:

> You're going to hear from David Radler. I told you Radler pled guilty. He's accepted responsibility for his fraud and he's going to jail. And David Radler will give you an inside look at how they went about stealing $60 million; how he and Black and Atkinson and Boultbee and Kipnis, how they all stole $60 million. Radler will tell you how it worked. And he'll give you a view into it. He'll tell you what they did — what memos they pro-duced. And David Radler, you'll have a chance to judge him; he will be supported by the other witnesses who testify; and, he will be supported by documents.

David Radler will be supported by documents? Am I at the same trial as these prosecutors? If there is one matter that is abundantly clear from Radler's lengthy testimony, it is that there is not one single document, whether it be a fax, memo, email, or letter, that supported the word of the star prosecution witness. Did such documents simply disappear after Mr. Cramer gave his opening? It seems that the prosecutor perhaps mis-spoke. There will be no objection by the defence for poor form. I strongly suspect, however, that the jury will be reminded in final argument by the defence that the only document supporting David Radler is his plea agreement with the prosecutors. He has already used his lifeline.

THE BOWERY BOYS

I contacted Tom Bower at his home in London some time after the jury returned with its verdicts against Conrad Black and his co-defendants. Bower was the author of a book, *Conrad and Lady Black: Dancing on the Edge*,[22] which had resulted in an extravagant $11-million libel lawsuit commenced by Black against Bower. Bower's conduct was referred to in the statement of claim as being "vindictive" and "high-handed." Tom Bower attended portions of the Black trial and covered aspects of it for a British newspaper while the libel lawsuit remained ongoing.

When I indicated that I wanted to interview him for my book about the trial, Bower set a most unusual condition for our discussion. I was first required to declare my reasons for predicting Conrad Black's acquittal. I instantly replied with one word — "disclosure" — and I was then permitted to proceed with my questions. Bower agreed to a subsequent telephone interview a few weeks later. I wondered if there would be another skill-testing question.

I discovered a piece of information during the course of my interviews of Tom Bower that actually startled me as I reflected upon its significance. Bower described meeting with key prosecution witness David Radler each and every day during the course of Radler's eight days of testimony on the witness stand. Every morning before Radler testified, they would meet at the swimming pool of the Peninsula Hotel, where Radler was staying, and speak together about the case. The luxurious Chicago setting served as the suitable rendezvous point for all of their frequent chats. I probed the matter further:

> Q: All right, and you were speaking with him, what, every
>   day that he testified at his hotel? Is that right?
> A: I'd meet him in the mornings …

And later:

Q: But you said you met him each day, though, that's what you said.
A: I did, I met him each day in the … in the … swimming pool.

Bower did not seem to feel that there was anything untoward in his meeting with the star witness of the trial regularly during his evidence and speaking freely together about features of the case. As Bower noted to me, it was all handled in a polite manner.

The possible blending of the duo's waterside discussions may have produced a toxic brew of testimony. That is precisely the reason that defence counsel needed to sample the content of those conversations for their acerbic flavour. From a defence point of view, Bower's repeated day-of-testimony conversations with a star witness — with the potential for those conversations to affect Radler's testimony — would have to be a legitimate concern.

David Radler informed Bower during their discussions that he was determined to save Kipnis and chose not to incriminate him. Radler's argument was with Black and not with Kipnis. According to Tom Bower, the prosecution had mishandled Kipnis. Bower was adamant that Radler conveyed to him that he was unaware of the prison conditions after he was sentenced. I then asked Bower what Radler's view of the prosecutors was. He had posed that very question but Radler had refused to tell him. He was "trying to save his deal."

Bower also indicated that Radler noted that "he did the plea bargain to put Black in because he and Black did the deal together." As for Boultbee and Atkinson, Radler told Bower that "he had no direct relationship with them about the conspiracy."

I asked Bower if Radler had provided an explanation for his professed desire in their discussions not to place Mark Kipnis in the fraudulent scheme:

Q: Oh, when you said that he was trying not to put Kipnis into it, into the fraudulent scheme, was that, did he ever convey the reasons for that, why he didn't want to put him in the scheme?
A: Um … he said it had nothing to do with Kipnis.

Did the swimming pool encounters play any part in shaping or changing the substance of David Radler's testimony? Any thoughts on the matter can only be sheer speculation and conjecture. However, what is abundantly clear is that none of the defendants' attorneys at the trial had an opportunity to explore the possibility of any tainting (or chlorination) of Radler's testimony.

MAY 15–16

Defence attorney Gus Newman, representing Boultbee, attempts to demonstrate how deeply involved Radler was in the day-to-day operations of Hollinger's American interests and how removed he was from the Canadian side. Judge St. Eve rebukes Radler for being evasive and uncooperative.

Radler admits to Ron Safer, representing Kipnis, that the $150,000 Kipnis received from Hollinger was not a non-compete payment, but merely a bonus for his hard work. Observers agree the defence has effectively diminished Radler's credibility.

MUSINGS OF A LEGAL ANALYST

I once had the occasion to defend a man charged with murdering his wife on the very night that O.J. Simpson was alleged to have killed his ex-wife Nicole Brown Simpson and her friend Ronald Goldman. The junior prosecutor at the trial in Napanee, Ontario, was Ivan Fernandes. We became friends, and when Ivan was appointed as a judge in downtown Toronto, I would stop by his chambers for a chat. On one occasion I was saddened to learn that Ivan was suffering from cancer and that his prospects were poor.

In our meetings that followed, I learned the story of Ivan's life before he came to Canada as a teenager. His high school years were spent in Uganda while the ruthless dictator Idi Amin was in power perpetrating a genocide that led to the slaughter of hundreds of thousands of Ugandans.

Ivan described one day when he was officiating at the East African Safari Rally in Kampala and he had a gun placed to his forehead by one of Amin's henchmen. Ivan was fortunate to escape from Uganda with his family unharmed. In their own neighbourhood, one man was brazenly shot in front of his wife and three daughters while another set of neighbours were abducted from their home in the middle of the night.

During my frequent visits to Justice Ivan Fernandes's chambers in the last weeks of his life, we devoted considerable discussion to the clash between civil liberties and public security. Ivan would become quite animated as he spoke of the complacency of North Americans to the emerging threat of terrorism. Many Americans incorrectly assumed that the bombing of a federal government building in Oklahoma City in 1995, he noted, was the work of Islamic fundamentalists. The notion of home-grown terrorism was a difficult pill for a democratic nation to swallow.

Ivan believed that Canadians still clung to a false belief that their country was immune to the spreading problem of global terrorism. He pointed out that the bank towers in Toronto could easily have been the target for the hijacked airplanes if the architects of the 9/11 attacks had been diverted from American airspace. Ivan and I engaged in fierce debates about whether safeguards for civil liberties needed to be redefined in these perilous times. I made the argument that security couldn't be a free pass for the unchecked authority of the state. Ivan admonished me for being terribly naïve for underestimating the pressing lethal threat. He related to me that he had read an interview with a senior Scotland Yard inspector who recounted that London police had thwarted major attacks that involved Al Qaeda. In the winter of 2005, Ivan expressed surprise that England, America's closest ally, had not yet been attacked by terrorists. Only few months later his dire concern became a tragic reality in the transit system of London.

I look back now on those meetings with Ivan fondly. I always left his chambers feeling richer as a human being and inspired by his deep conviction in the face of tremendous adversity.

In every aspect of our lives, we find ourselves regularly touched by people who inspire us. It may surprise you to learn that even in the spectacle of the Conrad Black trial, with its focus on accusations of greed and corruption, there are a select group of inspirational individuals.

The first of them is Ed Genson. I have rarely seen Genson outside court without a smile and friendly greeting for the court staff or a lonely Canadian trial lawyer. When I complimented him on a tie he recently wore, he told me that his wife had purchased it. "Fat people only get ties for gifts," he said. "It's the only thing you can be sure will fit."

Genson suffers from dystonia, a genetic disorder prevalent in Ashkenazi Jews. The illness leaves him with a limp and makes his head bob slightly. He moves around the courthouse in a motorized cart. When he cross-examines a witness, he uses a cane to slowly drag himself to the lectern. "I'll take my time getting up there," he once told the *American Lawyer.* "It's frightening to watch me coming."

Genson told one writer that jury trials wear him down and that his limp becomes more severe as he tires.[23] The Conrad Black trial must be a physical ordeal for him. Yet he remains consistently ebullient and an impassioned advocate for his client.

Then there is Genson's co-counsel, Gus Newman, who is representing Jack Boultbee. Newman cross-examined David Radler yesterday for almost the entire day. His sharpest questions came at the very end of his cross-examination. That may not seem particularly impressive until you realize that he is eighty years old. For an eighty-year-old man to undertake a gruelling three-month trial where there is no permissible margin of error is truly something to marvel.

The final inspirational figure is one of the co-defendants, Mark Kipnis. That may seem surprising. It shouldn't be. Kipnis could easily have cut himself a sweetheart deal with the prosecutors similar to Radler's and become a convicted felon in the process. Instead, Mark Kipnis risked decades in prison to stand trial with absolutely no guarantee of success.

Ron Safer told the jury that his client was innocent in his opening address. That is generally a risky strategy for a lawyer to employ because it sets the bar higher than it needs to be. The state has the burden to prove guilt beyond reasonable doubt. Even if a jury finds that a defendant is probably guilty, it still must acquit. In the Scott Peterson case, Peterson's attorney, Mark Geragos, foolishly promised the jury that he would expose Laci Peterson's true killer during the trial. He wasn't counting on it being his client.

It was clear today in court why Safer could safely make such a bold statement proclaiming his client's innocence to the jury. The government's case against Mark Kipnis is one of the flimsiest cases that I have ever observed in a major criminal prosecution. After today, it is virtually non-existent. Radler agreed that the bonuses of $150,000 Kipnis received were exclusively in recognition of the exceptional legal work that he did on both the CanWest deal and the U.S. newspaper transactions. It had nothing to do with the non-competition payments. In terms of benefits accrued from a $60-million alleged fraud scheme, the prosecution was unable to connect a single dollar to Mark Kipnis.

The most significant question that Safer posed to Radler in cross-examination was as follows: "Each time the government asked you, you said the bonus had nothing to do with the non-competes and was solely based on Mark Kipnis's hard work and the money he saved Hollinger International in legal fees?" Radler agreed that Safer's suggestion was correct. In other words, the prosecution has always known from interviews of Radler prior to trial that it could never connect the bonuses to anything fraudulent or, in particular, the non-competes. Yet in his opening statement to the jury, Jeffrey Cramer was prepared to leave that very unfair and inaccurate impression: "But what you're going to hear, ladies and gentlemen, is that Mark Kipnis received about $150,000 in bonus money. He got $150,000 in bonus money to help do their crime. Mark Kipnis had a fiduciary duty, I told you, just like the others. And he breached that duty, just like the others. His price was just a little bit lower. That's all. That's the only difference."

There is a steep price that the prosecution will pay, however, for including Mark Kipnis in the indictment. After today it seems clear that Radler planned from the outset to insulate himself from any blame by ensuring that it was Kipnis who signed the documents that were part of the fraudulent scheme. Radler was crafty enough to divert the attention to an unsuspecting subordinate. The prosecution bought the story. As Cramer noted in his opening, "If there is a document to be signed to complete this scheme, you will see that Mark Kipnis has a pen in his hand." That is precisely the devious *modus operandi* of Radler.

The implication for the jury is that David Radler was prepared to build a safety net for himself in the event that he needed it later. He was prepared to sacrifice Kipnis to suit his own nefarious purposes. The question that follows for the jury, then, is this: wouldn't Radler employ the same strategy to sacrifice Black, Atkinson, and Boultbee? By including them in the U.S. non-competes, he could invest in a stock that he could later cash in when the fire sale began. The defence can argue that the stock was their clients' culpability and that Radler cashed in by trading in the commodity that was dearest to him. As Safer suggested in his final booming question today, that commodity was Radler's liberty.

RAT SOUP

"The deal's dead." According to the *Chicago Sun-Times*, the comment was made by a veteran scribe, but I have heard similar statements made throughout the week by courtroom aficionados. There is about as much chance of Radler's deal being broken as there is of a Michael Jordan comeback in the NBA. The reason is simple. There is much more at stake than the singular plea negotiation of David Radler. The wheels of justice in America are lubricated every day by a litany of rich plea deals struck with accomplices and informants. If the government can't be trusted to honour its part of a bargain, the sweet fruit that is dangled as bait will be quickly rejected by rogue witnesses as the product of a poisoned tree. Perish the thought! We may actually see other trials being conducted in the courthouse.

Even with all of the bloated preparation of Radler and the exclusive company of two and sometimes three attorneys in court, Radler's witness meltdown was a ghoulish spectacle for the prosecution. It exceeded their worst fears. It can now be stated with relative certainty: Conrad Black will not be testifying at his trial.

The defence also has a new battle cry for their closing addresses: "Remember Radler." There was a declaration of war today in the Conrad Black trial. It didn't relate to Eddie Greenspan's halting his client's barrage of hallway tirades against his former business partner. Conrad Black today publicly concluded that no jury would convict him on the say-so of David Radler. Now there is a startling revelation from an unbiased observer of the proceedings.

The battle lines that were drawn today in court came from a former assistant United States attorney, Ron Safer, as he concluded his cross-examination of David Radler. The jury watched intently as Safer honed in on his prey.

The draconian federal sentencing guidelines were introduced by Safer to demonstrate the lucrative deal that Radler had secured with the government. It was all documented on a simple chart that the jury could follow beside them.

Radler reluctantly conceded that under the sentencing guidelines, his twenty-nine-month sentence was conditional on a motion being raised by the prosecutors. The following vitriolic exchange then took place.

"All you have to do is stick to the script?" Safer asked, referring to Radler's grand jury testimony.

Radler: "The story [is] the facts. I've got to stick to the facts."

Safer: "The facts the government wrote for you, right?"

Radler: "The facts I gave the government."

The accusation by Safer of a prosecution script was a direct attack on the integrity of the prosecutors at the table across the room. The group was being dramatically vilified by Safer for shaping and packaging the testimony of their star witness for the jury.

The prosecution is now down to the final four witnesses in their lengthy case. The first of them, Jonathan Rosenberg, began his testimony shortly after Radler left the stand. He was a lawyer for the special committee set up to investigate Hollinger International shareholder complaints in 2003. He has already related a few incriminating statements that certain of the defendants made to him. Peter Atkinson, for example, told Rosenberg that it wasn't a requirement of the CanWest deal that he be personally compensated. The prosecution has carefully chosen Rosenberg to do some clean-up after the Radler debacle.

LIKE A ROLLING STONE

Trial lawyers are wonderful storytellers. On my first day of teaching at the Benjamin N. Cardozo School of Law, I was paired with an affable personal injury lawyer from Georgia, Roger Dodd. In one memorable trial, Dodd's client informed him during jury selection that he intended to raise a motion on his own with the court. "What is it?" the judge demanded. "I want my lawyer executed," was the quick reply. "I think you mean terminated," the judge stated before dismissing the motion. The jury seemed unfazed by the exchange. It was Dodd's impression that the jurors felt that his disgruntled client got it right the first time.

I learned early in my career that there are few popularity contests to be won in the justice system. I clerked for a judge, Lloyd Graburn, whose censure was sought in the House of Commons by a former prime minister. Judge Graburn was a former senior prosecutor in Toronto who was highly respected by prosecutors and defence lawyers alike for his exquisite decency and even-handed approach to cases. He was also not a stranger to bold decisions, and it was one such controversial sentence that attracted some undesired notoriety.

The Rolling Stones had arrived in Toronto to relax and record some new music. There were reports in the local newspapers that Prime Minister Trudeau's wife, Margaret, had spent part of the weekend partying with Mick Jagger and the rest of the band. The police subsequently executed a search of Keith Richard's hotel room and discovered one ounce of high-quality heroin. Richards insisted that the narcotic was acquired for his personal use.

He pleaded guilty to the possession of the heroin before Judge Graburn. Rather than send Keith Richards to prison, the judge made the unorthodox decision to order him to perform a concert for the blind as part of his probation. Eventually, the entire band played the concert with Richards.

The decision was appealed and severely criticized. It led John Diefenbaker, the former prime minister, to stand up in the House of Commons and call for Judge Graburn to be formally censured. The judge was deeply hurt by the swirling controversy about the favoured treatment of a celebrity. It was unfounded and misdirected.

Criminal defendants can choose to follow an unpopular path as well. I recall that in my last meeting with Ivan Fernandes in his judge's chambers, he told me about a case that he had prosecuted in Kingston. The individual charged was being cross-examined by Ivan and eventually refused to answer one of his probing questions. Witnesses in criminal trials in Canada do not have the luxury of seeking the protection of the Fifth Amendment. The trial judge became quite exasperated as she sternly reminded the accused man that he was required to answer. The man's ill-advised and stubborn attitude sealed his doomed fate with the jury.

Conrad Black has joined the pantheon of unpopular causes. The unusual feature in his case is that he has managed to ostracize his own attorneys! Black may be the first defendant in modern history to exploit his criminal trial as an opportunity to launch a book tour.

It makes perfect sense to strike now. The international spotlight is shining brightly on Lord Black and journalists are tripping over each other in the Chicago Ritz-Carlton lobby incessantly seeking interviews about his scholarly book. My good friend Seamus O'Regan will be featuring an interview with Conrad Black on *Canada AM* early this week. By the end of the trial, however, the spotlight will predictably move elsewhere. Perhaps Paris Hilton will release her next bestseller, *Safe Driving Tips for the Drunk Driver*. That one will have to compete with Al Gore's new book, *Global Warming Is Going to Make Me President Again*, as well as Tony Blair's much anticipated *Bushwhacked*.

To quote Socrates, has Black gone daft? There are a group of seventeen men and women, otherwise known as a jury of his peers, who are scrutinizing every flinch of His Lordship's cheekbone in court. Does he really think that they will overlook a concerted public relations campaign while they place their own lives on hold for months to determine his legal fate?

If I were conducting an interview of Black, I would ask him only one question: Is his book a biography or an autobiography of Nixon (in the Freudian sense)? Revisionist history may sell books, but the sordid tale of Nixon's legacy is that he caused incalculable harm to the institution of the American presidency. He also paved the way for a raucous media skeptical of government and the office of the special prosecutor. Does the name Patrick Fitzgerald leap to mind?

Allow me to share another pertinent fact with you. The judge is likely reading the newspapers too. Recall the start of the trial when kibitzer Eddie Greenspan was practically ordered to the courtroom corner for giving an ill-advised interview in the *New York Times* decrying the fact that the judge had officially certified him as being stupid. Judge St. Eve will not be impressed with Conrad Black's media blitz. Count on it. If the agitated prosecutors ever have occasion to introduce the scrapbook of Black's press clippings at a sentencing hearing, expect the boom to fall hard.

The interviews with Conrad Black stray by design into discussions about his trial woes. And so we read in the Saturday edition of the *Guardian* that Black is publishing his Nixon book in the very midst of his case with a firm point in mind: "I'm sending everyone a message. I'm saying this is war." He further maintained that he had been "attacked in a violent manner by the U.S. government" and that it was "complete and total rubbish" that both he and his wife, Barbara Amiel, enjoyed an extravagant lifestyle. (It might be more accurate to say that even Conrad Black's rubbish was extravagant.)

The *Guardian* also refers to the "mounting speculation" in Chicago that Conrad Black may possibly testify in his own defence. Tom Bower must be squealing with delight. It is in this spirit that I have recorded the following simulated cross-examination of Black by the lead prosecutor, Eric Sussman.

Q: My name is Eric Sussman, Mr. Black.

A: I know exactly who you are.

Q: That's right. One of the Nazi prosecutors you spoke about to the *Toronto Star* reporter, correct?

A: I have no comment about that.

Q: Well, you would agree with me that you haven't had any problem making comments to the media before you took the witness stand?

A: That is correct.

Q: Of course those were free shots, weren't they?

A: That is your interpretation.

Q: Mr. Black, did you tell the reporter from the *National Post* that this was never a criminal case except possibly against David Radler?

A: Yes, and I stand by that statement.

Q: So you agree with me that you aren't even sure in your mind that Radler committed any fraud on the shareholders of Hollinger International?

A: That's right.

Q: And certainly no one else did?

A: Yes.

Q: So there may be no crime committed at all, correct?

A: That's exactly right.

Q: I'm curious. Is it your view now that it was quite possibly a genuine condition of closing for the sale of the American community newspapers that non-competition agreements be entered into with Hollinger Inc. as well as with the senior executives?

A: Yes.

Q: And so it was only a coincidence that all of the buyers for these papers testified in this courtroom that they
never requested such non-compete agreements?

A: I suppose it was.

Q: When you took the thirteen boxes of documents from
your office on 10 Toronto Street, was it also just a coincidence that it was the same day that the SEC had asked
for your documents?

A: Yes, it was.

Sussman would then end his cross-examination with a broad smile.
"No further questions."

MAY 21

Paul Healy, Hollinger's former vice-president of investor relations, testifies (under an immunity deal with prosecutors) he received complaints from shareholders about "excessive" executive perks as early as 1995, when he joined the company. Healy provides his insight into the New York City apartment Hollinger bought for Black in 1994 and then sold to him at a "discount" prosecutors allege was illegal. Black contends the price was fair because he put millions into renovations.

ANTIQUES ROADSHOW

I spent Victoria Day in an American courtroom. Although the holiday is named after a forgotten queen who can't even claim enough fame to have her face on any Canadian coin or currency, I still felt slightly unpatriotic walking into the Dirksen courthouse today. I am constantly reminded that I am in a foreign country. Today it was Jeffrey Cramer's common refrain of "hearsay" to questions that are patently not hearsay north of the border. Of course you only have my hearsay assertion to rely upon.

It was quite helpful to the jury to learn today in court that Conrad Black kept a separate apartment in his Park Avenue co-op to house his staff. The service apartment, at the expense of Hollinger International shareholders, also occasionally housed company executives. However, it mainly served as the sleeping quarters for the butlers, maids, and service staff. It must have been reassuring for the jurors to know that merely on a whim, Barbara Amiel could invite a few of her society set friends over for crumpets and Moroccan tea.

This trial is beginning to resemble the set of *Gosford Park*. All that is missing is the elaborate costume design. Ed Genson had the temerity to remind the trial judge that the posh Manhattan residence was perfectly legal and properly authorized by the shareholders. It was all part of a series of things, Genson alleged, that the government hoped would make Black look bad. Concerned that the jury would be overwhelmed by prejudice, Genson was correctly emphasizing that his client was drowning in a flood of bad character evidence.

Judge St. Eve responded to Genson's impassioned protests by reminding him that the evidence fell under the umbrella of count ten, the perks charge. The perks are the aromatic spices that the prosecution is relying on to flavour their non-compete feast. There is the Bora Bora paprika, the La Grenouille garlic, and now the spicy Park Avenue pepper. Conrad Black is cooked. (For the record, I am standing by my prediction of a not-guilty verdict.)

The prosecution called the perky Paul Healy today to testify about the tangled web of real estate intrigue involving the luxury co-op at 635 Park Avenue. Healy was a former head of investor relations at Hollinger International and lectured the jury about the importance of vigilantly protecting shareholder rights.

"Any one of us may have an investment," Healy declared with a tinge of sincerity in his voice. The messenger of fiduciary duties chosen to speak for the impoverished Hollinger International shareholders also had to concede that he had requested and received the protection of a court order of immunity for his testimony. A sound choice for victims' rights!

The very witness who lectured the jury about the virtue of treating all shareholders fairly and maintaining a level playing field also left his position at Hollinger International to join Breeden Partners. That is the firm headed by Richard Breeden, the corporate governance raider of the lost arc. I imagine that Ed Genson might have a few questions for Healy in cross-examination tomorrow to determine if he was forthcoming with Breeden about taking instructions to dummy up a memo that deliberately misstated the fair market value of a couple of Park Avenue apartments. This was accomplished to the financial detriment of the shareholders. Jeffrey Cramer referred to this flawed memo in his opening by stating that the shareholders' "pocket just got picked for a couple of million dollars for an apartment because of one memo."

Healy's reason for his deliberate malfeasance was heart-warming. He professed sheer delight at taking the apartment off the books. After the CanWest deal, Healy approached both Jack Boultbee and Conrad Black separately with a similar plea. "Wouldn't it be a great time to get the apartment off the books?" he asked both men. Black apparently readily agreed. The irritating complaints that Healy fielded from beleaguered shareholders such as Ira Gluskin and Tony Campbell would finally cease. If ever there was a plausible motive for a multi-million-dollar fraud with all of its attendant risks, that surely hits the mark.

It is curious that Healy repeated the prosecution's mantra today that Black's involvement with Hollinger International wasn't limited to certain parts of the company or the globe. It is also surprising that Radler didn't substantiate this claim. Perhaps Healy was too preoccupied with his investor road shows to have noticed the true division of responsibility.

When a witness's dubious credibility surfaces in the prosecution's own questioning, it usually foretells that disaster lies ahead. Healy had the jury laughing at him derisively as he explained his actions initially as "an intentional mistake." Rather than admitting to lying, Healy couched his actions in the more palatable description of "hyperbole." The only example of hyperbole in Healy's evidence today was his claim that he could still be prosecuted for perjury if he was untruthful. Which side of the courtroom decides if you're candid and truthful, Mr. Healy?

I actually don't mind listening to more hyperbole from Paul Healy tomorrow as long as I don't have to hear anything further about non-competition payments. The prosecution is finally finished that part of its case. It's all about perks and boxes now displayed in a veritable antiques road show. Its last stop will be at 10 Toronto Street, where the jury will watch Conrad Black removing the thirteen boxes from the office in a *Candid Camera* moment. The event took place on the Victoria Day weekend of 2005. I am beginning to miss Canada again.

MAY 22

Prosecutors introduce emails to Healy in which Black openly defied shareholder discontent over executive spending. They play audiotapes of Black's testy responses to shareholder questions at Hollinger's 2002 and 2003 general meetings. Healy says he tried and failed to convince Radler, Kipnis, and Black to inform the board of the shareholders' grumblings.

LIVE FROM NEW YORK: IT'S CONRAD BLACK!

I watched today at the Conrad Black trial as portions of the shareholders meetings in New York City from 2002 and 2003 were played for the jury. As the transcript appeared on the screen on the wall, the exchanges between Black and various angry shareholders could be heard in the background. Black sat in court with his back to the jurors as they were riveted to every word on the screen.

The jury conducted themselves very differently today. There was no slouching in their chairs or the occasional nodding off by one of the jurors in the back row. I didn't even observe any obvious signs of protracted gum chewing. It was a special moment in the courtroom. Black was effectively testifying at his trial.

One view of the audiotapes heard today was that Black was confronted by a series of angry shareholders giving voice to their protests and woes. From management fees paid to Ravelston to the non-competition payments paid to Black and other senior executives, a panoply of complaints was laid bare before the jury. On this view the tapes were highly incriminating. Clearly that was the prosecution's purpose in introducing them.

My view, however, is dramatically different. The jury heard Conrad Black's voice for the first time today. It was helpful to Black for the jurors to witness him being probed vigorously on some of the very issues that they will have to determine. The shareholders, including Gene Fox of Cardinal Capital Management and Chris Browne and Laura Jereski of Tweedy Browne, were essentially surrogate cross-examiners. "Since your only vehicle for competing in the newspaper business is our company," he was asked in a prelude to the first meeting, "why do you feel it was appropriate for these individuals [the senior executives] to pocket that money instead of our company?"

Black handled the withering challenge in a reasonably composed and forceful manner. He addressed every question that was asked. The theme of his defence was represented in one statement: "We haven't sat here feathering our own nest."

For example, Black reminded one recalcitrant shareholder that the agreements were presented to the independent directors. The management fees were not disproportionate to the industry norm and it was laudable to have owners involved with the management of the company. The millions of dollars of non-competition payments (and clearly the shareholders were previously aware of the payments relating to the American community newspaper sales) were justified, Black argued, because they were demanded by Izzy Asper in the CanWest sale and rendered the senior executives ineligible buyers in the future.

In addition to the shareholders meetings, Paul Healy presented the jury with a disparate image of Conrad Black. He was a man resistant to transparency and respect for the company's shareholders. Healy seemed anxious to help the prosecutors. His immunity deal lurks in the background. Ed Genson and the remaining lawyers cross-examining Healy tomorrow will have an opportunity to undermine and erase his suspect credibility. It marks yet another pivotal moment in the trial. Next to David Radler and Governor Thompson, Paul Healy may be the prosecution's most important witness.

MAY 23–24

Healy testifies he secured a proxy vote for Donald Trump at the 2003 meeting, so the celebrity real estate mogul could appear in support of Black's corporate stewardship.

The defence hammers Healy over his account of the New York apartment transaction.

DONALD DUCKS

The names Donald Trump, Bruce Springsteen, and Conrad Black all received prominent mention in court today. This is a very different trial.

Patrick Tuite made the courtroom erupt in laughter by establishing that the "boss" Healy made constant references to wasn't Springsteen. The "boss" wasn't even born in the U.S.A. He was the chairman of Hollinger International, Conrad Black.

The boss of the apprentices, Donald Trump, was heard at an audiotaped 2003 shareholders meeting lending his vocal support to the company and management. He declared his great respect for David Radler and Conrad Black. Trump's appearance followed a written entreaty by Black for "a rather esoteric favour" to help quell an "insurrection" by certain institutions.

The jury may yet see Donald Trump testify as a witness for Conrad Black. Black's lawyers must have paid careful attention during jury selection when a number of prospective jurors pointed to Trump as a symbol of their respect. In the jury's mind, he may be the antidote to Enron to prove that a billionaire businessman doesn't have to accumulate his wealth through excessive greed or corruption. Trump would be risking a great deal by arriving in court to testify in support of Black. The jurors would appreciate that. If Black is found guilty, Trump's lofty stature will be tarnished by association. The optics of his mere appearance as a defence witness therefore resonates favourably for Black.

I predict that if Trump does testify, he won't be followed by a single lawyer into the courtroom. Donald Trump doesn't need a supporting cast. That will also be a refreshing change for this jury.

Paul Healy may be spending the night huddling with his attorneys preparing for the continuation of his gruelling cross-examination. In Canada witnesses are strictly forbidden from speaking to anyone in the midst of cross-examination about their testimony. The lawyer who breaches this fundamental principle of professional responsibility can be severely sanctioned. In America it presents a billing opportunity.

Paul Healy, however, could be spending the evening at a bar association meeting preparing for the continuation of his cross-examination and it wouldn't revive his credibility. It has already been significantly punctured.

It is obvious to the jury that Healy is a fair-weather witness. His choice of sides has largely been dictated by his own self-serving interests. His immunity agreement is the most glaring example of that pattern. He could continue to be on the payroll of Hollinger International and yet work for Richard Breeden's management firm in Connecticut. Healy could write moving letters of heartening support to Conrad Black and then have breakfast with a disgruntled Tweedy Browne representative before an annual shareholders meeting.

While spreading raspberry jam on his croissant, Healy was leaking information to assist with the feeding frenzy that followed against his boss.

In a testy exchange, Ed Genson pressed Healy on his pronounced bias against Black. "You're an advocate, sir, not a witness, isn't that right?" Genson asked.

"An advocate for whom?"

Genson pointed specifically to Breeden and Jonathan Rosenberg, the lawyer for the special committee.

"I'm an advocate for justice," Healy answered.

Genson countered with the suggestion that he was an advocate for a cause.

The general rule about cross-examination is that no question should be posed unless the answer is known in advance. That isn't quite accurate. There is also no danger in asking a question in cross-examination where the answer can't come back to bite you.

Patrick Tuite, Jack Boultbee's attorney, asked Paul Healy to name the several friends in the real estate business whom he claimed in his examination that he had consulted about the $3-million fair-market value of the Park Avenue apartment. Healy could not recall the "two or three names" but noted in passing that they were in his Rolodex in his New York apartment. Healy may come to regret volunteering information about his Rolodex. Tuite was aware that if a couple of real estate agents had indeed been contacted, Healy would surely have mentioned them in his questioning by the prosecutors. They certainly would have been included on the government's witness list. It was a perfectly safe avenue of cross-examination for the curious attorney to pursue.

Tuite didn't end the matter there. In cross-examination, when the witness is staggering on the ropes, you never retreat back to your client's corner. Tuite has subpoenaed Healy's Rolodex. It will likely be featured in cross-examination tomorrow as Tuite presses the issue to its conclusion.

The prosecution indicated that the long and winding road of its case is nearing the end of its journey. The jury may see Donald Trump on the witness stand as the first defence witness as early as Wednesday of next week. He may yet be one of Conrad Black's trump cards in the case.

HEALY AND THE COMMENTS

Conrad Black is saying a prayer tonight that none of the jurors are Rosie O'Donnell fans. Donald Trump appeared at a press conference in Chicago today and continued his customary trash talk about the co-host of *The View*. The worst insult he hurled at her was a childish claim that O'Donnell is self-destructive.

How, then, would Trump describe his buddy Conrad's weekend diatribe against the prosecutors at his trial?

Trump told the horde of press that he wasn't following Black's trial and that in his hometown of New York City there wasn't a lot of coverage.

If he wasn't going to be a witness in the case, he would certainly have thrown some effusive bouquets to Black. Shyness is not a Trump family trait. His calculated silence is compelling proof that indeed the defence will be calling him. The coincidental timing of the press conference may have been the needed cover for a subsequent meeting with Black's lawyers to review his testimony. The prosecutors will be spending the Memorial Day weekend reviewing old tapes of *The Apprentice* as fodder for cross-examination. If they don't return it is because they were all fired.

Paul Healy resumed cross-examination today as the defence pursued a game of "follow the Rolodex." There were a few introductory comments made to the court by one of the legion of attorneys present for Healy's evidence. Apparently, there was no physical Rolodex in Healy's possession, as he had steadfastly told the court a day earlier, but rather only a Microsoft electronic address book. Rolodexes are like toasters. They are resorted to frequently by their owners and therefore not easily forgotten. In other words, Healy's credibility was burnt toast.

Healy also accepted Patrick Tuite's suggestion today that it was misleading to refer to the Park Avenue apartment as being worth $3 million, the price that Black paid for it some six years earlier. Healy admitted that "it seemed logical" to consider the $2 million that Black personally spent on renovations into the purchase price. Park Avenue was not quite as perky as Healy initially portrayed it to be. Ed Genson isn't prepared to accede to Healy's latest revelation about the purported Rolodex mix-up.

Judge St. Eve warned Healy at the conclusion of his testimony that he was subject to recall by the defence. Genson has that instinctive trial lawyer's sixth sense that if he follows the yellow brick road, Healy's address book can only generate even greater dividends. It is a gamble without any risks.

The value of a lawyer's sixth sense should never be underestimated. It can win cases.

I once represented a rookie police constable, Jeff Pearson, who was charged with assault. He had been issuing tickets to speeders on a portion of Lakeshore Boulevard where the Molson Indy was held each summer in Toronto. In one routine stop, the driver suddenly became belligerent and lunged at Jeff with his car keys and pen. A struggle ensued and soon Jeff found himself rolling over the hood of his police cruiser with his assailant and falling to the pavement. Fortunately, an Ontario Provincial Police officer was in the area and interceded to rush to Jeff's assistance while both men were on the ground.

The belligerent driver was charged at the police station and eventually released. About a week later, Jeff was informed by two officers with the internal affairs unit that he was also being charged with assault. It was alleged that before the second officer arrived, Jeff had thrown the driver to the ground and yelled, "Go home, Paki. We don't need your type here." The accusation of racism guaranteed that Jeff would lose his job if he was found guilty and he also faced a possible jail sentence. It was a completely fabricated account.

A couple of days before the trial was to commence, I received a disturbing call from the prosecutor on the case. She indicated that a "good Samaritan" witness had come forward, and her independent version confirmed the driver's account of my client's conduct. She had witnessed the incident and then left the scene quickly without leaving her name. Her conscience had bothered her, and as a result she had contacted the police with her belated statement.

Jeff was close to tears when I shared the bleak news with him. We could adjourn the trial, but the effect of this new witness would be like a stealth bomber to the case. It would be deadly.

On the day set for trial, I looked back and studied the independent witness carefully. She fidgeted in her seat nervously and refused to make eye contact with me.

On a big hunch, I asked the police union for an unlimited budget to retain a private investigator to follow Jeff's complainant day and night. Hundreds of hours of surveillance were completed before the investigator photographed the complainant and witness together. It turned out that they were in fact business partners and in a budding romantic relationship.

I took the photographic evidence to two senior prosecutors and a decision was quickly made to drop the criminal charge against Jeff. The two conspirators were charged with attempting to obstruct the course of justice. The driver ultimately went to jail for nine months for his contrived account. The so-called independent witness claimed that she acted under his duress and was spared a prison sentence.

The story does have a happy ending. Jeff Pearson eventually left the police force and attended law school. He is now an accomplished assistant Crown attorney in Newmarket, just north of Toronto.

The story demonstrates two incontrovertible truths: hunches can be fruitful, and there is at least one Canadian prosecutor who likes me.

Conrad Black's defence team relied on their lawyerly instincts to set up a roadblock for the prosecutors to introduce invoices for lavish purchases made by Black, including a twenty-six-carat ring. The invoices were discovered in the thirteen boxes that are the subject of the obstruction of justice charge. Judge St. Eve ruled late today that special certificates are required before the invoices can be introduced since the documents were obtained outside the United States.

The thirteen boxes are lined up in the courtroom for the jury to see. With the clock ticking to the end of the prosecution's case, they may end up as stools for the jurors to use during the deliberations. The jury is down to sixteen today. Only three more jurors need to be excused and the boxes will be a perfect fit in the jury room.

OPEN AND SHUT?

Now that the prosecution in the Conrad Black trial is about to rest its case in a day or two, I propose to return to a few select statements made by prosecutor Jeffrey Cramer in his opening on behalf of the government.

1. *Bank robbers wear masks and use a gun. Burglars wear dark clothing and use a crowbar. But these four — three lawyers and an accountant — dressed in ties and wore a suit.*

As Janet Whitman correctly highlighted in the *New York Post* yesterday, after some ten weeks of testimony and the evidence of five central witnesses, prosecutors have yet to place a single victim on the stand to claim that Conrad Black defrauded them. Bank robbers and burglars have real and identifiable victims left with indelible emotional and sometimes physical pain and suffering. The comparison made by Cramer to violent criminals carrying guns and crowbars was unfair.

2. *So, they'll go to the buyers. The buyer is buying a newspaper from Hollinger International. The buyer clearly doesn't want International to compete with them;*

*because again, if you're buying a newspaper, you don't want International set-
ting up a new newspaper right next door to you. So, you want to make sure
International doesn't compete with you.*

*They'll go and say, "Well, how about Inc.? Let me give you Inc., that
Canadian company."*

"Fine." The buyer doesn't care. It doesn't change the purchase price.

*So, they insert Inc. Now, they have got to go back to the company. They've got
to go back to the board of directors. And they provide false and incomplete statements to the board.*

The prosecutor has introduced Conrad Black into the scheme by implication when the evidence doesn't support his direct participation. Black
never approached a single purchaser in the sale of the American community newspapers. He never negotiated a deal or even had a conversation
with any of the buyers about the sale of the papers.

3. *Ladies and gentlemen, these are some of the most sophisticated businessmen
you will ever see. They are the most sophisticated businessmen you will ever lay
eyes upon.*

An interesting observation, but what evidence was there at the trial to
support it? The most sophisticated businessman that the jury will see at
trial may yet be Donald Trump.

4. *Keep remembering this was the shareholders' money when they sold this business to the public. It's the woman who put Hollinger International stock into
her retirement account. That's who owns this company. It's the guy who bought
Hollinger International stock and put it into the college fund. That's who owns this
company. It's not their company.*

Again there was no evidence to support such a bold statement about
sympathetic victims. Mark Steyn made the point today in his blog for
Maclean's that the government will never call any of the so-called victims
as witnesses because they have a shared antipathy to the members of the
audit committee (Burt, Kravis, and Thompson) as well as to the successor regime at Hollinger. Gordon Paris oversaw the company as its stock
fell from $20 to $4 before escaping with a bonus of almost $3 million.

Corporate governance has cost the shareholders $200 million, and the tab is still soaring with mounting legal fees for witness representation.

5. *But these are hundreds of millions of dollars in deals. One of these deals was several billion dollars. I will tell you what. If you take a little piece from deals that are worth hundreds of millions of dollars and billions of dollars, you can get to $60 million pretty darn quick. And that's what they did.*

The deal for billions of dollars that Cramer was referring to was the CanWest deal. It is not alleged that Black's hefty non-compete payment was anything but legitimate. It undermines the prosecutor's point and provides powerful dissimilar fact evidence for the defence to refute the government's theory that Black was aware that the non-compete payments were part of a fraudulent scheme.

6. *Someone's got to look out for the shareholder because it can't be the officers. They can get some money from the transactions. At Hollinger International, it's the audit committee. It's the audit committee. It's the subcommittee of the board of directors that is set up to review these; to make sure that the shareholders are given a fair shake; to make sure someone's looking at these transactions; to make sure the shareholders' interests are taken into account and that there's fair dealing.*

Cramer is actually telling the jury that the audit committee was set up to make sure that someone is examining these transactions. The defence will endorse this statement and argue that this is precisely what occurred when they independently approved the transactions. They will argue that the *ex post facto* excuses of convenience by the members of the committee of "skimming" and "missing it" don't mesh with the role outlined by Cramer.

7. *And David Radler, you'll have a chance to judge him; he will be supported by other witnesses who testify; and, he will be supported by documents.*

This statement about Radler was unfounded and will come back to haunt the prosecution in the four closing addresses of the co-defendants. There will be a harmonious chorus urging jurors to rely exclusively on Radler's own testimony to judge his credibility.

8. You're also going to hear from the outside lawyers and outside accountants. And it's going to be a similar story as the audit committee. They were not told the truth. They were not told about the non-competes. They weren't told.

The defence will challenge the position that no information was provided to the outside lawyers and accountants about the non-competes. On the contrary, they will argue that there was an abundance of disclosure, which vitiates any notion of criminal intent.

MAY 29

Real estate expert Jonathan Miller contends Black paid well below market value for the apartment he bought from Hollinger. Hollinger Inc. controller Monique Delorme testifies to seeing Black and his personal assistant, Joan Maida, remove thirteen boxes from the Toronto offices. Under cross-examination, she concedes she was aware Black had been evicted from the offices and had to remove his property from the premises.

JE PARLE FRANÇAIS

It feels good to be back in my bilingual country. I took an Air Canada flight from Chicago to practise my French with the air safety instructions. Canada is a peaceful country where it is actually possible to jaywalk without being run over by a cab.

I have to confess that I extended my stay in Toronto past the Memorial Day weekend. The prospect of returning to court to watch a videotape of Conrad Black removing several boxes from his office wasn't enticing enough to draw me back to the Windy City. The alleged crime in connection with the boxes confounds me. It's like the game show *The Price Is Right*. The prosecution picked the showcase with the thirteen boxes and hoped that they were filled with incriminating fodder. I have tried to imagine a similar case in Canada where someone was charged with obstructing justice for moving boxes in Philadelphia. It doesn't compute yet.

My stay in Toronto has been most productive. My eleven-year-old son has signed a non-compete clause with me. He won't be able to set up a law office within twenty miles of mine until after his bar mitzvah.

My teenage daughters have decided to accept their father's sound advice and have enrolled in perks school. It has a specially designed course where there is a series of lectures on "Choosing an island for that half-million-dollar getaway" and "Trading in your annuity for a dinner party at Scaramouche."

I travelled to court today in Toronto as I reacquainted myself with my city. I was an actual *flaneur*. Prosecutors and defence lawyers greeted me with such enthusiasm and always with the same cheerful refrain: "What are you doing here?" It felt good to be wanted. I went on *The Verdict* with Paula Todd. Paula asked me for Conrad Black's position on the boxes. I told her that he claims they were being moved because they were "evacuating" the building at 10 Toronto Street. Paula laughed. That's not a good sign for the defence.

I met a fellow defence counsel, Jonathan Rosenthal, in the green room at the show. "Conrad is going down," he said to me with some confidence. He blamed it on the American jury that will determine Mr. Black's fate.

Jonathan has a point. A jury in the U.S. convicted Martha Stewart. I defy anyone to explain her crime to me.

After the show, I telephoned my mother and interrupted her bridge game with Rita and George Davies. My dad was overflowing with praise for my performance. Then he added, "You're still predicting that Conrad Black is going to get off. There are fourteen charges. Aren't you pushing it?" I told my dad that there are worse things in life than looking like a blubbering fool in front of half a million people by making a silly prediction. Like saying it front of 2 million people, for example.

My dad has seen my predictions fall flat before. I once made the quote of the week on Court TV's website when I was defending the hip-hop star Ja Rule. "Ja Rule will be pleading not guilty and you can underline that three times," I emphatically announced amid the crush of the media outside the Old City Hall courthouse. Although Ja Rule eventually pleaded guilty to assault and receive a small fine, the judge did apologize to my rapper client for the abusive manner in which the patrons of the after-hours club treated him prior to the punch-up. I consider that a victory. And you can underline that four times.

TILTED

I ended the night with a cappuccino at my neighbourhood pizza place, Sette Mezzo. The owner, my friend Sol, keeps reminding me that he would have been a great lawyer. He certainly knows how to react with aplomb to dangerous situations. He once explained to me that in a former career he had acted as a court interpreter at a refugee hearing for a prisoner who had already stabbed an immigration officer. There was an armed guard posted outside a glass window poised to strike if necessary during the hearing. Sol was asked by the adjudicator to translate his final ruling denying the violent prisoner refugee status in Canada. Sol's interpreting skills were suddenly creatively stretched. "Look," he told the burly inmate, "I want you to know that if it was up to me, I'd let you stay in this country. But it's his call and he says that you lost the case."

MAY 30

The prosecution rests its case.

AROUND THE WORLD IN EIGHT DAYS

The defence was handed a hollow victory today. One of the money-laundering charges against Conrad Black was withdrawn without a whisper of a reason today from the attorneys for the U.S. government. The silence was out of character with the robust nature of the prosecution. Their case was ending with a whimper rather than a bang.

Judge St. Eve granted her approval for the charge to be dropped in the absence of the jury. The move was likely anticipated by the defence. The government was essentially conceding that the jury properly instructed on the correct law would be incapable of finding Black guilty of that count. Marc Martin made it clear that he will be seeking to have further counts against Black dismissed. The racketeering charge is a prime example of a suspect charge. The obstruction of justice charge is another. The indictment may yet prove to be an enormous sandcastle.

Eric Sussman put an end to ten weeks of the government's case today when he advised the trial judge that the prosecution was resting its case.

The much bigger news of the day is that it is estimated that the defence for all four co-defendants will be completed in eight days. If Conrad Black were to testify, his cross-examination would take longer than the entire allotted time. Black is finally behaving like a choirboy and abiding by his lawyers' counsel. He was about to drown and at the last moment reached out to grab the lifebuoy thrown to him. Eddie Greenspan must have prepared an encyclopedia of written instructions for Black to sign if he insisted on testifying. That is now safely tucked into the waste bin.

The news of an abbreviated defence is significant for a number of reasons. The impact of four defendants taking an average of two days apiece to mount their individual defences will reverberate with the jury as a sign of supreme strength in the defence position. The corollary is that the prosecution has failed miserably to meet its burden of proof in the case.

It also strongly suggests that none of the other three defendants will take the witness stand. The defence has obviously reassessed the faltering strength of the government's case and pared down its list of potential witnesses considerably. There's a breeze of confidence filtering through the defence camp. There appears now to be a united front. That must be discouraging news for a lagging prosecution.

It is unlikely that there will be any fresh explosive testimony from any of the defence witnesses. Instead they can be expected to chip away at the edges of the prosecution's case. For example, Black's former executive assistant, Joan Maida, who will likely be called as the first witness for Conrad Black, is expected to verify that there was an innocent explanation for the removal of the thirteen boxes from 10 Toronto Street: the company was being forced to vacate the premises. The next witness, Ken Whyte, the founding editor of the *National Post*, will speak to the issue of Black's and Radler's separate roles at Hollinger International. Black had an extensive hands-on role at the *Post* that would have prevented him from supervising the American operation of the company.

Eddie Greenspan advised the court today that he had earlier planned to call the leading parole lawyer in British Columbia as a witness to explain the law relating to parole eligibility in Canada. At this point in the case, the jury has only Greenspan's suggestion to Radler that he would be eligible for parole after serving just six months of his impending twenty-nine-month sentence. Radler feigned ignorance of the possibility of an early release date in cross-examination.

The bombshell that Greenspan dropped on the court was that this very parole lawyer in British Columbia had already been contacted by David Radler. In other words, not only was Radler fluently versed in his earliest exit date from prison, but he had also taken proactive steps to retain counsel to ensure that it would happen. Greenspan had stumbled on even a bigger lie by Radler than he could ever have dreamed of. It was the equivalent of Dorothy's discovery that water melted the Wicked Witch. Or Johnnie Cochran's revelation that Mark Fuhrman used the n-word. The jury will hear all about Radler's parole lawyer and his role in the case. That is a virtual certainty in the land of Oz.

The attorneys for each of the defendants will take every precaution to avoid calling a witness who can damage their case rather than advance it. That is a perennial danger for the defence. There are two questions that the defence must consider before calling any potential witness: (1) Does the witness help my client's case? (2) Is there any risk that the witness has information that can hurt my client?

The trial is marching to its conclusion. If Conrad Black loses, he will surely regret giving up his Canadian passport. If he is acquitted, he should be singing the Canadian national anthem. He can recall that the true north is strong and free.

THE DEFENCE

MAY 31

The defence gets off to a bumpy start with Maida, who testifies about the removal of the boxes from Hollinger Inc. but contradicts parts of her testimony under cross-examination. She is followed by *Maclean's* editor and publisher Ken Whyte, who was editor of the *National Post* under Black. He claims to have had next to no contact with Radler at the Post.

Whyte describes parties Black used to host at his Toronto home as "A-list," but work-related. Defence lawyers believe this bolsters their claim that Barbara Amiel's $54,000 birthday party — of which Hollinger paid two-thirds — was a business event.

JOAN OF ARC

Today was a big news day in Chicago. Universal Studios announced that a new Harry Potter theme park was in the planning stages for Orlando, Florida. David Radler is apparently hoping to finish his prison sentence in time to land the role of Dumbledore. When asked by a reporter to confirm the rumour, Radler replied, "I have to check with Greenspan first. Only he can tell me if I'll be out of jail."

Starbucks issued a press release today announcing that it is switching to 2 percent milk for all of its coffee drinks by the end of the year, although customers will still be free to ask for whole milk for their triple lattes. Weight Watchers seized the opportunity and hired Governor Thompson to lobby alongside its barristers and baristas for an even healthier move to skim milk.

In other major news, former vice-presidential aide Scooter Libby's attorneys will be seeking probation for their client when his sentencing hearing takes place early next week. One of their anticipated arguments will appeal to pragmatists everywhere. If the judge in the case sentences him to jail, then President Bush will have to step in immediately and issue a pardon. "Is it really necessary to embarrass our president?" will be the lawyers' plea.

Patrick Fitzgerald, the special prosecutor, is seeking up to a three-year prison sentence for Libby. Three years for lying about some conversations with reporters about CIA operative Valerie Plame. Libby's attorneys countered by arguing that Fitzgerald is seeking a hefty penalty to sentence their client for a leak that he was never charged with.

There may still be time for Scooter to roll over and offer up Vice-President Cheney for his involvement in Plamegate to drastically lower his sentence. It won't matter if there is a single memo, fax, or email to back up any claim he makes. There is excellent precedent for that.

The news in the Conrad Black trial was that after ten weeks, the defence was finally underway. Joan Maida was seen in the parking lot of the courthouse after she finished testifying selling the remainder of her "Conrad Will Win" T-shirt collection. During her testimony, she had admitted distributing some of the T-shirts while noting her desire to see Black win his trial.

Having just watched Paul Healy challenged by the defence as a partisan and biased witness, the jury now watched as the prosecution portrayed Maida as his bookend. The day after a money laundering count was dropped, the first witness for the defence was a wash.

The day ended with an image of Conrad Black intricately involved with the management of the *National Post* at its inception. Founding editor Ken Whyte testified about post-midnight phone calls from Black inquiring about aspects of the paper's operation. Black's preoccupation with the paper was contrasted with the virtual absence of David Radler.

Court is adjourned until Monday, when cross-examination of Whyte will continue. Conrad Black didn't say a single word the entire week. That was the biggest news of all.

Center The Defence

TRUMPETS AND TROMBONES

I spent much of today watching the jurors in court. There have been a number of misconceptions about the jury in this case, including a notion that the evidence would be too complex and technical for them to absorb.

Here are ten observations that I have made in my study of the jurors:

1. They are still involved in the case.

   After almost three months of trial, the jurors are remarkably attentive and conscientious. They pay particular attention to the demonstrative evidence used by the attorneys. There wasn't a single juror napping or doodling today in court. The jurors are a focused group.

2. There is no revealing body language.

   There was no rolling of eyes, nodding of the head in obvious approval or disapproval, indignant crossing of the arms, or — the ultimate sign of impending defeat — turning away from the lawyers. This jury is inscrutable, and it is impossible to detect the direction that it is leaning. Perhaps the jurors are conscious of being in a bubble and the subject of intense scrutiny by the media. I have never seen a jury that is so difficult to read.

3. The note taking has dwindled.

   Barely a note was taken today by the jurors. This suggests that the evidence was not very helpful to them in their ultimate decision. They are becoming selective about what they are recording. There appears to be an unspoken consensus among them about what information is relevant. This may signify that the jury deliberations will be significantly shorter than might be expected in a case of this length and magnitude. I am predicting that a verdict will be reached in four to five days.

4. The jurors rarely smile or laugh.

   This is in marked contrast to their collective behaviour only a couple of weeks ago. There were obvious moments of humour today, and only a couple of the men in the front row smiled intermittently. This signifies a jury that appreciates that the trial is reaching its conclusion and that their solemn task of reaching several verdicts is quickly approaching. Discard any notion that the case will be decided for frivolous reasons like class prejudice or a dislike of Conrad Black's stridence and arrogance. This impressive group of jurors is firmly resolved to follow the evidence and to avoid extraneous reasoning.

5. The jurors were not surprised to see that Conrad Black wasn't going to testify.

   After Ed Genson called his last witness today, there wasn't a single noticeable reaction. The jurors likely concluded that in view of the judge's previous announcement of a late June ending to the trial, Black was not going to be a witness. They knew that Radler's evidence occupied almost two weeks of the trial; Black's certainly would have been at least that long and perhaps even longer.

6. The jury addresses will be enormously important.

   In close cases, the jury addresses can be the deciding factor. My observations of this jury tell me that they are still undecided.

7. There is no identifiable banding of groups of jurors.

   Unlike in a Canadian jury trial, the jurors change their seating after breaks during the day. They rarely communicate or gesture with each other during the trial. They are largely a group of sixteen individual voices. An individual holdout to create a mistrial is certainly a possible outcome of the trial.

8. The jurors are fully aware of the media's presence in the courtroom and the profile of the case.

   Several jurors peer over at the area where the media is congregated. They recognize the regular contingent of Canadian and New York journalists who are seated about twenty to twenty-five feet away from them. I expect that they have nicknames for all of us.

9. There is no clear choice for jury foreperson.

   My own choice is the woman who sits closest to the witness stand and is the most intent and expressive of the jurors. She has her optimal position staked in the jury box and has enough authority with her fellow jurors to maintain it.

10. The jurors respect the trial judge.

   There is clear evidence of excellent rapport between the judge and all of the jurors. The fact that they are routinely punctual under arduous conditions is a testament to their respect for her. They will follow her jury instruction meticulously.

JUNE 4–5

Having learned Radler retained one of Canada's foremost parole lawyers before discussing his plea bargain, the defence files a motion requesting that he be recalled to the stand.

James Reda, a New York–based expert on executive compensation, testifies the non-compete fees Boultbee received were "within market range." Jinyan Li, a law professor at Toronto's Osgoode Hall, testifies about the tax status of non-competes in Canada.

TEA TIME

Barbara Amiel refused to ride an elevator with me on two occasions today at the courthouse. I wish I had the opportunity to tell her that I am wonderful elevator company. I can cheerfully discuss the weather or the results of the French presidential election. My versatility has no bounds. I know the characters in *La Traviata* and I'm fluently bilingual. I am not profane or discourteous and can be ebullient or maintain stoic silence if that is requested. After listening to the evidence in court today, I can report that in Canada the top court is the Supreme Court of Canada, lottery winnings are non-taxable, and the system of tax laws is exciting.

I must be free of any charges of legal bias if both sides of the courtroom are less than enchanted with my presence. The prosecutors looked at me askance today as well. I suppose that being quoted in the *National Post* on the weekend describing the prosecutors' decision to tie their case's fate to David Radler as "scandalous" didn't boost my chances of being invited to the District Attorneys' annual ball.

A trial is not a tea party, as any trial lawyer will share with you. Ron Safer has laid down the gauntlet on behalf of his client, Mark Kipnis. In motions for a mistrial and for a judgment of acquittal that will be argued before Judge St. Eve tomorrow morning, Safer explicitly accused the prosecutors in the case of a lack of good faith. Specifically, he noted that "the government proceeded during opening to refer to evidence it knew would be unsupported at trial."

A claim of bad faith against opposing counsel is not brought without a lot of forethought by experienced counsel. It is a serious allegation that courts are loath to recognize. It is equally incumbent on an advocate to fearlessly raise the issue when the evidence clearly supports it. However, when it is made frivolously and without merit, it must be harshly rejected by a court.

The prosecutors are not sleeping well tonight. Safer is a former member of their office whose integrity and skill are above reproach. He would be their last choice of anyone in the courtroom to be advancing a claim of prosecutorial misconduct. Safer's argument on both motions will undoubtedly be taken very seriously by Judge St. Eve. She has already expressed her desire to hear the motions expeditiously because Kipnis is "differently situated than the other defendants." While ultimately rejecting the motions, the judge will likely indicate that she will ensure that Kipnis has a fair trial by firmly repudiating the false suggestions made by the prosecutor against him in his opening in her jury instruction. That is indeed good news for all four co-defendants.

Safer's principal argument for a mistrial is a fairly simple one. David Radler had numerous meetings with the government during which he consistently maintained that Kipnis received a bonus of $150,000 for legal work in connection with the U.S. community newspaper sales. Kipnis's exemplary work, by Radler's admission, also saved Hollinger International millions of dollars in legal fees. In reply, the prosecution has argued that Kipnis's bonuses did not take place in a vacuum and that Safer is unfairly casting a "sinister light" on their opening statement.

When Jeffrey Cramer opened to the jury at the outset of the trial, he emphasized that the bonus was Kipnis's payoff for his crimes in connection with the non-compete payments. According to Cramer, "his price was just a little bit lower" than that of his co-defendants. That was patently false. The stark reality is that Kipnis cannot be traced to one penny of illicit gains in the alleged $60-million fraud scheme.

According to the government's theory, he risked his liberty, his profession, and his reputation for absolutely nothing.

As Safer pointed out in his written argument, it was the direct result of his client's efforts that all of the individual non-competes in the American community newspaper sales were disclosed. The accountants at KPMG and lawyers at Torys were kept fully in the loop about these non-compete payments by Kipnis.

If Kipnis is found guilty by the jury (and no verdict is ever certain), the bitter irony is that he will serve a prison sentence much lengthier than David Radler's. As an American citizen, he will be required to serve the sentence without the relaxed parole eligibility that Radler will enjoy. It would be a travesty of justice.

The prosecution is scrambling in the final few days of testimony. After days of wandering through the desert, the attorneys for Boultbee and Atkinson finally touched on a pressure point that mattered to the jury today — the non-competes. The jury was as enthralled as they have been at any time in the trial as they heard a number of defence experts testify about the subject of non-competition payments. Their thirst was quenched.

The prosecutor's opening address once again came back to haunt them. Jeffrey Cramer had urged the jury to remember the five magic words in relation to the non-competition payments: "The buyer didn't request it."

The unshaken testimony that the jury heard today was that given the tax advantages in Canada after 1999, when non-competes were held by the Federal Court of Appeal to be non-taxable, it was perfectly proper for the seller to propose the non-competes. Whoops!

Matters only got worse for the prosecution.

James Reda, an executive compensation expert, had studied non-competition payments made to sixty-five executives from twenty-five different companies and found that various non-compete payments made to Conrad Black and three other Hollinger International executives were "within market range." Those three magic words, "within market range," will be repeated by defence counsel as their mantra in their closing addresses.

JUNE 6

Judge St. Eve dismisses the defence's request to recall Radler.

MOTION SICKNESS

The defence lost two motions today, and upon reflection they may actually be pleased with the results. First, there was a motion brought by Conrad Black's attorneys to recall David Radler about retaining a parole lawyer. The jury's memory of Radler right now is of a bruised witness whose credibility has been eviscerated. Why assume the risk of providing the prosecution with a chance to rehabilitate him? In other words, unless the defence was convinced that the ball would substantially clear the fence, it was risky business to bring Radler back. I imagine that the questioning of Radler would have proceeded as follows:

Cross-examination (continued)

Greenspan:	Mr. Radler, you told this jury that you didn't know anything about your chances for early release on parole, isn't that correct?
Radler:	Yes.
Greenspan:	And that you didn't know until I told you that you would get out of a Canadian prison in six months?
Radler:	Yeah, I agree with that.

Greenspan: Isn't it true that you retained a parole lawyer before you came to this court to testify?

Radler: I'm not sure, Mr. Greenspan. You will have to check with my lawyers in British Columbia. I trusted them to look after my matters.

Greenspan: You're actually telling this jury that you didn't even know that you had a parole lawyer until this very moment?

Radler: No, I didn't say that. After I finished testifying, the first thing I did was confirm that I would get out in six months. That's when I spoke to Mr. Martin about the situation. I was very relieved afterwards when I realized that I had the best parole lawyer in the province now on my team.

Greenspan: No more questions.

Redirect

Sussman: Mr. Radler, when you were questioned by Mr. Greenspan a few weeks ago, did he ever ask you if you hired a parole lawyer?

Radler: No, he didn't.

Sussman: What would your answer have been at the time if he asked you?

Radler: I would have told him that I wasn't sure because I left the details of my case to my own lawyers to take care of.

Sussman: Why was that?

Radler: I knew that I had some of the best lawyers in Vancouver.

Sussman: Nothing further.

Let's now turn to the other motion — the motion for a mistrial for Mark Kipnis. Judge St. Eve rejected the notion that the prosecution acted in bad faith in their opening. The judge never satisfactorily explained how she reached such a result. Indeed, she seemed to provide some credence to Ron Safer's position by stating her surprise when Radler agreed that the bonus received by Kipnis was legitimately obtained. She further noted that she watched the jurors' reactions during Safer's effective questioning and they were paying very close attention. It would provide a very powerful argument for Safer's closing.

Did Ron Safer really want a mistrial for his client? It was a calculated risk that, if his motion was successful, the government wouldn't seek to try Kipnis again on perhaps a more streamlined indictment than the eleven counts he presently faced. In the event that the government chose not to retry Kipnis, with an undecided and unsettled verdict, would he have any chance of regaining his professional livelihood or his reputation? None of his defence evidence had yet been called. All that presently remained for the public was the lingering image of Kipnis being one of the four men in suits likened by the prosecution to bank robbers with guns or burglars with crowbars.

A mistrial was not in the interests of Mark Kipnis. As Safer told Judge St. Eve, he doesn't want to be giving a closing address. He was implicitly reminding her that he is hoping to be successful with his motion for an acquittal. That is the motion that Safer really wants to win — not a mistrial and certainly not severance.

After court concluded early today, all of the journalists covering the Black trial met for lattes and cappuccinos at Intelligentsia. Some of the discussion related to the chase for jurors after the verdict is given. It will be a mad dash for exclusive interviews for everyone except the legal analyst. In Canada, the interview of a juror about the deliberations is a criminal offence.

I have compiled a list of the top ten questions for the jurors in post-trial interviews:

1. What did you think the lawyers and the judge were whispering about in the sidebars?
2. Would you vote for Governor Thompson if he ran for governor again?

3. If you had to choose between Barbara Amiel and Marie-Josée Kravis to guest host *Fashion Television,* who would you choose?

4. Were you disappointed when Donald Trump didn't show up?

5. Are you planning a family vacation to Bora Bora?

6. Will you be attending David Radler's sentencing hearing?

7. Which attorney would you hire if you ever got into trouble a) in the U.S., and b) in Canada?

8. Did you pay attention to Eric Sussman smirking at the prosecution table?

9. Which juror does the best Gus Newman imitation?

10. Did you ever wonder why all these Canadian journalists kept showing up for the trial day after day? (I was wondering about that myself!)

JUNE 7–8

The defence calls Hollinger International's external auditor, Patrick Ryan of KPMG, as a hostile witness. He testifies he called the non-competes to the attention of the audit committee, which appeared untroubled with the revelation.

Chris Paci, a lawyer who worked on a Hollinger debt offering in 2002, testifies the financial records of previous Hollinger transactions had gaps. He says when he raised his concerns with Thompson, he was told the disclosures were correct and had been approved.

TORNADO WATCH

There is a tornado watch in effect this evening for Chicago, as the western area of the city is expected to be confronted by some severe weather conditions. The tornado already touched down in the Dirksen courthouse earlier in the day. The havoc and devastation that it brought to the prosecution's case at the Conrad Black trial was palpable.

Patrick Ryan, a lead partner with KPMG, was on the witness stand to describe a meeting that took place in February of 2002 with Hollinger's audit committee. Along with Ryan, present at the meeting were other representatives of KPMG, as well as David Radler, Mark Kipnis, Richard Burt, and Jim Thompson, the chair of the audit committee.

A central purpose of the meeting was to seek confirmation of the audit committee's approval of over $15 million in non-compete payments to Conrad Black and other senior executives of Hollinger International.

These payments had not been disclosed in prior SEC filings on Canadian counsel's advice.

Ryan clarified that the audit committee approved the non-compete payments that related to the sale by Hollinger International of forty-five U.S. community newspapers for approximately $215 million.

He was asked if Jim Thompson said anything to indicate that he had never heard about the non-compete payments. "Not a word," was Ryan's reply. So much for skimming and being kept in the dark.

Ryan was not a friend of the defence, which made his evidence even more compelling for the jury. While refusing all requests to meet with Ron Safer, he'd had several meetings with prosecutors and spent a couple of hours with Julie Ruder the day before his testimony began.

The question du jour is this: why didn't the prosecution seek to call Patrick Ryan as its own witness? Is it entitled simply to pick the grapes on the vine that produce the vintage case that leads to Conrad Black's conviction? There is little dispute that Ryan punches a gaping hole through the heart of the prosecution's theory about the non-competes. Follow the bouncing ball in Jeffrey Cramer's opening to the jury: "The next thing you have to do is you've got to tell the — you don't tell the audit committee about non-competition agreements. You can't. You can't tell them … Did the audit committee get full and accurate disclosure? They thought they were being told the truth because they had no reason to doubt these defendants. But they weren't."

Cramer was plainly wrong when he made the assertion that the audit committee wasn't told about the non-competition agreements. Cramer suggested that "you can't tell them." The inference is that if these poor victims of flawed information were provided with the truth, they would never have approved them. *Au contraire, mon frère.*

The prosecution selects the witnesses that support a conviction, marshals unlimited resources at its disposal to build its case, and then finally makes a deplorable sweetheart deal with an insider that it can dangle over his head until he toes the prosecution line faithfully to help secure a conviction. Plead guilty or pay the trial tax. It is hardly surprising that the conviction rate hovers somewhere between 95 and 97 percent.

Only someone as outrageous as Conrad Black would be prepared to take the risk.

RUNNING SHOES ON THE MOON

The rumours began swirling about me early in my legal career. There were voices of disbelief and dismay. "Can it be true," one of my classmates pondered at our fifth-year reunion, "that Skurka doesn't play golf?" I had left the party briefly to get some raspberry Kool-Aid, and when I returned I was greeted with sombre silence. I had tried desperately to hide my aversion to golf. There was a putter stored in my locker at the Osgoode Hall courthouse and I brandished it at every opportunity. I secretly studied *Golf Digest* magazine at the local Indigo bookstore and learned to bluff my way through my co-counsel's discussions about golf strategy in court. I even attended the Canadian Open in Oakville every summer and made sure that I was seen on TSN. I was outed, however, when I was asked to identify my golf handicap and I responded that I had sprained my left ankle in university.

I was further distressed to learn at this trial that my lack of golfing skills was something that I had in common with David Radler. Radler could at least console himself with the knowledge that he was not a member of the legal profession. I had no such excuse. I further understood that if I ever engaged in a $60-million fraud scheme involving the shareholders of a public company, golf therapy sessions in prison would have to be skipped.

I now freely admit that I hate the game of golf and find it particularly boring and unstimulating. My deep feelings were reinforced several years ago while I happened to be working at my law office one Friday afternoon in the summertime. I took an urgent call from a frantic young man searching for my associate, Bill Horkins (now Justice Horkins). Bill subscribed to the proper lawyerly rituals and had left for the day to play golf at St. George's, one of the finest golf courses in Canada.

The young caller insisted on meeting with a lawyer urgently.

"What is this about?" I asked.

"Have you heard about the police officer's gun that was stolen from his squad car?"

"Of course," I quickly answered.

The story about an undercover officer's gun being stolen had been widely broadcast on the news that morning. There was a phalanx of anxious police officers swarming the city searching for the perpetrator and the weapon before any lethal mischief could arise.

I listened as Bill's twenty-year-old client described stealing a bag from the trunk of a car only to discover later that it contained a set of handcuffs, a police notebook, and a gun. He was terrified that he might be killed if the police found him with the gun, and he ultimately decided to bring it wrapped in newspaper to our law office.

My associate was enjoying a lovely round of golf at St. George's while I stayed back to await the delivery of a loaded police revolver. The golf lords were making certain that I paid for my transgressions.

The gun was ultimately turned over to the police with the assurance of a senior prosecutor that counsel wouldn't be charged with possession of the gun or interviewed about the manner that it arrived at the law office. I retained a respected lawyer, Bob Carter, to help me facilitate the challenging transfer of the gun to the police. In the interim, I drove Bill's client to the police station in Scarborough to arrange for his surrender.

There was one final lesson in the case. After Bill's client was charged, Bill was advised by a police officer involved with the investigation that his young client's fingerprints were on the newspaper wrapping. Bill insisted that the related fingerprint chart be produced. It soon became clear that it was a ruse and there were in fact no traces of fingerprints. The matter was resolved favourably, with Bill's client spending only a few weekends in jail for stealing a loaded firearm.

There wasn't a single piece of paper, contract, or undertaking signed by the senior prosecutor from the Attorney General's Office guaranteeing that Bob Carter and I wouldn't be charged with possession of the gun. It was simply a verbal agreement that we genuinely accepted would be followed. There is an immutable honour system that permeates the criminal justice system in Canada. Plea discussions are regularly conducted between opposing lawyers affecting every facet of an accused person's liberty. There is rarely a confirming letter ever exchanged. I can recall only one instance in my entire career.

Only the diamond trade in Belgium operates on such a high degree of mutual trust. The honour code among lawyers to keep their word is breached only at great peril. This brings me to a moment in the Conrad Black trial a couple of weeks ago. I noticed that Earl Cherniak was in the courtroom observing the proceedings. Earl is regarded as one of the pre-eminent civil litigation lawyers in Canada and I was curious to learn more about his presence. Rather than the warm greeting that I had expected from Earl, I received a rather perfunctory hello at the break. I later saw him huddled with Eddie Greenspan in the hallway in discussion and thought nothing of it.

Upon my most recent return to Toronto the mystery of Earl's presence was finally solved. I now understood why he was avoiding me like I had leprosy. He knew that I would naturally ask him his reason for landing at the Black trial and he wouldn't be permitted to cloud the truth. Indeed, Earl Cherniak was in Chicago to conduct a mock cross-examination of Conrad Black. The implications of this development are significant. Black must have expressed a desire to take the witness stand and testify. It likely took a mock questioning by one of Canada's foremost litigation lawyers to persuade him that the decision would be imprudent, if not catastrophic. If Black wins the trial, he will never appreciate the enormous debt of gratitude he owes to Earl Cherniak.

There was also a suggestion by Ron Safer that Mark Kipnis still might testify. Safer had at one point in the trial a real dilemma. I have stood on record previously as suggesting that Kipnis would be the one defendant likely to testify at the trial. I believe that it was his intention to do so. However, the case has proceeded so favourably that it would be shocking if Kipnis now testified on his own behalf. It is the government's burden to prove the case against him. Their case has fallen woefully short of establishing his culpability.

I expect that many trial observers are wondering why only Mark Kipnis introduced evidence of good character. His former paralegal, Margaret Bajzek, described her boss and friend as the best boss she had ever worked with, "100 percent above-board," and "totally law-abiding." She concluded by stating, "I would trust him with my life."

Clearly Black, Boultbee, and Atkinson had a number of excellent character witnesses ready and willing to appear in Chicago on their behalf. Recall that Allan Rock, the former minister of justice and Canadian ambassador to the U.N., was on Atkinson's list of potential witnesses. However, the attorneys for the three co-defendants realized that they would be triggering the prosecution's right to call bad character evidence if their clients' good character was raised at trial. It was a calculated risk that they decided they could not take.

Kipnis's cupboard of bad character evidence was totally bare. With all of the vast resources of the state, the prosecution couldn't muster a single witness to counter the powerful testimony of Margaret Bajzek. It is one of the last pieces of evidence that the jury will hear at the trial. I wonder if the defence will close its case by establishing that former governor Jim Thompson gave the thumbs-up sign to the prosecution on his way out of the courtroom. The jury might have a better appreciation of why he tried to fool them with his skimming excuse. Good character followed by sinister character.

I am looking forward to the jury addresses beginning next week. I was alarmed to learn that the prosecution has the right to reply to the defence closings. No such right is given to a prosecutor in Canada,[1] and for good reason. It is blatantly unfair to the defence. The four defence closings in the Black trial will be sandwiched between two prosecution closing statements. The Canadian and American systems of justice really are two distinct planets. I have repeatedly stumbled as I catalogued the many differences. It is difficult to wear running shoes on the moon.

NORTHERN BULLY

> *Ms. Grubar scoffed at suggestions the case has been too difficult for jurors to understand and she had some blunt assessments of the various lawyers including Edward Greenspan, a Toronto lawyer representing Black.*
>
> *Mr. Greenspan's aggressive style ticked off some of the jurors, she said.*
>
> *"I could not stand the way he hammered away at people. He did more harm than good."*
>
> — "Ex-juror thinks Lord Black will walk,"
> *The Globe and Mail*, June 11, 2007

Let's see now. Sandra Grubar, who sat on the jury for three weeks before asking to be dismissed to care for her ailing father, believes Conrad Black will walk free of the charges. The juror didn't see a single member of the audit committee testify or the star prosecution witness, David Radler. She heard none of the perks evidence about the Park Avenue apartment or the surprise birthday party for Barbara Amiel.

And she never watched the video of Black removing the boxes from 10 Toronto Street.

My question for Ms. Grubar would be a simple one, if I were permitted to ask it: how is possible that Eddie Greenspan's cross-examination did more damage than good if you are prepared to acquit his client? It is fairly easy to join the chorus of Greenspan critics at this trial. It has been rising to a crescendo after courtroom observers watched him being painfully burned by Gord Paris at the outset of the trial.

If Conrad Black happens to win in the trial, it will now be impossible to blame it on a stupid jury. As Grubar highlighted in her interview with the *Globe and Mail*, the jurors are "sharp and common sense" people who have managed to follow the evidence even with a few dry and sleepy patches along the way.

If Black is successful at trial, it will have been achieved despite his best efforts to torpedo his own defence with the reckless public tirades he continued to make against his lawyers' advice.

If he is acquitted, Black will have overcome a formidable prosecution team with unlimited resources to build its case and tear down the defence, a team with the success rate of former Dodgers superstar Sandy Koufax and with the immeasurable assistance of an army of lawyers fronting virtually every prosecution witness.

Don't Eddie Greenspan and Ed Genson deserve at least partial credit if the verdict conforms to this ex-juror's assessment and Conrad Black walks?

My dad took a straw poll of his morning workout group at the Jewish Community Centre. Merv Lass handed my dad the verdict. It was not guilty for Conrad Black on all charges. Greenspan and Genson should be relieved. They can now forego the joint five-hour jury address they have planned for next week.

It has been a bad week for Canada. The Anaheim Ducks beat the Ottawa Senators handily to claim hockey's holy grail, the Stanley Cup. One of Canada's top criminal lawyers was reduced to being compared on the front page of a national newspaper to an overbearing hammer thrower. And finally, on the last episode of *The Sopranos*, a Canadian television station cut away to a light beer commercial before the ending was shown. (What do you mean that there was no ending?)

I recommend that Eddie Greenspan look at the glass as being half full rather than half empty. I leave him with these inspiring words by the great

American humorist Mark Twain, who offered this insight into his obliga-
tion to pay the government income tax: "I am taxed on my income! This is
perfectly gorgeous! I never felt so important in my life. To be treated in this
splendid way, just like another William B. Astor. Gentlemen, we must drink!"

Greenspan likely feels that he has never been so prominently in the
public eye as he has been in this case. He has also never felt so important
in his life. Does it matter that it was derived from a case that may tarnish
his reputation if he loses? The answer is yes. Greenspan is standing by the
former juror's opinion that Black will walk free from the courtroom. That
would be a perfectly gorgeous sight for the defence.

Whatever the verdict, it will also mark Greenspan's last trial in America.
Gentlemen, we must drink to that.

JUNE 11–12

Journalist and long-time Black associate John O'Sullivan testifies that Amiel's birthday party was more of a business event than a social occasion, noting that eleven of fourteen Hollinger directors were in attendance, along with business contacts such as Trump and broadcaster Charlie Rose. Genson reads the court a threatening email Black received in 1999, to support claims that he used company aircraft for security reasons.

Accountant and former FBI agent Alan Funk testifies that, having reviewed 400,000 pages of documents relating to Hollinger's affairs, he found "no significant evidence that is consistent with fraud."

Each of the four defendants declines his right to testify. The defence rests its case.

FUNKY MUSIC

Eddie Greenspan gained at least ten grey hairs today. The inauspicious moment arrived when Judge Amy St. Eve inquired of his unpredictable client if he had been advised of his right to testify.

Conrad Black stopped to consider the question. Why should he rush his answer? After all, he certainly didn't want to act impetuously. Should he or shouldn't he? The seconds ticked away on the clock. "I … I decline my right to testify," he announced to the court.

While Greenspan was sighing in relief, Eric Sussman must have been privately rueing the lost opportunity to slay the dragon and cross-examine Conrad Black. To dream the impossible dream. It remained his one last glimmer of hope to demonstrate to the jury that it was possible for someone to be more untruthful than his star witness, David Radler.

The evidentiary portion of the trial ended today (with none of the defendants testifying), but not before the jury was treated to some unintended comic relief. Alan Funk, an expert fraud examiner called on behalf of Mark Kipnis, admitted to spending nearly eight hundred hours reviewing some four hundred thousand documents provided to KPMG. However, it was the staggering amount of his fee that riveted the courtroom. Calling an expert witness whose compensation undermined his perceived objectivity was an unnecessary risk for Kipnis's attorneys to make. It was also an inopportune time for their first glaring mistake in the case.

Kipnis was poignantly captured in the jurors' minds as a tragic and sympathetic underdog struggling against the unbridled power of the United States government. How then does it make sense to call a witness who is paid an almost obscene amount of money to testify in his defence? Funk's evidence was clearly not crucial to the case. Indeed, the attorneys for the co-defendants undertook not to rely on his evidence in their closing statements. The recipe for Kipnis's successful defence had been carefully prepared and was almost spoiled by a bitter after-dinner mint.

Jeffrey Cramer's trial lawyer's instincts told him that he was hitting a pressure point with the expert's fee. He asked Funk pointedly when he would reach his ballpark figure of $800,000. "As soon as you sit down," Funk replied. When Michael Schwartz, one of Kipnis's attorneys, stood up to ask a few last questions, he quipped, "Okay, Mr. Funk, I'll keep the meter running." I am confident that Mark Kipnis wasn't laughing at his counsel's poor choice of humour.

I suspect that the jury was preoccupied with one lingering question as they listened to Funk's testimony: how did Mark Kipnis raise $800,000 to call this fraud examiner?

The jury already had a laundry list of perks at the trial to compare to the $800,000 expert fee of Alan Funk:

- the trip to Bora Bora: $600,000
- the surprise birthday party at La Grenouille restaurant: $54,000
- a Chinese carpet (Park Avenue apartment): $33,000
- heated towel racks (Park Avenue apartment): $4,300
- Louis XVI painted stools (Park Avenue apartment): $9,000
- a three-drawer commode (Park Avenue apartment): $12,000
- a mother-of-pearl box (Park Avenue apartment): $9,600
- a diamond vault (Park Avenue apartment): $9,800
- a mahogany shaving stand that belonged to Napoleon (Park Avenue apartment): $12,500

Total cost of perks: $744,200

The defence in the Conrad Black trial began with Joan Maida and ended with Alan Funk. It "maida funky noise" but added little to the case for the defence.

JUNE 14

Granting a prosecution request, Judge St. Eve agrees to instruct jurors to consider whether Black and his co-defendants intentionally avoided knowing about alleged crimes at Hollinger.

OSTRICH FEATHERS

You know it's a slow day in the trial when the major discussion among the journalists covering the case is that they will only have thirty minutes' notice of the jury's verdict.

The other big news, of course, was the trial judge has ruled in favour of the prosecution's appeal for an "ostrich instruction" to the jury. Also referred to as conscious avoidance or deliberate ignorance, the instruction will permit the jurors to consider whether the defendants deliberately chose to avoid acquiring knowledge of the fraudulent non-compete payments in the American community newspaper sales. A similar instruction was also allowed in the Enron and WorldCom cases.

I must profess to being confused about this new position. I thought I actually heard David Radler recount at trial a series of conversations with Conrad Black in which it was plainly Black who hatched the non-compete fraud scheme. Radler played the part of "easy rider" and gleefully went along with the lucrative plot that made more money than *Ocean's Thirteen*. As the principal actor, how then can Black be accused of playing the supporting role of an ostrich?

Essentially, the prosecutors' position can best be encapsulated in the following manner:

David Radler was a prolific liar under oath at trial and was solely responsible for creating a $60-million fraud scheme involving the sale of the American community newspapers. It was he alone who inserted the contrived non-compete clauses into the transactions that enriched the various senior executives and parent company of Hollinger International. It was only David Radler who initially set out to defraud the shareholders of Hollinger International of their rightful claim to the proceeds diverted in the non-compete payments.

Yet at some point the clever muser Conrad Black figured out the illicit scheme but chose to close his eyes and accept his share of the millions regardless.

The prosecution advanced a clear theory in its opening statement about the defendants' direct complicity in the fraudulent scheme that it never deviated from during the course of the trial. The defence should have been able to rely on that position. Instead the attorneys for the four defendants are now confronted by this new and conflicting "ostrich" theory that was presented by the prosecution only after the conclusion of the evidence. The case hadn't been defended on that basis.

In my opinion that doesn't seem terribly fair to the defendants.

That the prosecutors appealed for the ostrich instruction is an implicit recognition that their case has crumbled and that David Radler's testimony is wholly unreliable. It basically comes down to a "Hail Mary" pass by the prosecution to salvage a case that is beaten and crushed. Their final chant to the jury is "Go, ostrich, go!"

CLOSING ARGUMENTS AND JUDGE'S INSTRUCTIONS

JUNE 18

Presenting the prosecution's closing arguments, Julie Ruder attempts to simplify the government's case for jurors. "The crime in this case is the defendants hid and lied about the true reasons why money was paid," she tells the court. "Don't fall for the cover story. These defendants have done these crimes and we have proven it beyond a reasonable doubt."

HOME RUN TROT

I have already been severely challenged about my prediction that Conrad Black will be found not guilty on all counts. The case is over, I am told. The prosecution gave a smashing closing statement that was viewed as an absolute home run. The female prosecutor, Julie Ruder, connected with the eleven women on the jury. She is going to be followed by a few good old men. I suppose that the jurors should close their notebooks and put down their pens, because there can't possibly be anything useful to hear from the defence. The vultures are circling the Dirksen courthouse ready to strip the vestiges of flesh from Conrad Black's body after the slaughter in the courtroom today.

There is little doubt that the prosecution's closing statement was a masterful performance. Consider, for example, the manner in which Ruder treated Izzy Asper's letter requesting a non-compete agreement with Conrad Black for the CanWest deal:

Why did Mr. Black go out years after the fact and years after the deal was done and get Izzy Asper to write up that handwritten letter, that scrawled letter you saw that says, "Yes, I did request and require non-competes from Conrad Black."

The reason that that happened, the reason why Mr. Black emphasized it at the shareholder meetings, the reason why he got the letter and the reason why Mr. Black's counsel emphasized it to you in openings is because that's the most important thing. Unless the buyer required that non-compete, there is no justification for taking the money away from the shareholders.

I would suggest, however, that final judgment on the prosecutors' success be reserved until the attorneys for the four defendants have completed their final addresses over the next three days. I am not prepared to waver yet from my prediction.

I might remind any dubious readers that my opinion is simply that, my honest and objective assessment of the result in the case. If I'm wrong, it won't lead to an outbreak of typhoid fever or be the cause of a stock market crash. It won't lead to border closings at Niagara Falls, either. Judging from the fiery antagonism that my prediction has precipitated in some quarters, I might be expected to fall down on my sword and crumble into a pile of goose dust if my prediction in the case is incorrect and Black is convicted. For the record, I intend to do neither.

I have tabulated the number of people who have read or heard my prediction about Conrad Black's not-guilty verdict. Let's see now. There is the *Chicago Tribune*, *Maclean's* magazine, *Canada AM*, *NewsNet*, *The Stafford Show*, *Adler Online*, and the breakfast club at the Jewish Community Centre. I would calculate the total to be in the area of roughly 4 to 5 million people who will witness my belly flop if Black is led out of the courtroom in handcuffs.

If only I possessed psychic powers to read the jurors' minds rather than having to rely on intuition. A former Toronto homicide squad officer, Mark Mendelson, once related to me that in virtually every high-profile murder investigation that he conducted, a special file designated for psychics had to be opened. These various psychic files sometimes contain tips from as many as twenty individuals claiming psychic powers. The tips come personally delivered, sometimes with aliases, or by fax, email, or phone.

The visions described by the psychics come in many different forms. It might be water, trees, and a tall man with long grey hair. Or it could be a victim crying for help while buried in the mud. In some cases, the psychics point to particular suspects. For example, the police might be asked to investigate the ex-husband in an investigation after he was seen in a vision brandishing a knife.

There is finally a small category of rogue psychics who scheme to fool the police. They seek out information about a major crime on the Internet, in blogs, and in newspaper accounts. They then contact the police with their disingenuous prophetic vision to claim a monetary reward.

I have often wondered what would happen if psychics appeared on a jury panel for a criminal trial. Would they automatically be excused? They hold an advantage over the other jurors: they already know what the jury will decide. Jury deliberations might become unruly and messy.

I had my own premonition about the two Eddies' jury address tomorrow. They will attempt to match Julie Ruder stride for stride. I expect that by the end of the day tomorrow, we may be speaking about a defence home run. A single won't bring the tying run home to the plate. Greenspan and Genson are fully aware of that fact in the case. If they aren't, the case really is over.

JUNE 19

Beginning the defence's closing arguments, Greenspan apologizes to jurors for his aggressive style. He accuses prosecutors of trying to prejudice the jurors against Black by detailing his lavish lifestyle, attacks their failure to produce a "smoking gun," and criticizes Radler's plea bargain. Greenspan also contends all payments to the defendants were disclosed to the audit committee.

DAVID LAWYERMAN

I have some news for the prescient observers of the trial who are already preparing in earnest the obituary for the ill-fated Lord Black of Crossharbour. Eddie Greenspan weaved a bit of magic in the courtroom today and rescued his client's prospects for a happy outcome of the trial. I have compiled my own Lawyerman top ten list of the reasons that Greenspan was successful.

Number ten:
> Eddie Greenspan put the prosecution on the defensive from the out-set by posing two questions: "Where are these [irate] shareholders?" and "Where are the victims?" Not a single Hollinger International shareholder was brought to testify to explain to the jury that the non-competes mattered to them. By way of contrast, Greenspan played a portion of the 2003 Hollinger International shareholders meeting at which the second-largest shareholder, Mason Hawkins, praised a

"very capable management team" that "created approximately $2 billion of intrinsic value from virtually nothing."

Number nine:

Greenspan portrayed his client's wealthy lifestyle, vocabulary, and opulent tastes ("a rich man with expensive things") as a distinct disadvantage that the prosecution was trying to exploit by distracting the jury with images of heated towel racks, champagne, and caviar. "He is different from you and me," Black's lawyer acknowledged to the jury.

He further urged the jurors to treat Conrad Black like any of their neighbours. "You don't reward people in America for their fame and fortune, but you don't punish them either," he told them. Equal justice was required even for people disliked by the jurors. Conrad Black may have missed the slight, but the jurors certainly got the message. The subtle reference was to his client's strident arrogance amply evidenced in his emails and musings.

Number eight:

Greenspan recognized that his client is in a struggle for his life and that he needs to push the envelope. In a bold and correct move, he advised the jury that even if they find that Conrad Black is probably guilty, it is not enough to convict. A highly skilled lawyer never makes such a concession unless he is worried about the outcome.

Number seven:

There is no smoking gun in the case. "David Radler is all they got," Greenspan stated, and in order to "get the big fish," Radler was willing to point the finger at Black to save himself. In ten sessions with the government, Radler learned to read a script that was sculpted by the prosecutors. The jurors heard that the trial judge will instruct them that they must approach their assessment of Radler's testimony with great caution and care. I suppose that means that all the other witnesses should be evaluated in a frivolous and capricious manner.

Number six:

Greenspan wasn't put off by Eric Sussman's repeated and very un-Canadian discourteous objections to his jury address. At one point Sussman even suggested a sidebar. There is nothing quite as helpful to sustaining momentum in a jury address than a protracted sidebar. Sussman had brought an espresso machine to court and was prepared to make Eddie a tall double while they chatted with the judge. Greenspan ignored the interruptions and ploughed ahead with his closing.

Number five:

The audit committee's approval of the non-competes raised a reasonable doubt on its own. It was "hard not to be insulted," Greenspan argued, by the government's position that Thompson, Burt, and Kravis should be believed. Rather than missing the disclosure of the non-competes as they steadfastly maintained, the members of the odd audit committee read and approved them. These "Olympic liars" and "Olympic skimmers" lied to the jury because they were "trying to salvage their reputations."

Number four:

The prosecution witnesses refused to speak to the defence. Bad breath was not offered as an excuse. Only one government witness, a lawyer for one of the buyers of the American community newspapers, was prepared to meet with the defence. Greenspan asked pointedly, "Why is that?" The answer, my friend, is that they prefer the prosecution wind.

Number three:

The prosecution didn't deliver on its promises in the opening address. Time after time, Eddie Greenspan demonstrated that Jeffrey Cramer failed to deliver on the hyperbole that marked his dramatic, headline-grabbing opening statement. Case in point: Greenspan asserted that if the prosecution's theory is correct, the defendants were the "dumbest bank robbers in the history of the world."

Number two:

> Greenspan apologized to the jury for being a bit gruff with the prosecution witnesses in the rough-and-tumble of the trial. There was also the rather insignificant explanation that he was defending a man whose life was at stake. However, if the jury wanted a refreshing injection of humility from this brash bully from the northern lights, it was forthcoming.

Number one:

> And the number one reason that Conrad Black's counsel vitiated the impact of Julie Ruder's closing on behalf of the government: Eddie Greenspan finally connected with the jury in a stellar performance. It was advocacy at its best and he was awarded the first star. The jurors were attentive, taking notes and absorbing Greenspan's message. The jury clearly has not decided this case. Ed Genson began his portion of the closing by sharing with the jurors the predicament that both he and Greenspan "had a lot of sleepless nights lately." Perhaps they will be sleeping soundly tonight thinking about Ron Safer getting his anti-fraud pen ready.

HITMAN

The day ended with Judge Amy St. Eve informing Eddie Greenspan that all of the attorneys in the case were following his lead and using the term "I submit" in their jury addresses. Jack Boultbee mentioned outside of court that he wondered if robes would follow next.

The day began with Eric Sussman's feeble attempt to embarrass Theresa Tedesco by scolding her in the presence of her colleagues for daring to interview Julie Ruder's father. He had told Tedesco after hearing Greenspan's closing that there are usually two sides to every story. Sussman demanded to know if Tedesco had advised Ruder's father that she was a member of the press. In a courtroom where the media represents approximately half of the people in the uncomfortable wooden rows of seats, it shouldn't be surprising to a prosecutor's parent (who also is a lawyer) that a reporter was the source of the inquiry. Her press pass might have been a good clue too. Perhaps Mr. Ruder was simply being fair with his assessment.

It seems to make perfect sense that the team of prosecutors gathers each morning to monitor all of the Canadian news accounts and blogs. There may be all kinds of useful trial tips that can be used in the courtroom. I realized that many of the defence counsel in the Black case, the defendants, the RCMP, and even some of the witnesses are avid readers of my blog, but I am now encouraged to learn that representatives of the U.S. government follow it as well. I shall try to add useful tips periodically for the eager prosecutors to follow for the duration of the trial.

Today's tip: While the defendant's attorney is making his closing argument, it is best not to carry on conversations with fellow prosecutors, roll your eyes, or stare at your watch.

I was in the hallway today when I was approached by a CBC radio reporter, Mike Hornbrook. "Can you do a hit for me?" Mike asked. "Sure," I replied.

Eddie Greenspan overheard the conversation. "You agreed to do a hit and you don't even know who it is?" he asked with a grin. For a seasoned criminal lawyer, the mention of a "hit" immediately raises the spectre of a contract killing.

It is a good thing that Eric Sussman didn't overhear my conversation with the Hornbrook. While being led to the basement of the courthouse in handcuffs, I would be shouting, "There are two sides to the story!"

Conrad Black approached me at the morning break to complain about the panel discussion featured in the latest issue of *Maclean's*. Our panel included three former federal prosecutors. I told Black that if he is acquitted, he can claim that the magazine cover proclaiming him "GUILTY!" could be this century's version of the newspaper headline "Dewey Defeats Truman." He didn't laugh. His lawyer has a better sense of humour.

The jury is anxious to begin their deliberations. They declined an opportunity for an afternoon break in order to keep the case moving along.

The jurors will listen to the equivalent of nine separate jury addresses by the time they receive their final instructions from Judge St. Eve. Some of the defendants have various attorneys splitting their closing addresses. The jurors will be swimming with information by the time they retreat to the jury room. By then the only thing they may remember from the various addresses is that Pat Tuite brought his daughter to court to watch and Gus Newman's wife was also present. It is like visitors' day at camp with all of the family visitors to court.

Only in an American courtroom can you listen to defence attorneys accuse the prosecutors of manipulating the evidence and being biased and yet also describe them as wonderful and hard-working people. Perhaps they are wonderful manipulators.

JUNE 20–21

Genson makes his closing argument, belittling the prosecution's evidence supporting each of the thirteen charges against Black and accusing them of manipulating the facts. Newman closes on behalf of Boultbee, leading jurors through the paper trail and concluding there was no cover-up.

Michael Schachter, representing Atkinson, argues against the government's "baseless accusations," noting neither Radler nor any other witness implicated Atkinson in any criminal act.

WE ARE THE CHAMPIONS

The prosecution strategy of divide and conquer in the Conrad Black trial appears to have been extinguished. One of the striking features of the jury addresses on behalf of Black, Boultbee, and Atkinson was that their attorneys strayed some distance from disparaging any co-defendant in the case. While certainly reminding the jurors that they were judging four separate trials, the defence presented a united and cohesive front.

Black was in the most precarious position, as his counsel proceeded first with their submissions. He would be helpless to fend off an attack by a co-defendant. Black could conceivably be confronting the equivalent of four prosecutors in the courtroom if all of the remaining defence attorneys turned their backs on a mutual defence strategy.

The jury still can find that the fraudulent non-compete scheme was a Radler-Black operation and acquit Boultbee, Atkinson, and Kipnis.

However, the harmonious joint strategy employed by the defence seriously diminishes that prospect.

"Our system of justice is the envy of the world," Michael Schachter, Atkinson's lawyer, told the jury today.

Americans sincerely believe this self-aggrandizing claptrap and the jury was lapping it up. Which part of the world is it precisely that cherishes the ideals of the American criminal justice system? You can strike Canada from the list.

There is so much to admire, starting with the notorious Guantanamo Bay detainee facility. It was announced today that the Bush administration may be seeking to close it down permanently and transfer the terror suspects to other military prisons.

Then there is the American policy of extraordinary rendition, which was used to smooth the transfer of a Canadian, Maher Arar, to a Syrian jail cell where he suffered prolonged torture. Arar was exonerated in a public inquiry held in Canada and yet remains on the no-fly list in the U.S. without a suitable apology there.

America endures as one of the few democratic countries with widespread support for the death penalty. Inmates in several states languish on death row waiting their turn to die inhumanely at the hand of an anonymous executioner.

Prison sentences measured in decades rather than years are routinely meted out by American judges guided by the draconian federal sentencing guidelines. The State of Illinois has one of the highest wrongful conviction rates in the United States. In the year 2000, Governor George Ryan declared a halt to executions in his state, noting his "grave concerns" about its "shameful record" of shipping innocent men off to death row.

Is the trial of Conrad Black the envy of the world? According to Schachter's jury address today, the goal of the prosecution is "to win regardless of the facts."[1] That seems like a damning indictment rather than high praise. The trial is accordingly regarded as a competitive sporting event where winning is the supreme goal.

It's a criminal case and not a game, Schachter indignantly told the jury. What, then, can be said of the claim that Mark Kipnis was included in the fraud scheme charges with the expectation that he would fold his tent, accept a plea, and convert into a co-operating witness? If that was indeed their hope, the prosecution took a big chance by rolling the dice and including Kipnis. His presence has damaged the overall case. The prosecutors will have all of Monday to think about that predicament as they listen intently to Ron Safer's final address to the jury.

CANYE WEST

I can now add the *Guardian* newspaper in England to the list of print and broadcast media that have cited my dicey prediction of wholesale not-guilty verdicts at the Conrad Black trial. The numbers are rising faster than donations at a Jerry Lewis telethon. The grand total now stands at about 7 million people.

A senior assistant Crown attorney pulled me aside in court on Friday in Toronto. He was visibly angry about the overbearing conduct of Conrad Black's prosecutors at the trial. He expressed dismay that they had relied on the word of David Radler without a shred of supporting evidence. It wasn't the first dissent that I had heard from a shocked and less-than-awed Canadian prosecutor.

In his testimony, Radler had described four telephone calls with Conrad Black that hatched the scheme. Radler was based in Chicago in the *Sun-Times* building, while Black was separately based in New York, London, Toronto, or Palm Beach. There would surely be telephone records to corroborate the existence of long-distance calls between the two men if they occurred, Greenspan noted to the jury. Why were such records not submitted as evidence?

I was reminded of something that Greenspan told the jury at the end of his address. If Conrad Black accepted the word of David Radler, it was a crime. If the prosecutors followed his word, it was justice. The missing part of the trilogy that Greenspan planted in the minds of the jurors was this: "If you believe the word of David Radler, it will be a miscarriage of justice."

All roads in this trial lead to Radler. It is inconceivable that without his turncoat testimony the case would even have been prosecuted. The plea agreement with Radler was born out of desperation rather than reasoned professional judgment. Radler's attorneys exploited this leverage to full advantage in structuring a sweetheart deal that rivals the purchase of Manhattan Island in 1626 for $24 worth of merchandise.

As Michael Schachter theatrically dropped the transcripts of Radler's eight days of trial testimony with a thud in front of the jury, he virtually shouted to the jurors that his client, Peter Atkinson, hadn't been implicated by Radler in the fraudulent scheme. "You can read every word of David Radler's testimony on the stand," he emphatically told them, "and you will see he never testified, never testified, that Peter ever did anything wrong."

If we can properly assume that Schachter's statement is indeed accurate, the implication is that Radler took the enormous risk of looting the Hollinger safe without seeking a single assurance that Atkinson wouldn't expose the scheme to the authorities rather than becoming a co-conspirator in the plot.

Dice roll #1:

> The prosecution argued that Boultbee and Atkinson were both falsely inserted into the CanWest non-competition agreement and yet decided not to call Leonard Asper from CanWest to support this position.

Dice roll #2:

> In addition to victims and irate shareholders, the prosecution chose not to call a single member of the Hollinger board of directors other than the audit committee members. Why weren't Henry Kissinger and Richard Perle, for example, called by the prosecution to claim that they were misled about the disputed non-competes?

Dice roll #3:

> Why wasn't a single member of David Radler's inner sanctum (e.g., Todd Vogt) called by the prosecution to substantiate any of Radler's claims about his misdeeds?

Dice roll #4:

> The prosecution rests on a theory that Radler and the co-defendants were prepared to expose the misbegotten non-competition payments in the American community newspaper deals to a series of auditors at KPMG, lawyers at Torys, the Securities and Exchange Commission, and the three venerated members of the Hollinger International audit committee with a responsibility to the shareholders.

TILTED

Dice roll #5:

> The prosecution also rests on a theory that Radler conscripted an in-house lawyer for the company, Mark Kipnis, and placed him on the front lines of a $60-million fraud, even making him the point of contact for the audit committee, without taking the added precaution of compensating him with a single shekel as hush money to appease him and to purchase his loyalty.

This is a prosecution built on a wing and a prayer. A bed of feathers has a firmer foundation. Even ostrich feathers. Mark Kipnis would be foolish to be overconfident about the result in his case. He was the only defendant located in Radler's *Sun-Times* sanctuary and he was directly involved with the wire transfer of the proceeds of the non-competition payments to Hollinger Inc. and to the senior executives.

Julie Ruder devoted a considerable part of her closing to connect the dots to Kipnis's guilt. Kipnis has decided on an approach that it is "better to be Safer than sorry." Ron Safer, his distinguished lead conductor, will deliver a stirring rendition of "Requiem of Innocence" on Monday to an audience of rested jurors. Safer will assume the moral high ground in the case and forcefully make the government's ill-conceived prosecution of his client appear abusive and vexatious. The rest of the defence closings will seem like a Tupperware party by comparison.

Kipnis has been described as "the forgotten man" with a quiet sympathy building in his favour and the defendant who is most likely to walk free from the courtroom. His enviable prize for winning will be a soiled reputation, the destruction of his professional career, and near destitution.

I have come to know Mark Kipnis over the months of the trial and my impression of the man has remained consistent. He is a kind and decent person. I have also been consoled by the fact that he is a non-golfer. Unfortunately for him, it isn't my view of him that matters but the jurors'. Other than the glowing praise they heard from a former assistant, they know nothing about the man's character. I am certain that the decision not to call Kipnis to testify was as challenging a decision as any Safer has had to make in his career. His jury address will have to personalize his client's plight and the treacherous path of injustice that his client has been forced to overcome.

One of Mark Kipnis's favourite books is *To Kill a Mockingbird*. That hardly seems surprising since he is reprising the role of Tom Robinson at his trial. The legal manoeuvring at Kipnis's trial, like Robinson's, has twisted and contorted the facts to skewer his innocence (Jeffrey Cramer's opening: "He [Kipnis] got $150,000 in bonus money to help do this crime"). It will be up to a Chicago jury to deliver a fate to Kipnis that is different from Tom Robinson's tragic ending. Tomorrow Ron Safer will have the opportunity to take on the venerable role of Atticus Finch and wear his mantle.

JUNE 25

Kipnis's lawyer, Ron Safer, reminds jurors that even Radler testified that the $150,000 bonus his client received was awarded for good work, rather than for assisting in any impropriety.

A $60-MILLION STEAM

Criminal lawyers grow accustomed to a special look when complete strangers discover their vocation. Their faces scrunch up in apparent disgust and then they invariably add the following comment: "I suppose *someone* has to do it."

We are treated much like the garbage man picking up the smelly trash or the hotel maid assigned to cleaning bathrooms. There are also the less charitable individuals who are unforgiving when they discover our profession. I met one such couple recently at a social occasion. The husband recognized me and whispered to his wife that I was the lawyer who defended the Maple Leaf Gardens sex abuse case. My client was a former usher alleged to have molested scores of children and teenaged boys at the acclaimed hockey rink in Toronto.

The woman chose to direct her comment to my wife seated beside me at the table.

"How do you sleep at night?" she asked with the customary scrunched-up face. This was something new, I thought to myself. Criminal lawyers, however, are skilled at the quick retort and I instantly replied on behalf of my shocked wife.

"She actually doesn't sleep," I stated matter-of-factly. "We have wild sex all night and there just isn't time for that."

I thought the poor woman was going to spit out her wine, she was so aghast. The rest of the women at the table, however, were all smiling. I have cultivated a brand new reputation as a Don Juan.

Ron Safer had the ultimate comeback to prosecutor Julie Ruder's decision to mock his anti-fraud pen in her closing. "There are usually two sides to every story," he told the jury, borrowing Ruder's father's statement to the *National Post*. Safer could have started a sauna with all of the steam rising from the prosecutors' table after his clever remark.

The baton was passed from to Safer from Michael Schachter today in closing arguments. The defence has become a four-member relay team with a seamless transition from each respective set of attorneys. Eddie Greenspan, Michael Schachter, and Ron Safer have particularly shone and are treating the prosecution's case like a piñata stuffed with American community newspapers.

The prosecution counted on Peter Atkinson to fold and take a Radleresque deal — wrong.

They then relied on Mark Kipnis to fold his hand and wave the white flag — wrong.

With a doomed pre-trial strategy, the prosecution counted on Boultbee, Kipnis, and Atkinson to pile on Conrad Black to selfishly salvage their own tenuous positions — wrong. Schachter and Safer instead aimed their slings and arrows firmly at the prosecution. If the jury can't trust the sneaky prosecutors, they won't give much credence to their reply tomorrow.

The message was summed up best by Safer. "The prosecution started with a conclusion and then worked backwards," he told the jury. "When the evidence doesn't fit, they ignore it." That was a damning indictment of the prosecution team. In Canada we describe that as tunnel vision and it has the potential to create the setting for a miscarriage of justice.

As he hovered over the prosecutors' table mockingly at times, Safer accused the government of being selective with their witness list. He added that they were trying to get the jurors to forget about intent and making repeated arguments with superficial "surface appeal" to make them stick.

Schachter suggested that the prosecution was attempting to "squeeze out any possible negative spin from the documents to make Peter look bad" and "twisting and straining" to build a case against him. Will the prosecution take the bait and respond? I suspect that Eric Sussman won't be able to resist the challenge. The more time that he devotes to Kipnis's and Atkinson's arguments, the less time he will be able to devote to dismantling Conrad Black's position in closing arguments.

The inclusion of Mark Kipnis in the case has another negative spillover effect for the prosecution. It makes them appear to be mean-spirited to the jurors because there isn't a scintilla of tangible evidence against Kipnis. It was a disastrous decision to include him on the same indictment as Conrad Black and the other defendants. In the end, the real beneficiaries may be Black, Atkinson, and Boultbee. Their prospects for success soared today.

JUNE 26

Prosecutor Eric Sussman begins his lengthy rebuttal of the defence's closing arguments, urging jurors to "follow the money" and scoffing at defence claims that as many as thirteen government witnesses had perjured themselves. He admits that the audit committee may have failed in their duties, but "just because the security guard is asleep does not mean you can rob the bank." He also downplays Radler's importance, telling jurors they have enough evidence to convict without the purported star witness's testimony.

HOP ON THE BUS, GUS

Ron Safer chose to quote from a Paul Simon song today in the final hours of his closing argument. "All I want to tell you is that a man hears what he wants to hear and disregards the rest," he told the jury with reference to the members of the audit committee that has been nominated for the Hall of Shame.

His address was summed up on placard that he held up before the jury. It read simply, "Why would Mark risk everything for nothing?" Safer would have been better served to hold up a blank whiteboard and describe it as the total sum of the evidence against his client.

The prosecution followed Safer by making its reply argument to the more than twenty-five hours of defence addresses. I asked an assistant U.S. attorney in the courtroom why the government is given such an enormous tactical advantage. I was told that it was the result of carrying the burden of proof in the case. I then explained to him that Canadian prosecutors managed to get their fair share of convictions without the added benefit of reply.

It is not fair to describe Eric Sussman's three-and-a-half-hour rejoinder today as a reply. (It will be followed by about an hour and a half tomorrow.) I prefer to call it a pile-on or a defence sandwich. It doesn't matter if the prosecution could have anticipated the argument for its initial closing from the cross-examination conducted at the trial. The only issue is whether the defence touched on the issue in any of its closing addresses at trial. That leaves the door wide open.

Allow me to share a few examples from Sussman's reply argument of what should have been confined to the initial closing argument of the government:

- Sussman told the jury that the perks are a window into Conrad Black's attitude towards the shareholders and their money. It permeates all of the transactions.
- "Why do you think this guy [Conrad Black] was lugging boxes out the back door?"
- "How does Conrad Black know about every penny at a birthday party and not about millions in non-competes?"
- Peter Atkinson's $2-million non-compete payment in the CanWest deal is like winning a lottery in Canada that is tax-free.
- "David Radler only has to make the judge happy."
- "Radler's every incentive under the plea is to tell the truth."
- "No sackcloth and ashes for Mr. Black."
- "Black was involved with every deal."
- The audit committee dropped the ball and failed the shareholders. However, "just because the security guard is asleep does not mean you can rob the bank."
- "We don't pick the witnesses in this case. Who picked David Radler? Conrad Black ..."
- "He's David Radler, not Santa Claus."
- "Don't you think if David Radler was reading from a script, he would have done a much better job? Don't you think he'd have times and dates and notes for his telephone calls?"

The expansive reply afforded to Sussman continues tomorrow morning, and then the jury will receive its final instructions from Judge St. Eve. This will not be a lengthy jury deliberation. There weren't many notes taken by the jurors today. They seem to share a collective sense already of the right and just resulting from the case.

JUNE 27

Sussman concludes his rebuttal. The jury is charged by Judge St. Eve, and deliberations begin.

FIREWORKS

> *Black remains confident of his acquittal, his lawyer, Edward Greenspan, told reporters outside the courtroom. Greenspan said the Black family is holding up well through a trial he described as "tense and very nerve wracking."*
>
> *He said he's not impressed by the reported 95 percent conviction rate of the U.S. Attorney's Office in Chicago.*
>
> *New York Yankees baseball pitcher "Roger Clemens loses the occasional baseball game," Greenspan said. "This is a unique case."*
>
> — *Chicago Tribune,* June 27, 2007

It must be comforting to Conrad Black to know that his lawyer believes that his chances of winning his trial are comparable to those of a seven-time Cy Young Award–winning pitcher losing a baseball game. A British journalist handed me a form this morning for the press sweepstakes for the Conrad Black verdict. The winner must accurately predict all thirteen charges. There is no indication of the grand prize. Since I have carefully followed the expert testimony at the trial, I realize that the winnings, whatever they are, will be taxable in the United States. I respectfully declined to enter. I can't afford to win.

Canada has the right idea about jury deliberations. Twelve people are placed in a room from morning to late evening (with convenient breaks) and sequestered in the evening in a ratty hotel. Their use of newspapers and television is carefully monitored.[2] The process continues each day until a verdict is reached. It is the perfect ambience to encourage speedy but just verdicts.[3]

The Conrad Black jury began its deliberations today under very different conditions. There will be no evenings, no weekends, a half-day on Friday this week, and an early adjournment today for a juror's prior engagement. I am waiting tomorrow for a juror to suggest breaking early to attend a Cubs game or a taping of *The Oprah Winfrey Show*.

Allow me to share a few final observations of the government's rebuttal argument today and Judge Amy St. Eve's final instructions:

1. Eric Sussman's rebuttal was six hours and fifteen minutes long. Julie Ruder's closing jury address for the prosecution was seven hours. Given that Sussman merely repeated everything that Ruder said, we are left to conclude that Sussman speaks more quickly.

2. Sussman waited for his rebuttal to drop the bombshell that Radler was no longer essential to his case. The timing was calculated to leave no opportunity for the defence to take him to task for such a dramatic statement. The jurors will appreciate this cunning strategy. They will adopt Ron Safer's suggestion and imagine his response to the prosecution's falling star witness.

"Did I hear Mr. Sussman correctly?" he would begin, with hands on head. "I checked the transcript and he really did say that the government didn't need to rely on David Radler to succeed with their case. He must have kept it a secret from Jeffrey Cramer, because that certainly wasn't his position in the prosecution's opening.

"It makes perfect sense for the prosecutors to offer a deal to an accomplice to spend a few months in a Canadian horse farm in a $60-million fraud scheme. Of course this isn't a man whose evidence they need. They are simply demonstrating that they have a generous and charitable side.

"I suppose that it must be a coincidence that Radler hasn't been sentenced yet. The reason can't be that the government was waiting to see how he performed for them at this trial, because he isn't necessary to prove their case. His attorney must have a busy court schedule.

"Mr. Sussman has a point. Why should you waste your time considering the only witness in the case who claims he discussed the fraud scheme with any of the defendants?"

3. Sussman spent an inordinate amount of time dismantling Mark Kipnis's defence because he realized that Kipnis is the umbilical cord that connects all of the defendants to the alleged non-compete scheme.

Ron Safer expressly told the jury that the approval by the audit committee of the non-competes raised reasonable doubt on its own. If Kipnis is acquitted, like a set of dominos, his three co-defendants could be acquitted as well!

4. The possible motive attributed to Kipnis by Sussman could apply to virtually every single human being on the planet who works for a living and who depends on an employer for his salary and bonus. Kipnis purportedly risked everything in a $60-million scheme for nothing tangible because Conrad Black and David Radler controlled his salary and bonus.

Another Sussman line from his rebuttal about Kipnis: "In the land of the morally bankrupt, the nicest guy is innocent." The trial is now a morality play to the prosecution. I can return home to Toronto. Morality is for priests and rabbis. I am only a legal analyst.

5. Sussman tried another clever tactic. He introduced statements on a screen from three shareholders, Laura Jereski, Lee Cooperman, and Chris Browne, expressing concerns at a shareholders meeting about the non-compete payments paid to Conrad Black and others. On the eleventh hour of the trial, the jury was being left with the words of actual victims to digest.

The problem of such reply, however, was that the statements were hearsay and not admitted for the truth of their content. Was this an honest mistake by the lead prosecutor or had he put his head in the sand and discounted any issues of unfairness to the defence?

6. If the theme of "follow the money" ensnared Richard Nixon in the Watergate scandal, Sussman deemed it poetic justice to use the same theme for the trial of Nixon's biographer, Conrad Black. The jury was urged to

follow the money trail to show that Black, Radler, Boultbee, and Atkinson profited handsomely from the fraud.

7. Sussman mistook Conrad Black's email to Paul Healy sent a few days after the 2002 shareholders meeting. It read: "Two years from now no one will remember anything about this." He was referring to Sussman's underachieving rebuttal.

8. The judge's instructions took exactly fifty-seven minutes to read to the jury after a three-month trial. We know the time because the judge told the lawyers that she had complied with her estimate of one hour. By Canadian standards, the instruction was sparse. There wasn't a single word spoken about the respective theories of each side or a meaningful review of any of the evidence. There was no opinion expressed about any feature of any of the testimony, and there was no application of the law to the evidence in the case. Conrad Black can forget about an appeal if he loses the trial.

9. There was no "bubkas instruction" to the jury for David Radler. The jury was told only to exercise great care and caution in assessing his evidence. In a "bubkas instruction" the judge would have charged as follows: "You have heard from the prosecution's witness, David Radler. He is an admitted liar who even lied to the government. He has a deal for his sentence that hangs over his head until he finishes testifying. Not a word of his evidence is backed up by a single document in the case. It is not clear that he engaged in any crime with any of the defendants. Ladies and gentleman of the jury, Radler is worth bubkas to you. To rely on anything he told you would be as dangerous as playing with dynamite in a firecracker factory."

10. The jury was not told anything by the judge in her instructions about the use they should make of Mark Kipnis's one character witness. It simply rests with the jury that she was prepared to trust her life with him. Does that mean that Kipnis was less likely to have committed a fraud?

Although the jurors understood that they would receive a printed copy of the judge's instructions, they stared at her intently as she read every word to them. They appeared anxious to begin their deliberations.

Conrad Black is a lucky man. His jury is concerned about getting it right and reaching a just verdict. The stakes are enormous. It will be the most important day of an illustrious life. If Black is found guilty of a single charge, he will be led out of court in handcuffs and will be in custody until his sentencing. If there is an acquittal, there will be a fireworks display in honour of Canada Day. It will be sponsored by the Canadian libel bar.

STRAWBERRY SHORTCAKE

I witnessed first-hand the novel influence of blogs and BlackBerrys in this trial. One of the attorneys for a defendant in the Black trial approached my colleague Mark Steyn at the break to discuss one of the blogs he had prepared that morning in the courtroom. In this new world of Black blogs, an attorney can review an instant evaluation of his performance. Did the cross-examination hit its mark? How are the jurors reacting to the presentation of the evidence?

Another novel feature of this trial are jury consultants. I have been told on good authority that attorneys routinely use them in major trials in Chicago. They are about as common as BlackBerrys, but they mystify me. I wonder what special expertise they possess to interpret a person's body language or personality. Do they teach this skill at Harvard or Yale? About half of them are psychologists but they also come from a variety of fields including theatre, marketing, and communication.

I asked Eddie Greenspan about jury consultants and he informed me that in thirty-eight years, he never used the services of a consultant in one of his criminal cases. If he was defending a client charged with robbing and killing a taxi cab driver, he wouldn't choose a cab driver as a juror. He didn't need to pay an expert to tell him that.

The *Toronto Star* reported today that the prosecution hadn't retained any professional help to choose the jury. I was therefore curious to learn if jury consultants had been retained for Conrad Black's defence. "None," Greenspan informed me. "I don't believe in them." Apparently some of Black's co-defendants did have jury consultants in the courtroom during jury selection, but they couldn't always agree on the same suitable candidates.

Black's defence team did hire a special consultant to conduct mock jury addresses with three separate focus groups of twelve randomly selected people over a one-and-a-half-day period. Greenspan and the rest of his team watched in a booth through a one-way mirror. The goal was to test how jurors from different backgrounds reacted to the presentation. The experiment was hardly a resounding success in Greenspan's opinion, but it provided the defence with some useful information about juror profiles.

Jury consulting has grown into a major industry over the past few decades. There are hundreds of firms involved and profiting several hundred million dollars a year. In the spring 2007 issue of *Psychology Today* magazine,[4] there was a story about one of the jurors in the 2004 murder trial of Scott Peterson. Her name was Rochelle Nice, and she was given the nickname of Strawberry Shortcake because she came to court every morning with her hair dyed a different shade of red.

Jury selection took three weeks to complete. Both Peterson's lawyer, Mark Geragos, and the prosecution wanted Nice on the jury and she was subsequently chosen. The jury consultant retained by the prosecution, Howard Varinsky, described changing his clients' initial outlook on Shortcake. "The prosecutors didn't want her," he noted, "because she looked more outlaw than the nice straight homeowners with three kids and a picket fence. When they asked her about the tattoos, it was really code for 'How can I trust you, looking the way you look?'"

Varinsky claimed to have observed a brief expression of rage exhibited by Strawberry Shortcake before she answered the question about her tattoos and he persuaded his dubious client to accept his advice and take her. Varinsky claimed to know that she would never acquit Scott Peterson. I suspect that the true reason may relate to the fact that the case against Peterson was utterly overwhelming. His wife's body washed ashore with their unborn child only a few miles from the place in San Francisco Bay where Peterson told the police he had mysteriously gone fishing alone on Christmas Eve.

I asked Eddie Greenspan if he was truly worried about the 95 percent conviction rate of prosecutors in Chicago in federal cases. He replied that his statistics are actually better. He has never lost a case in the Dirksen courthouse. His answer was entirely truthful. Of course, this Canadian barrister and Queen's Counsel has also never tried a case in the courthouse before.

TILTED

Eddie Genson had a slightly different take on the formidable success rate of prosecutors in Chicago. "In this building, you usually need lightning to strike," he told me. "You don't need lightning in this case," he maintained. It will be ironic if one of the few successful defences in a federal courtroom results from Conrad Black's trial, in which a jury consultant wasn't hired by his counsel to assist with jury selection. Genson and Greenspan have more than sixty years of experience trying criminal cases between them. It is a safe prediction that their instincts can match the very best jury consultants. If I was in Atlantic City, I would place my bet on them.

TEA LEAVES

It is sometimes far easier to read tea leaves than to speculate on the jury's decision in a particular case.

Permit me to provide you with a couple of examples from two fascinating Canadian murder trials that illustrate the point.

I describe the first case as "the sleepwalker." Ken Parks fell asleep on the couch in his home. When he awoke a few hours later, he put on his shoes and jacket and walked to his car. He brought with him a hatchet and two knives. Parks's destination was the home of his in-laws. After driving nearly twenty-five kilometres, he arrived at their home and entered with a key.

Later that night, Ken Parks walked into a police station with several cuts to his hands and with blood dripping from him. He was extremely upset and distraught as he exclaimed to the desk sergeant, "My God, I've just killed two people. My hands."

The police soon discovered Ken Parks's mother-in-law dead and her husband in dire condition. Charges were laid against Parks for first-degree murder and attempted murder. There was no apparent motive for the violent episode and Parks told the police that he had no memory of an angry exchange with his in-laws. Ken Parks's inexplicable actions were attributed by a series of experts called at his trial to sleepwalking. He had been experiencing problems at home that were making sleep a formidable challenge.

The jury deliberated for some ten hours before returning a not-guilty verdict. The decision was subsequently appealed and the Ontario Court of Appeal agreed that the result was extremely troubling but refused to tamper with the perplexing verdict.

The second case is called "the dreamer." Julie Bowers was charged with the murder of her eleven-month-old son, Dustin. Bowers had reported to the police that her infant son had been kidnapped from her car while she conducted her banking. Eventually, she led the police to Dustin's body, explaining that she had a dream where she visualized her son lying in the snow in the precise location where he was found.

In an incredible decision that was not appealed, Julie Bowers was found not guilty by a jury in Kincardine, Ontario.

Unpopular decisions by juries often lead to unfair, derisive criticism. After Michael Jackson was cleared of all charges of sexual abuse, a former prosecutor suggested on the Fox News Channel that intelligence tests were desirable for all jurors.[5] David Letterman's top ten list dealt with sample greetings left on Michael Jackson's answering machine after the verdict. The number one message was as follows: "Hi, it's Saddam Hussein. How do I get one of them idiot juries?"

No one has suggested that Conrad Black has an "idiot jury." At least not yet.

I have already heard two conflicting sets of assumptions about the looming verdict in the case as the jury enters its fourth day of deliberations: a) a quick verdict in the case is good for the defence — if the jury has to exhaustively review all of the non-competes, it is welcome news for the prosecution; and b) a lengthy jury deliberation is good for the defence — with a 95 percent conviction rate, if the jury needs more than a day to ponder its verdict, the balance has tilted back in favour of the defence. All of the possible permutations and combinations that flow from the length of deliberations and the nature of questions asked by the jury can leave a court watcher's head spinning like a Ferris wheel.

The jurors in the Black trial have asked for the prosecution's chart summarizing the American community newspaper non-competes as well as the transcript of the testimony of Jonathan Rosenberg. What does it all mean? Does it shine a bright flashlight into the jury room and provide a peek into the jurors' mindset?

Wading through the heavenly scented tea leaves, here is my guarded opinion of the current state of the jury's deliberation. Warning: the following material may offend anyone who harbours illusions of a shackled

Conrad Black sinking to the bottom of Lake Michigan while buzzards fly above shouting, "Is he dead yet?"

Jonathan Rosenberg was the New York lawyer who was charged with the responsibility of investigating complaints from Hollinger International Inc.'s shareholders in 2003. He turned out to be more potent than truth serum because remarkably he managed to extract a few damaging statements from some of the defendants. Conrad Black, on the advice of counsel, had refused to co-operate with the special committee's investigation.

During Rosenberg's testimony, Black's counsel, Ed Genson, asked the trial judge to instruct the jury that his evidence did not pertain to his client. I am therefore surmising that the jury has decided to start with a consideration of the legal fate of Mark Kipnis, the defendant with the most compelling case for reasonable doubt. Atkinson, Boultbee, and Black will follow.

The broad consensus among virtually every legal analyst covering the trial is that Kipnis will be acquitted by the jury. The jury will therefore have to disregard Rosenberg's testimony that Kipnis related to him that the non-compete payments from American Publishing Company (APC) were "silly." He further allegedly stated to Rosenberg that the only newspaper that APC had left was the *Mammoth Times* and a non-competition payment didn't make sense. The company didn't get value for it. It was Rosenberg's impression that Kipnis thought the whole thing was "silly."

This was ostensibly an admission by Mark Kipnis that he was aware of the fraudulent scheme involving the non-competes. It is the only direct evidence in the case against him. The same is true of his co-defendants Peter Atkinson and Jack Boultbee. As Judge St. Eve instructed the jurors, they will have to rely on their own independent recollection of Rosenberg's testimony rather than a transcript.

In cross-examination by Michael Schwartz, Rosenberg agreed that he interviewed Kipnis over thirteen hours during his investigation in a free-flowing discussion. Memos were kept of detailed summaries rather than verbatim transcripts. The conversations were not tape recorded.

Rosenberg used the same unorthodox approach in his meetings with Atkinson and Boultbee.

In his finest moment at the trial, Pat Tuite made a convincing case that Rosenberg was "arrogant and biased" and was unworthy of belief by the jury. He held up an inexpensive tape recorder and asked rhetorically why one hadn't been used at the interviews. There was no court reporter, no tape recorder, no note taker or a typed-out statement. In testimony from Rosenberg that Tuite called "chilling," he claimed that it wasn't appropriate to keep precise records because it "could come back to bite the company in some future litigation." "How does the truth bite the company?" Tuite asked in a biting and sarcastic tone.

The interviews were deliberately set up, Tuite added, to not allow for anyone to refute Rosenberg. The jury should perceive this behaviour, he maintained, as an insult. Tuite's harangue about a manifestly unreliable process certainly provided the jurors with ample fodder to disregard Rosenberg's evidence and continue on the road to acquit Mark Kipnis.

Rosenberg will then become a non-entity in the case against Atkinson and Boultbee. Their so-called confessions will be discarded by the jury. The three co-defendants have arguably overcome the most damaging testimony in the case. The tea leaves favour the defence presently. I say this, however, as a dedicated coffee bean worshipper.

GONE WITH THE WINDY CITY

I have never quite accepted that the prosecutors in Patrick Fitzgerald's office commanded a 95 percent conviction rate. I finally had the opportunity recently to question a federal prosecutor about the near-perfect success rate that compared favourably to the achievements of Lance Armstrong and Roger Federer.

"It's not true," he told me.

I just knew that such an alarmingly high rate of guilty dispositions was blatantly false. I was feeling quite vindicated. I was about to expose this charade forever. My heart was beating quickly with anticipation of sharing the news with the esteemed journalists covering the trial.

"You see, Steve," the prosecutor continued, "we never lose a single case."

My jaw dropped, and for the first time in my life since my circumcision (eight days after birth), I was speechless. These prosecutors never lose. I was on record predicting before about 7 million people that Conrad Black and his co-defendants would walk free from the courtroom and my chances of being accurate were now deemed by an insider to be non-existent.

I have chosen upon reflection not to waver from my outlandish prediction. It was so hot in Chicago on Sunday (almost 38 degrees Celsius) that you could fry an egg on concrete. May I suggest my head?

The jury is only a day or two away from deciding this case. There will be no hung jury or undecided verdict. The mere fact that over the course of seven days of deliberation not a single question of substance has been posed by the twelve jurors suggests a remarkable cohesiveness and sophisticated level of understanding on their part. This jury has been underestimated by everyone except for the lawyers and journalists who have watched them diligently perform their task in the courtroom.

Conrad Black has told the *National Post* that he has reserved judgment on the jury until his verdict is delivered. Allow me to gauge the manner in which this British subject will carefully construct his delicate conclusions about the jury in his case. If he is acquitted of all thirteen counts, the jurors will be portrayed as Mensa members who would be suitable senior editors at the *Telegraph* when Lord Black assumes control and ownership immediately after the satisfactory verdict. If, however, he is found guilty of any of the charges he faces, the jurors will be viewed as unduly rushing to judgment only to be prepared for the simultaneous arrival in America of both Harry Potter (with a new book and movie) and that icon of British song and fashion, Victoria Beckham. The jubilant jurors need some spices to rouse their dormant senses as they ponder Harry and Victoria bending it like Beckham.

JULY 10

Jurors twice declare themselves unable to reach a unanimous verdict on "one or more" charges. Judge St. Eve admonishes them to continue their deliberations the next day.

DYNAMITE BLAST

I had a nice surprise today. One of my very favourite people in the world, Justice Harry LaForme, from the Ontario Court of Appeal, was visiting Chicago with his family. He has authored landmark rulings as a trial judge on the legality of same-sex marriage and the authorized use of medicinal marijuana. Harry, as he insists on being called, became the first Aboriginal judge appointed to any appellate court in Canada. He will one day be the first (of many) Aboriginals to sit on the nation's highest court, the Supreme Court of Canada.

After a leisurely lunch, we strolled over to the courthouse only to be surprised to learn that the jury in the Conrad Black trial had just sent a note to the judge. Before court was convened, Eddie Greenspan introduced his noteworthy client to Justice LaForme.

"We have something in common, you know," Conrad Black noted with some pride as he shook the judge's hand.

"We are both called 'Your Lordship'," he remarked.

Where are those vomit bags that the airlines carry when you need them?

The jury's note presented the first insight into their lengthy deliberations. They have decided a number of the counts but remain deadlocked on "one or more" of the charges. The judge repeated her "dynamite instruction" urging them to make every reasonable effort to break the logjam. They were asked to reach a verdict without surrendering their honestly held beliefs about what weight or effect should be given to the evidence.

It was revealing that the defence huddled to consider the jury's note and promptly asked for the jury's verdict. They clearly were enamoured with the expected verdict. By contrast, the prosecution team, with Patrick Fitzgerald in court, appeared visibly shaken and wanted the jurors to be afforded a choice of resuming their deliberations or announcing their verdict.

What do the fresh mint tea leaves tell us? The note was a bombshell in the trial. Here are the ramifications that flow from it:

The jury's verdict in the case is merely hours away. None of the journalists covering the trial are prepared to stray far from the courtroom. Stay tuned.

Kipnis, Boultbee, and Atkinson will be free men tomorrow. Their ordeal will soon be over. The verdict of the jury will be not guilty on all counts. Conrad Black has beaten the core charges he faces, including the racketeering and fraud charges relating to the $60 million in non-competition payments. The remaining charges relate to some of the perks or more likely to the obstruct justice charge.

The deadlocked jury will either return with no verdict on the remaining charges tomorrow or perhaps return with a sweeping acquittal on all counts. It will not matter because the government will never retry Black on any of the peripheral charges. There was a discussion of a forfeiture at a hearing this morning that I deliberately boycotted. I defiantly protest any notion of determining a procedure for forfeiting millions of dollars of assets while four defendants retain their presumption of innocence.

The irrepressible Tom Bower joined my courtroom boycott (I presume) and volunteered that one of Conrad Black's good friends told him that Black was resigned to defeat in his criminal case. His gregarious colleague, James Bone, suggested a mock trial where I would play the part of Eddie Greenspan and Tom Bower the part of Eric Sussman. James would carry the gavel and portray Judge Amy St. Eve. Given that this proposed judicial officer had previously confided in me that Conrad Black would be found guilty by the jury of every charge but the Bora Bora holiday perk, his impartiality might be slightly skewed.

On the tenth day, the jury will finally rest. The trial of Conrad Black will soon be over. I will miss the British press.

BLACKS IS PHOTOGRAPHY

*In executing the former head of its food and drug agency Tuesday,
China made its most dramatic gesture yet to show it is serious
about ensuring the safety of its exports.*
— Chicago Tribune, July 11, 2007

They certainly take their corruption cases seriously in China. Conrad
Black can take some small comfort that his vast media empire hadn't
expanded to the *Shanghai Express*. I have heard a wide range of possible
sentences that Judge St. Eve might impose on Lord Black if the jury
returns guilty verdicts on the substantial fraud counts. The word "decades"
is the most common reference. Is it possible that he actually faces a nine-
ty-year sentence as has been suggested?

I decided to consult an expert on the federal sentencing guidelines
with considerable familiarity with the case. Good news for the finger-
wagging defendant. He is seriously looking at only a twenty-year sentence. With parole eligibility, he can be released before the hundredth
anniversary of the stock market crash.

I admit to being puzzled about one facet of the trial. David Radler, by
all accounts in the prosecution's theory, was alleged to be Conrad Black's
co-pilot and principal in the looting scheme perpetrated on Hollinger
International. It was critical for the defence to puncture a gaping hole in
his shaky credibility by exposing the favourable deal that he had secured
with his self-serving guilty plea. Yet when he was cross-examined by
Mark Kipnis's attorney, it was put to Radler that all he faced under the
federal sentencing guidelines was approximately seven years in prison.
How would he have been in any better position than Conrad Black if
they had been tried together as co-defendants? Surely Radler would
have faced a similar twenty-year sentence if he had gambled on a trial
and lost. Why was this facet of his potential risk seriously minimized by
the defence? This remains one of the great mysteries of the case.

There can be no mystery about the motivations harboured by
Conrad Black. He conducts himself as if he is wearing a sign that reads
"I want to be convicted." The latest episode involves the confrontational
gesturing of his third finger at a belligerent cameraman. (Black later
informed Eddie Greenspan in my presence that he would have hit the

rude offender in the face if he had the opportunity.)

My colleague at CTV, Rosemary Thompson, witnessed the debacle and described a scene of pandemonium when Conrad Black arrived alone at the courthouse to learn of the jury's note. Black emerged from the unfamiliar terrain of a taxicab sans socks. As he entered the revolving doors of the courthouse, he was filmed and photographed gesticulating with his finger defiantly raised. The photo made the front page of the *Toronto Sun* with the bold headline, "LORD, THAT'S RUDE."

This isn't simply a matter of the correct etiquette for entering a courthouse. In the firing line of the kind of adversity Conrad Black confronted, Emily Post would surely counsel restraint and stoic resistance to a heated and overwrought reaction.

The consequences for Black were potentially far more severe. It was his good fortune that the photo was not picked up by a single Chicago media outlet. In fact the *Chicago Tribune*, by contrast, carried a photograph today of Black with his daughter both smiling as they left the courthouse together. What if the jurors caught the *Toronto Sun*'s front-page headline and accompanying photograph? They would have viewed it in a critical moment of their deliberations when the final result hung precariously in the balance. The impression it conveys is the odious notion that Black is giving the finger to the entire American system of justice.

Guess what, "Your Lordship"? The jurors have sacrificed four months of their lives to uphold those very virtues that you were eschewing. The jury would chew you up and toss you to the coliseum lions for such a silly transgression.

Today Conrad Black walked alone with his wife at lunchtime along the very area of the Chicago Loop where the classic car chase scene in *The French Connection* was filmed. He sternly berated a cameraman for following him as he tried to enjoy a few private moments under extraordinarily trying circumstances. He asked if it wasn't possible to have a few moments alone with his wife. Conrad Black should understand the exigencies of the media better than anyone. For several years it was a focus of his life. His wife is a noted journalist as well.

However, Conrad Black isn't accustomed to being the subject of the media's scrutiny. He will have to adjust quickly. I suspect that the Chicago media was embarrassed that they missed a lordly photo opportunity. They won't allow another chance to capture his one-finger salute to pass.

THE VERDICT AND SENTENCING

JULY 10–11

THE JURY RETURNS A VERDICT

It was late on a Thursday and almost two weeks into the jury's deliberations when the twelve jurors in the case reached a unanimous verdict. The jurors had exhaustively waded through the trial exhibits as well as the detailed narrative contained in the indictment. The government's case against each of the four defendants had to be reviewed independently. The jurors had reached a consensus after the first couple of days that Conrad Black was guilty of obstruction of justice.

The jurors had pronounced views about some of the central witnesses in the trial. David Radler was seen as a shady character that was holding back information from the jury. The three members of the audit committee received unfavourable report cards from the jurors. Joan Maida floundered on the witness stand and lacked credibility. She was such easy pickings for the government that one juror faulted Jeffrey Cramer for taking advantage of a weak witness. "He could have done it without being a jerk," the juror stated.

There was a chart prepared by the foreperson listing the names of the defendants and corresponding charges, in prominent bold lettering, set up on an easel for easy viewing. The checkmarks and various Xs and Os in each column were now completed. If the jurors had found one more mail fraud guilty verdict, there would have been an additional X marking Black guilty of racketeering.

For a few minutes, only the group of men and women in that jury room knew the result that would soon be publicly announced for the four defendants in the case. A special precaution of drawing the blinds had been taken early in their deliberations after one juror had noticed someone peering into one of the windows of the jury room from the adjacent Monadnock Building.

Judge Amy St. Eve had permitted the jury the luxury of determining its own workday schedule and the jurors proceeded to discuss their next step. Some of the jurors (who were now being paid at a rate of $50/day) expressed a desire to "get it over with so we would not have to trudge back downtown on Friday." However, it was ultimately decided that instead of rushing to complete the elaborate verdict forms for all four of the defendants, the jury would return the following morning to complete its exacting task. It also provided any jurors with lingering doubts about their important decision to change their minds overnight.

In fact, none did. When the jurors returned the next morning, in business-like fashion, the foreperson read each charge out loud and the forms were then passed clockwise around the oval table for every juror to sign. When the forms were collected, there was an unusual stillness in the room. The court officer was alerted that a verdict had been reached and the jurors sat stone-faced and silent, awaiting the call to enter the courtroom. The sullen mood didn't change as they lined up to enter the courtroom.

The jurors were expecting that their faces would be studied for hints of the verdict as they entered the courtroom accompanied by a court officer's bellowing command of "All rise." During breaks in the testimony at trial, jurors became aware that their reactions were being scrutinized. As one juror noted, "it was disconcerting to have a pause in the testimony and turn and see the eyes from multiple faces boring holes through the jury." As the judge began to declare the various charges and verdicts, the jurors were now in a position to study the emotional reactions of the lawyers and defendants in the case.

The teams of four prosecutors seated closest to the jurors were observed flipping pages and checking boxes without any facial expressions. The lead prosecutor, Eric Sussman, might have betrayed a slight hint of disappointment at one point.

Conrad Black appeared to be in a state of disbelief as the first guilty for a mail fraud charge was read. He shook his head in pronounced disgust as the guilty verdict on the obstruct justice charge was announced by the judge. For whatever reason, the guilty verdict on this particular charge appeared to resonate with him more than his three mail fraud convictions.

The other defendants remained relatively still and revealed little of their reactions to the announcement of similar guilty verdicts for three counts of mail fraud. Both Jack Boultbee and Peter Atkinson were observed for the most part looking down. Mark Kipnis stood along the wall of the courtroom farthest from the jury next to his attorney, Patricia Holmes.

After the verdicts were read, the jurors left the tense mood of the courtroom and returned to the relatively peaceful sanctuary of the jury room. There was a sense of genuine relief that their arduous journey had almost ended. Judge St. Eve eventually arrived and extended her appreciation for the jurors' work. Over the course of the trial, the judge had earned the abiding respect of all the jurors who could plainly see that she appreciated their efforts. The trial judge had made periodic visits to the jury room, principally to relate issues of scheduling and court protocol. One of the jurors regularly baked desserts that were presented to the judge and her accompanying court officer.

Judge St. Eve spoke sincerely of the manner in which she took the best interests of all her juries to heart, but particularly so in this case. She presented the jurors with the option of meeting with the media if they wished. A special room had been arranged for individual members or the entire jury to answer questions from the press. None of the jurors opted to use the room.

The judge also asked for the jurors' positions on having their names released. She added that there was little value in objecting, as she would probably be compelled to release the list of names because of an impending court ruling on the issue.

Before leaving, one of the jurors, James Kirby, turned to Judge St. Eve and wished her good luck with the process. "Well, thank you," she replied. "And you're right. It is a process."

The jurors were invited to leave secretly through the Dirksen courthouse's sub-basement. They left in a blue mini-bus, which they were told was regularly used for the transfer of prisoners. The bus driver and the armed escort chatted casually with the jurors as they headed to their drop-off point in front of the famed Art Institute on Michigan Avenue.

The jurors listened raptly as the armed escort recounted a story about a jury address that Ron Safer, the lead attorney for Mark Kipnis, had given as a prosecutor a few years earlier in a gang trial. In a packed courtroom, Safer's eloquent closing address left everyone in the courtroom with tears in their eyes. In an inauspicious omen for their clients, it included the defence lawyers as well.

After saying their goodbyes, the jurors dispersed one last time in the trial. Kirby returned to the courthouse to retrieve his bicycle. Someone who he later learned was the British author and journalist, Tom Bower, approached him. Kirby politely declined to answer any questions about the trial. However, before he left on his bike, he made one parting comment: "To paraphrase Donald Rumsfeld, you go to trial with the jury you have, not the jury you want."

A ROLL OF THE DICE

When the jury's verdict in the Conrad Black trial was announced in the summer of 2007, many people greeted it with relief that a corrupt media titan had finally been tamed and beaten. A group of lawyers at the law firm of Bennett, Jones in Toronto toasted the result with glasses of champagne.

Bennett, Jones was the Canadian law firm acting for the special committee that was charged with investigating the alleged financial abuses of the shareholders of Hollinger International. For Lord Black's legion of detractors, the announcement of four guilty verdicts against him was indeed a moment to celebrate and savour.

Inside the courtroom, the reaction of Black's co-defendants and their attorneys was far more gracious. One by one, they approached him, patted him on the back, and wished him well. There was one notable exception. Peter Atkinson made a direct line to the courtroom door without even acknowledging Conrad Black. Years earlier, he had been urging Black to settle the Hollinger shareholders' claim but he had been firmly assured that victory lay ahead. The jury verdict in Chicago now told otherwise.

Mark Kipnis's handshake was the most gracious of all. Moments earlier, as he awaited the pronouncement of the verdict, he had held his lawyer Patricia Holmes's hand and squeezed it tightly. When the guilty verdicts were read out against him, all the life went out of his hand as if someone shot him. His only immediate concern was to check on his wife, Kay, in the courtroom to ensure that she was okay.

Conrad Black reacted stoically. He later heard that Tom Bower suggested that Black had locked eyes with him after the verdict. Black mocked the spurious claim. He would never consider granting Bower the satisfaction of believing that he mattered to him.

Black soon huddled after the verdict in a small room on the twelfth floor of the courthouse with his wife and lawyers. His wife, Barbara Amiel, was visibly angry. She hadn't been on speaking terms with Eddie Greenspan after a shouting match erupted between them during the trial. The atmosphere in the room was understandably sullen. Eddie Greenspan began the discussion by noting that Black had been acquitted of the heart of the indictment. Marc Martin, the Black team's respected expert on the law, had already informed him in court that the likely range of sentencing would be three to six years. They were strategically well placed for an appeal and Greenspan wanted to come out with a statement to the press that would place a positive spin on the results. He expressed his desire to claim that the verdict was a "serious embarrassment to the government."

However, Conrad and Barbara wouldn't heed Greenspan's advice. The trial was lost and it couldn't be spun in any direction that would ameliorate such a grim outcome. Like a soldier returning from a lost battle with many casualties, Black would accept defeat with dignity and aplomb. A neutral statement was then quickly drafted, which Greenspan proceeded to read to the media throng anxiously awaiting downstairs. He later regretted not following his own instincts, believing that a positive statement could have capped Black's sentence at least three years. That may have been a bit of wishful thinking on Greenspan's part. The sentencing for Conrad Black was adjourned for five months, which presented ample opportunity for feckless behaviour.

Ed Genson didn't say a word in the crowded room. He deferred to Greenspan, and in any event, Barbara Amiel wouldn't even acknowledge his presence. This was Greenspan's call, but Genson too had grave misgivings about accepting defeat. If the decision were his to make, he would speak defiantly to the media without a word of prepared speech. He would later receive as many congratulatory messages as sympathetic calls.

Later that night, Genson lay in his bed with his eyes open as the night passed. He didn't like to lose.

While Eddie Greenspan was reading his brief to the media, Mark Kipnis's legal team was already congregated in a boardroom in their law offices in the Sears Tower. Every lawyer in the group felt devastated by the verdict. There had been underlying concern that an American jury might be reluctant to acquit Kipnis, the sole American defendant in the courtroom, for the fear of being accused of playing favourites.

Ron Safer firmly took charge in a meeting. There was no time to wallow in the despair they felt in the conviction of an innocent they had represented. Every lawyer plunged immediately into preparing for a motion to have the jury's verdict set aside.

Eric Sussman was glad to have even made it to the courtroom in time for the jury's verdict. He had been stuck on a bus when he received a call that the jury was ready to deliver its verdict. A reporter had given him a warning that the jurors had been seen dressed up. It had been twelve days of anxious waiting for the lead prosecutor and he had been on edge. He spent some of the time watching movies and catching up with people. The jury's verdict on the perks had surprised him although he didn't regret including them on the indictment. They helped give the jury a true sense of who Conrad Black was and added some insight into his character.

Overall, Eric Sussman was satisfied with the verdict. He felt that the jury had agreed with the essence of the government's case and reached some fairly significant findings. It marked a victory for the government against Conrad Black.

The verdict that did surprise Sussman was Mark Kipnis's. He believed that he would walk free. After returning to the office after his rebuttal, he told a colleague that the jury really wanted to acquit Mark Kipnis. Sussman harboured no regrets about including Kipnis in the indictment, although he admitted that including Kipnis represented a big distraction during the trial. He noted that if anyone knew that the non-competition payments were a sham, it was Mark Kipnis. Sussman stated that he would have liked to see Kipnis co-operate and tried very hard to make that happen before the trial and even during the trial. Mark Kipnis had plenty of opportunities to make things more equitable for himself, Sussman observed, but "he wanted to roll the dice."

There were equally no regrets about making the deal with David Radler and the decision to call him as a government witness at the Black trial. The manner that Radler testified at trial surprised the lead prosecutor more than the nature of his evidence. The jury needed Radler's co-operation, and in its absence it would have been hard for the jury to convict Conrad Black. Sussman added that without Radler it might have been difficult for government to even indict Black. David Radler was that important to the prosecution. Without Radler tying Black to the non-competes, it would have been very easy for Conrad Black to stake a position at trial similar to Jim Thompson, the head of the audit committee, and claim that he only skimmed the relevant documents.

The charging decisions in the case were approached in a professional and lawyerly way. A prosecutor has the difficult call to sift through the rubble and determine what is criminal, what is negligent, what belongs in civil court, or with the SEC regulator. According to Sussman's candid assessment, "there were a lot of people who screwed up." A lot of people didn't do their job and were negligent. KPMG was a "nightmare" and Torys was a "nightmare." In many respects, Torys had more knowledge than the members of the audit committee who Sussman accepted weren't paying attention.

I suggested to Eric Sussman that if the audit committee members chose to turn a blind eye to material facts, a prosecutor could properly bring charges under a theory of deliberate ignorance. Sussman, however, rejected any contention that the three audit committee members should have been Conrad Black's co-defendants. Their conduct didn't rise to the level of willful blindness in his view because they still had to know what was going on was criminal. As for the couple of hundred million dollars of management fees, Sussman confirmed that they weren't included in the government's case because Conrad Black didn't obtain them fraudulently. The shareholders knew about the management fees, as did the audit committee. There was no crime to prosecute.

WHEN THE SAINTS COME MARCHING HOME

I finally had time to get a haircut. I am amazed how the last four months of my life have been consumed by the Conrad Black trial. I can now return to enjoying the simple luxuries of life, such as sleeping and eating. Chicago is a lovely city and I am certain that one day I will get to see it. Other than swimming in the same swimming pool where Johnny Weissmuller trained for his Tarzan movies, my days and nights have generally been spent sitting at the Dirksen courthouse or in my hotel room with my laptop.

TILTED

My barber, Kareem, greeted me warmly as I walked in the door. A couple of fellows were waiting their turn.

"Aren't you the CTV guy who predicted that Conrad Black would get off?" one of them brusquely asked me.

"Yes, that was me," I replied with the traces of crow's pie still dripping from my lips.

The same question was repeated at the carwash, the bank, the cleaners, and, to complete my circle of humiliation, on national television.

On the day of the verdict I appeared on CTV Newsnet to discuss the result in the case with Dan Matheson, Paula Todd, and former federal prosecutor Jacob Frenkel.

"So you made a boo-boo, Steve, with your prediction," Dan Matheson asked right away. About an hour or so later Paula Todd noted that I had made the flawed prediction on her show. "You're not suggesting that Eddie Greenspan and Eddie Genson now give up the appeal, are you?"

The public flogging was now complete.

Let me state that I have broad shoulders. As a trial lawyer I carry a burden so my client doesn't have to, so I'm prepared to carry the burden of my erroneous prediction for as long as it takes to live it down.

However, in the interest of full and complete disclosure, there are a few matters that should be addressed about the jury's verdict. The reality is that not a single legal analyst covering the trial predicted this outcome. That is nada, as in zero. The notion that Mark Kipnis and Conrad Black would be treated by the jury as equals in guilt in the alleged looting of the Hollinger International shareholders was never even remotely considered. I welcome the opportunity to be proven wrong, but it will not occur. I have maintained from the outset of the case precisely what his attorney stated after the jury's verdict: Mark Kipnis is an innocent man.

I feel that I have witnessed a miscarriage of justice and I have faith that one day that injustice will be corrected. Perhaps Judge St. Eve will reverse the verdict, or perhaps this will occur in an appellate court, but it will happen. It is the one immutable prediction that I make in this case. As Ron Safer astutely noted while affirming both his client's innocence and the fairness of the trial, the jury could not separate Mark's conduct from that of his co-defendant. In other words, Kipnis was doomed to be found guilty by association.

I was fascinated to read in an interview with one of the jurors, Monica Prince, that the jury struggled mightily to find an avenue to acquit Mark Kipnis, whom they dubbed "St. Mark."

"We tried to save Mark. We had a heart for him. He wasn't going for the big money ... We really tried to get him off, but just couldn't."

The evidence at the trial disclosed that Kipnis wasn't going after the big money or the little money. He didn't benefit at all from the fraudulent scheme. The juror's comment, however, touched on a theme that I have emphasized in the past and largely explains my previous prediction. I have always believed that Kipnis's complicity in the $60-million fraud scheme would be judged in the same manner as Black's. Indeed it was. The mistake that I made and acknowledge was to underestimate a jury's resolve to find Kipnis guilty. Once that occurred, Conrad Black's legal fate was sealed. All four defendants in the case were inextricably consigned to the same verdict.

A few words in defence of the much-maligned Eddie Greenspan. Jurors have been outspoken about disliking his bedside manner and have mocked him. Perhaps if he had shared the advantage that the four prosecutors enjoyed — that is, to be seated only a few feet from the jurors, facing them for the length of the trial — their comments might have been more gracious. The seating arrangement in the courtroom severely handicapped the defence and should be causing much embarrassment among those charged with the administration of justice in the State of Illinois.

The fact remains that Greenspan's client was acquitted of nine of the thirteen charges, including the central charges that he faced, and this was not achieved by the mere waving of a magic wand. Surely Black's lawyers deserve credit for executing a successful trial strategy, even if it was not 100 percent successful.

The verdict in the case was clearly a compromise. The jurors' deadlock was apparently a feature of that middle ground that was reached. The jurors' mixed verdict on the non-competes can be compared to a man jumping into a swimming pool and coming out with only his legs wet. Clearly there was division in that jury room, and to the jury's great credit, they resolved to overcome it and reach a full verdict. As the author Peter C. Newman related to me while we were both waiting to be interviewed on CTV in the Toronto studio, it is like an election where the results may not be satisfactory to some, but the people have spoken.

The result for Conrad Black will be a sentence measured in a few years rather than decades. He should ponder the advice that Martha Stewart was given after the disastrous end of her trial. Her appellate counsel, including my good friend Marty Weinberg from Boston, persuaded Stewart to take the high road forward and serve her rather lenient sentence. Black would be wise to take a similar approach unless the grounds for appeal are particularly strong. He has a beautiful family and a supportive network of caring friends who I suspect will not abandon him. My free advice to him is to cast his material ambitions aside and treasure his good fortune. There are still many chapters to be written in this man's larger-than-life history.

On a more personal note, I came into this trial never having communicated with Conrad Black. We met briefly once for an interview during the trial but other than that our encounters took place in the courthouse hallway and did not involve a lot of words. Occasionally he would approach me in court to whisper to me about a former prime minister being impressed with the fairness of my coverage or to rebuke me for a critical opinion that I offered. Like many others in the courtroom he read my blog on a daily basis. I am certain he preferred my prediction to the forecasts of the legion of journalists who were calling for a rather bleaker outcome.

A couple of days prior to the jury's verdict I received my first email from him, which included a polite rejoinder to a blog entry that I had written about the raised middle finger gesture he presented to a photographer. On the night before the verdict, his last gracious words to me were as follows: "If there is no movement from the jury tomorrow, please indicate a date when you would like a drink. If the jury acquits before we arrange it, let's have a drink in Toronto."

PASS THE PEERAGE

Conrad Black instantly went from being generally vilified to being radioactive after he was found guilty of obstructing justice and improperly inserting himself into various non-competition agreements with a series of American community newspapers. On the first day of August in 2007, Conrad Black arrived in the Chicago courtroom with every expectation that Judge Amy St. Eve would extend his bail order to allow him to return to his luxurious Bridle Path home in Toronto. "If the judge does the right thing," he wishfully observed, "I will be on the next plane to Toronto." All that Judge St. Eve required of Black to grant his request was an increase to the $21-million bond that he had previously posted as bail. The cupboard was bare and not a single former business associate or upscale comrade came forward to assist Conrad Black.

For a man who had once attended parties with prime ministers, presidents, and titans of industry, the harsh lesson that he had been abandoned by his elite constellation of notables portended an ominous future. He would be denied the opportunity to spend the minimum period of one year in Canada required to gain permanent residency in the country, a prerequisite to obtaining a Canadian passport.

Why would Conrad Black, a man who grew up in Canada and amassed his vast wealth in the country, need to apply for a Canadian passport? He had renounced his citizenship to nobly sit in the esteemed House of Lords in England. It was a decision that earned him the contempt of many Canadians. The majority of his former countrymen, I suspect, would prefer a bowl of porridge to a title of peerage.

Black's motives for wishing to reacquire his passport were less than pure. It was part of a campaign to allow him to serve his prison sentence in Canada with its comparatively relaxed parole system. Only Canadian citizens such as the star prosecution witness, David Radler, were eligible for this arrangement. Canada is the land of the brave and the land where you save. In this case, it could mean savings of years of life in a penitentiary.

Conrad Black had been foiled in an earlier attempt to get back his passport through diplomatic channels. Black's telephone call to the Prime Minister's Office was abruptly cut short when the Canadian official he spoke to reminded Black that they were former classmates at Upper Canada College, a distinguished private boys' school in Toronto. Black's successful schoolboy plot to steal some examination papers had been exposed, resulting in the entire class being forced to retake some of the examination. To Black's chagrin, the fury of at least one of his former fellow students had apparently not subsided during the intervening years.

Black will never surrender his attempts to regain his passport, just as he will fight to his last breath to cleanse his soiled reputation and appeal his convictions. It is the nature of the man.

Unfortunately for Black, his lawyers' quiet efforts over the course of years to regain his Canadian passport were recklessly wasted by Black's own conduct. When the Canadian television show *The Agenda* began on TVO with its host Steve Paikin, Conrad Black was the first guest to appear. Black volunteered the information that efforts were underway to regain his passport. The first Eddie Greenspan heard of it came when the media began calling him. Paul Waldie from the *Globe and Mail* called him a few hours before the show aired (it was taped) wanting to talk to Greenspan about his client's application for citizenship. "Why would he say that?" Greenspan wondered in dismay. If anything was close to a state secret, Black's application was it. Even members of Greenspan's own office were unaware of the ongoing quiet diplomacy.

Greenspan knew instantly that the bureaucrats would run away from the passport matter. Black's public statement had made it an electrically charged public issue. For all intents and purposes, the prospect of Conrad Black ever having a Canadian passport again had faded.

DECEMBER 10–17

SENTENCED TO DEBT

Conrad Black's prosecutors filed sentencing materials before Judge St. Eve denouncing Black's lack of remorse and his consistent demonstration of contempt for the judicial process and the jury's verdict in his case. *Men's Vogue* and BBC were cited as the sources of the defendant's disconcerting defiance. I understand the prosecutors' position perfectly. If Black had simply come forward after a gruelling four-month trial and candidly admitted that he had looted the shareholders of Hollinger International for millions of dollars, surely there would be no strident claim by the prosecutors that Black should be harshly treated for expending needless time and resources for a wasteful prosecution. There would equally be no suggestion that his belated pangs of remorse rang hollow and should be discarded by the court. Rather they would be welcomed and applauded by his grateful team of prosecutors. (The same logic applies to including Krispy Kreme donuts in your diet.)

A criminal defendant has every right to protest his innocence even in the face of a jury's resounding verdict to the contrary.[1] It is true that Black's assertions were sharply pointed and vitriolic, but his right to state them cannot be denied. The jury has long ago disappeared from the case and the risk of tainting Judge St. Eve's opinion is non-existent. However, even his own lawyers would have counselled him against denigrating the American judicial system on the eve of his own sentencing. Disparaging comments about the "shortcomings of the plea-bargain system" in America are unhelpful. It is akin to insulting the chef before ordering a meal.

Conrad Black's profound lack of insight once again materialized in a *Toronto Star* article that appeared a couple of days prior to sentencing.

Rick Westhead wrote that during the trial, the defence intended to call Donald Trump as a witness to testify that at Barbara Amiel's surprise birthday party, Trump met with Black and discussed a real-estate deal. The reason that Trump never testified can be traced to an ill-advised two-paragraph email sent by Conrad Black to Trump. "Black wrote too much, salting his email to Trump with his typical verbose description of the government's case. When Greenspan found out about the email, he had to tell Trump to stay home, as he worried prosecutors might claim he had tried to influence a witness."[2]

Indeed, Trump was prepared to testify. After the story broke in the *New York Post*, Judge St. Eve had ensured that the proper additional security was in place to accommodate the celebrity witness's arrival. It all had to be cancelled after the discovery by Greenspan of his client's reckless correspondence to Trump. Some time later Greenspan approached me about the subject.

"It's your fault that we couldn't call Donald Trump," he advised me. I was astonished to learn that I was entirely to blame for the salty email. Greenspan informed me that Black's email was written only a few days after I had prepared a purely imaginary and sardonic blog in which Black invites Trump to appear as a witness for the defence. It read as follows:

Dear Donald:

I wish to ask one final esoteric favour of you. As you may know, I am presently caught in the struggle of my life with the United States government. The Hollinger shareholder meeting that you attended was like an *American Idol* audition by comparison. Laura Jereski may be Simon Cowell's tweedy twin, but my criminal case is the Ultimate Fighting Championship. These Eliot Ness imposters have charged me with racketeering, Donald, can you believe it? Who do they think I am, one of the Sopranos?

You may recall a splendid surprise birthday party that was arranged for Barbara at La Grenouille a few years back. It used to be such a fond memory for me. Kissinger, Carmen, and Kravis all graced the party with their presence.

Barbara told me that she was thrilled to be seated next to you. You were such charming company and a fluid conversationalist. I had struggled mightily with the seating plan and nearly put Barbara at David Radler's table. What a disaster that would have been.

The U.S. government has charged me with bilking the shareholders for the portion of the party charged to the company. Can you believe it, Donald? Didn't we consummate a mutually beneficial business deal shortly after the party? What would the city of Chicago be without a Trump Tower? I look forward to a trip to the Holy Land after the trial to see your new Trump condo in Tel Aviv. Soon there will be monuments to Donald Trump around the world. I watch in glowing admiration as you have mastered the fine art of male reproduction.

One of the prosecutors actually had the audacity to ask one government witness if there was a sign at the restaurant with the Hollinger logo on it. The prosecutors should bring the maître d' from La Grenouille to court to ask if that would be permitted. They would be duly informed that a Michelin four-star restaurant would place itself at peril of losing one of its treasured stars for such a tactless and gauche violation of good taste.

I will keep my request brief, Donald, because my loquacious tendencies have already caused my own legal team much consternation.

Did I mention that my new Nixon book just made the top ten national bestsellers list in Canada? The verdict should be a huge boost to sales, don't you think? I digress.

Please consider my humble request in the spirit with which it is intended and RSVP at your earliest convenience.

Regards,
Conrad

On the topic of reproduction, more than one hundred letters of support were presented to Judge St. Eve on Conrad Black's behalf for his sentencing hearing. As Barbara Amiel noted, her husband "always sees the best in events and people. For Conrad, the glass is always half full no matter what life dishes out for him." As for America, according to columnist George Will, Black "loves this country with a deeply informed passion." There was a consistent theme of a man portrayed with a generous spirit. As his long-time friend Gerald Schwartz wrote, "[He] has always been courteous and helpful — not just to friends and acquaintances of high rank but to everyone I have seen him come in contact with in the course of daily life."

Noticeably absent from the claim of Conrad Black's abiding and long-standing devotion to the United States was praise for the American justice system. Indeed, in the days leading to Black's sentencing, the *New York Times* coincidentally published an installment in a series of articles examining commonplace characteristics of the American justice system that were actually unique in the world.

The latest entry in the series detailed the distinctively American legal doctrine of the felony murder rule that "makes accomplices as liable as the actual killer for murders committed during felonies like burglaries, rapes and robberies."[3] The article noted that countries following the common law such as England and Canada had abolished the doctrine, which one American attorney called draconian. An earlier article in the series explained that the United States stands alone in the world in convicting young adolescents as adults and allowing them to spend the rest of their lives in prison. "In its sentencing of juveniles, as in many other areas, the legal system in the United States goes it alone. American law is, by international standards, a series of innovations and exceptions. From the central role played by juries in civil cases to the election of judges to punitive damages to the disproportionate number of people in prison, the United States is an island in the sea of international law."[4]

I sought out that bright fellow on the Conrad Black defence team, Marc Martin, to unlock the confounding mystery of America's radical departure from legal convention. Why is the U.S. going it alone in the world? Martin attributed the erosion of civil liberties to a get-tough-on-crime mentality that began under Ronald Reagan as a feature of the war on drugs. It spread like a cancer, according to Martin, to a broad law-and-order agenda that eventually encompassed far more than the scourge of crack cocaine and other illegal substances.[5]

However, it wasn't an island to which Conrad Black had been confined for months while awaiting his sentencing but rather a lavish Palm Beach mansion. It hardly classified as the rough life. As he arrived in a Cadillac Escalade for his day of reckoning in a Chicago courtroom, I watched him engulfed by cameras and microphones as he manoeuvred the short distance from the sidewalk to the courthouse entrance. His wife and daughter were part of his coterie. One CBC reporter was slightly injured in the ensuing melee. It was reminiscent of Sherman McCoy's first appearance at the Criminal Courts Building in *Bonfire of the Vanities*: "The mob seemed to shake itself, like a huge sprawling dog, and came bounding toward the car. Some of them were running, and he could see television cameras jouncing up and down."[6]

Inside the courtroom, the tone was more collected and serene. Judge St. Eve finally heard from the first victim of shareholder plundering. The sole representative victim, named Gene, claimed to have been outfoxed by Black in the past but now lobbed blame freely in the direction of the defendants' tables. Conrad Black was seething inside but managed to contain his emotions.

As Black approached the front of the courtroom to deliver his statement to the court, he appeared nervous and the swagger from his step was gone. He emphatically declared that he had never spoken disrespectfully about the judge, the jurors, or the process. He then continued reading from a prepared statement: "The other thing I'd like to say is I do wish to express very profound regret and sadness at the severe hardship inflicted upon all of the shareholders, including a great many employees" — was it possible that Conrad Black had been humbled and his hubris expunged, I wondered — "by the evaporation of $1.85 billion of shareholder value under my successors."

As a former major shareholder himself, Black was telling the court that he in fact was a victim. The statement added a fresh dimension to the notion of a victim impact statement. It had never been uttered by a criminal defendant about himself before. It then dawned on me that Black must have watched the episode of *Happy Days* in which the Fonz was challenged to admit he was wrong.

"I was wr ... r ... r ..." The Fonz struggled repeatedly but without success to utter the one word that signalled defeat.

The day ended relatively well for Black.[7] He strode purposefully holding his wife's hand as he exited the courthouse. One court security officer whispered to me that "Black dodged a bullet." Instead of spending decades in prison as his prosecutors had urged, Judge St. Eve sentenced him to six and a half years and recommended that it be served at a minimum-security prison. The forfeiture order was for $6.1 million, which represented the calculated total amount of loss caused by his crimes. The judge rejected the $32-million loss claimed by the prosecutors. Black was permitted to retain his Palm Beach mansion and the U.S. government was further ordered to return the $9-million proceeds from the sale of Black's New York Park Avenue apartment that had been brazenly seized by the FBI.

It was already well past five in the afternoon when the sentencing hearing for Mark Kipnis took place. The mood in the courtroom was extremely tense and sombre.[8] Judge St. Eve had given his attorneys the option of returning later in the week to conduct the hearing, but Kipnis insisted on proceeding that very day. One side of the courtroom was filled with friends and family of Mark Kipnis. Everyone was fully aware that Peter Atkinson had been sentenced to two years in jail and Jack Boultbee to two and a quarter years. Ron Safer was seeking a probationary sentence for Kipnis that represented a marked departure from the sentence called for by the federal sentencing guidelines. His client had already turned down a sentence of three years that was available until the very moment that Safer stood to cross-examine David Radler.

Safer was the beneficiary of one incredible stroke of good fortune. On the very morning of his sentencing hearing, the United States Supreme Court released a decision that upheld a District Court judge's decision to impose a three-year probationary sentence when the guidelines called for a sentencing range of thirty to thirty-seven months' imprisonment. The judge had alluded to the counterproductive effects of imprisonment for a defendant who "understands the consequences of his criminal conduct and is doing everything in his power to forge a new life."[9] The U.S. Supreme Court agreed and rejected any rule that requires "extraordinary" circumstances to justify a sentence outside the guidelines range.[10]

Moments before the hearing began, Mark Kipnis nodded in my direction. I nodded back. I watched Judge St. Eve carefully as Kipnis's son, Blair, provided an emotional testimonial to his father's wonderful character. "Please don't send my dad to jail," he pleaded at its conclusion. Blair had credited his father for having the "courage to stand up here." Earlier the court heard from Ted Rilea, the head of labour relations at the *Chicago Sun-Times*. He expressed his belief that Kipnis didn't deserve to be incarcerated and that it "would be a horrible, horrible thing for Mark to be in prison."

Ron Safer's sentencing submissions were among the finest that I have ever heard in a criminal case. The words poured directly from his heart. After pointing to Kipnis's impressive "acts of random kindness and generosity," he attempted to explain the reason for the jury's verdict. "I failed him," he advised the court. "I should have been able to convince this jury they should treat differently someone who received no money." Safer was the former chief of the criminal division in the United States Attorney's Office. Among the trial lawyers who worked under his auspices was a brilliant and hard-working prosecutor named Amy St. Eve. Safer was now before her imploring her not to send his client to prison. "But the final word has not been spoken," he added. "You will speak it."

Mark Kipnis addressed the court and began by protesting that he wasn't a bank robber in a suit nor was he was St. Mark, as he was dubbed by some of the jurors. Kipnis remained adamant that he "never for a moment believed those non-compete agreements were illegal." As for the APC non-competition payments,[11] a purely innocent explanation was advanced. David Radler had approached him and told him that the APC non-compete was a vehicle to avoid paying taxes. Kipnis replied at the time that it was silly to take advantage of a tax loophole when so much money was already being made. His suggestion that Radler simply pay the taxes was shrugged aside.

The only contrition expressed by Mark Kipnis was that he "could have done better and should have done better." However, most significantly, he never abandoned the principle that he was wrongfully convicted. His voice trailed off as he admitted that he missed being a lawyer.

It was then Judge St. Eve's turn to impose Mark Kipnis's sentence. It was already past seven in the evening. Patricia Holmes placed her hand gently on Mark Kipnis's back.

"You were clearly the least culpable person in this scheme," Judge St. Eve stated. She noted the incontrovertible point that Kipnis had not profited from the scheme and indeed "didn't receive a penny."

As Judge St. Eve announced the sentence, there was a noticeable quiver in her voice. She was struggling to contain her emotions. Mark Kipnis was to be sentenced to five years' probation. There would be six months of electronic home monitoring, a $200 fine, and 275 hours of community service. Judge St. Eve noted that anyone who had sat through the months of the trial would fully appreciate why she was not sending Kipnis to prison. There were gasps of relief from Kipnis's friends and family. His mother, Jean, was literally rolling about in the front row demonstrating her delight. Holmes managed to keep her tears in check by reminding herself that she was an attorney.

Later that evening, I was invited to appear on *The Verdict* with two stellar American trial lawyers, Pat Woodward and Jacob Frenkel. They are both among the best of the best. We were followed on the program by two jurors from the trial, Jean Kelly and James Kirby.

"Did you hear?" Jean exclaimed to her fellow juror. "Mark got probation. Isn't that great?"

As we walked out together from the studio, Jean Kelly told me that she would have been offended if the judge accepted the prosecution's position that the loss in the case was in the $30-million range. She asked me what then would have been the point of having the jury's verdict. Touché.

A number of movies were mentioned by the various attorneys during the long day of submissions, including *It's a Wonderful Life* and *The Shawshank Redemption*. However, there was a scene in one of my favourite films that I instantly recalled after Judge St. Eve kept Mark Kipnis out of prison. I mentioned it to Patricia Holmes at the counsel table minutes after court was finally recessed forever in the trial.

The movie is *Philadelphia*. It was a poignant story of prejudice about a young lawyer's struggle for his life after discovering that he had been diagnosed with AIDS.[12] When he is fired from his law firm, the attorney (played by Tom Hanks) fights back to regain his self-respect and sues his law firm. When the dramatic moment comes for him to testify at his civil trial, his body is ravaged from the disease and his spirits are sagging. He is asked by his attorney (played by another great actor, Denzel Washington) what he loved most about being a lawyer: "It's every now and again. Not often. Occasionally. You get to be part of justice being done. It is quite a thrill when that happens."

I was lucky enough to be among the few in Judge St. Eve's courtroom on a cold December evening in Chicago to witness justice being done. The court had tilted back.[13]

The next afternoon I sat in Ron Safer's office and asked him about the tremendous advantages accorded to prosecutors in trials in America. He shared with me that when he was a prosecutor and stood up to declare, "I'm Ron Safer on behalf of the U.S. government," he felt the courtroom floor tipping in his favour at almost an eighty-five-degree angle. "With power," he added, "comes tremendous responsibility."

KING SOLOMONIC

In a sentencing proceeding that lasted about fifteen minutes, Judge St. Eve approved David Radler's plea deal with the United States government and sentenced him to twenty-nine months in prison and a $250,000 fine.[14] She had no harsh words for Radler about his testimony at the trial, nor was the emotional thermometer in the courtroom raised as she imposed her sentence. It was a perfunctory hearing where every single person in court knew in advance precisely what the outcome would be. As Radler strode comfortably out of the courtroom as the star witness with a five-star deal, the curtain closed on Conrad Black's case in Chicago.

Radler would no doubt be rushing back to his home in Vancouver to continue to build his burgeoning newspaper business. Black still retained shares with him in Horizon but advised me that he couldn't envisage the day when the two former media moguls would be in business together again.

Black continued to live in his comfortable Palm Beach mansion with Barbara while awaiting his surrender date in early March. Friends visited him and spoke to him often. He did miss his house and his books back in Toronto. His spirits were far from extinguished after his sentencing; he railed about the prosecutors' conduct as his biggest surprise about the American criminal justice system. His disappointment extended to his jury, "who were not a very Solomonic group." The U.S. government, he complained, had been on his back for four years. If they hadn't improperly seized the millions of dollars in proceeds from the sale of his New York apartment, he would have had Brendan Sullivan as his counsel at trial. Black's final words to me were, "I will win, either inside the system or by exposing the system, or both."

Eddie Greenspan and Ed Genson, their legendary status intact despite a journey that caused a few bruises along the way, went their separate ways to defend other celebrity clients and high-profile cases.

Pat Tuite retired from the practice of law. The Black trial was the final chapter in a distinguished legal career in Chicago. Darren Sukonick was due to return to handling client files at Torys. Ron Safer was back to his busy duties as the managing partner at Schiff Hardin, content that his client wouldn't spend a single day in prison.

The lead prosecutor in the Black trial, Eric Sussman, visited Toronto to speak at the International Fraud Investigators Conference, where he lamented the U.S. government's lack of access to particular pieces of evidence from Canada and suggested that Canadian law enforcement and the Canadian public would have to sort out these difficulties. Resolving these "difficulties" would require Canada to ignore the Charter of Rights, the Mutual Legal Assistance Treaty, and due process.

Mark Kipnis went to work at a sign shop with his son, struggling to make a living. He will never practise law again. However, all is not lost. During a challenging tempest in his life, he was embraced by a host of caring friends and family determined to carry him through his crushing ordeal. In the end he was not the forgotten man.

THE APPEAL-GO-ROUND

BAUBLES AND BEADS

CALL ME CONRAD

Within a few days of the jury's disappointing verdict, Conrad Black had met in Chicago with Andrew Frey, a high-profile New York based lawyer, and retained him for his appeal.[1] Frey was a former deputy solicitor general and Black may have been influenced by the literate description on his law firm's website noting that "in the pantheon of appellate practitioners, Andrew Frey occupies a vertiginous position."

Conrad Black's prison sentence was scheduled to begin on March 3, 2008. The trial judge, Amy St. Eve, refused Black's request for bail pending appeal. The decision was expected and Black continued to maintain that she was a very fair judge. A federal appeals court adopted a similarly rigid position on bail and the stage was set for Black to surrender at Coleman Federal Correctional Institution (part of the Coleman Federal Correctional Complex) in Florida. He set out with his wife for the three-hour drive from his home in Palm Beach. A crowd of reporters and camera operators surrounded his car as it left the gate of their mansion.

Upon their arrival, Barbara Amiel announced to the correctional officers: "my husband, Conrad Black, is self-surrendering." Black entered the facility at Coleman carrying only his spectacles and a small amount of money to be deposited into a commissary account.[2] Inside he was provided with a prison-issue green uniform, belt, and shoes with the option to wear a grey t-shirt during the summer. Administrative staff informed him that he would be treated as equal with the other 1,900 inmates at Coleman and that he was expected to act accordingly.

Garland Hogan was one of the first inmates Black met in prison. Hogan advised him about the possibility of obtaining a special work assignment, but Black expressed a preference to accept whatever job he was assigned.[3]

The other Coleman inmates were aware of his celebrity status and quickly accepted Black, observing that he never sought out any entitlement or privilege. The residents, as Black preferred to call them, were encouraged to call him Conrad rather than Mr. Black or Lord Black. They began to approach him as he walked the track, sat in the common area, or at mealtime for advice and encouragement on a range of topics. During the visiting period for inmates, Black would often be interrupted as other inmates eagerly introduced family members to him. A visitor once asked one of Black's lawyers (whose meetings lasted as long as seven hours) if he was "the rich guy's lawyer."

Conrad Black never showed any signs of bitterness over his confinement to prison and chose to endure his suffering privately. He was aided by his devout Catholic faith. Barbara Amiel described her husband as always displaying the positive side of things and never wavering in his faith. She visited him at Coleman weekly and on occasion more frequently. According to close family friend Bryan Stewart, Black's outward disposition masked a deep sadness that "inevitably lay heavy upon him." Black was a man in his mid-sixties with the grim prospect of spending almost six more years in prison. Soon after his arrival at Coleman, the Department of Homeland Security placed an immigration detainer on Black. He wasn't a U.S. citizen, and therefore wasn't eligible for early release or placement in a halfway house.

Conrad Black had access to an electronic message system to communicate with approved recipients. The prison first reviewed each message.[4] With the aid of his personal assistant, Joan Maida,[5] he began corresponding by email with hundreds of people around the world in spirited exchanges. In one case a woman with terminal cancer emailed Conrad Black seeking his view for suggested reading. His comforting reply, promptly delivered, included expressions of sympathy and support.

Black volunteered to lecture the inmates in Coleman about American history and social economics. The prison program was a flourishing success as inmates and prison staff attended in large numbers. Black also wrote weekly topical columns for the *National Post* and the *National Review* that built up a regular online following of over one million readers. Black received a subscription to the *National Post* in prison.

Conrad Black's most significant accomplishment at Coleman was tutoring many of the inmates in English. He estimated that he eventually tutored more than one hundred student inmates, assisting them to acquire a General Equivalency Degree. Many of them were deemed to be hopeless cases. Ernest Hemingway's *The Snows of Kilimanjaro* was introduced to the students as a lesson of the virtue of short, simple sentences. As the sessions grew in popularity, Black tutored up to four students at a time. A number of the inmates he tutored proceeded to take college-level courses in prison.

Conrad Black's conduct in prison had even impressed one of his jurors. "I tip my hat to him," James Kirby observed. "He has certainly made the best of it."[6]

THE FIRST APPEAL IN CHICAGO

Conrad Black's appeal was heard in Chicago on June 5, 2008, before a courtroom filled with media, interested observers, and members of Black's family. Along with Judge Richard Posner, the other circuit judges assigned to the appeal were Dianne Sykes and Michael Kanne. Ron Safer, Richard Greenberg, and Michael Schachter joined Andrew Frey in the section reserved for defence counsel. Ed Siskel, a member of the prosecution team at the Black trial, represented the government.

Frey proceeded first with his argument and began with the obstruction of justice conviction. He described it as likely the weakest case he had seen in forty-five years of practice. His claim was that there was simply no evidence that Black intended to conceal or destroy the documents when he moved them.

Frey focused his submission on the two mail fraud convictions for the Hollinger International subsidiary, American Publishing Company (APC), totalling $5.5 million. He began with an explanation to the judges about the interrelationship between two fraud theories that were left by the government with the jury at Conrad Black's trial. The first traditional fraud theory was directed to the theft of money or property. The second contentious theory only required proof of the deprivation of honest services and was arguably invalid. It could potentially involve the breach of fiduciary duties without any financial loss or misappropriation. Frey emphasized that there was no assurance that the jury's verdict rested on a legal theory. The jury had delivered a general verdict that failed to distinguish between the two prosecution theories.

Judge Posner interrupted Frey frequently during his argument. The finest appellate judges poke and probe at the litigants' arguments, pressing them with questions about the lingering issues in the case. Posner's approach was radically different. He preferred exclamation marks to question marks. The government's case was "very straightforward," Posner declared. "There was a lot of evidence of ordinary theft and presumably that is what the jury focused on."

Frey's challenge was to rid Posner of his embedded conclusion that there was an abundance of evidence of a conventional pecuniary fraud. The judge remained unshaken. Ron Safer listened to Frey's submission in an adjoining row and wasn't pleased. Frey had to carry the main argument but he had devoted only an incredibly small amount of time on the core issue with APC.

The four defence lawyers in the Court of Appeals that morning had never conducted a joint meeting to coordinate strategy or run though practice moot arguments. It was evident during the hearing that there wasn't a coherent position among the group. Inconsistent and tangential issues were pursued and the advocacy suffered as a result.

Ron Safer spoke last and had to overcome the disappointment of Judge Posner identifying him by an attorney's name from New York. Safer pointed to a critical conversation that David Radler had testified to at trial with Mark Kipnis. Radler asked the company's counsel to draw up the APC non-competes. He genuinely believed that the audit committee had already approved $5.5 million to Ravelston and its executives as management fees. The only evidence on the record, Safer forcefully asserted, was that Radler's request to treat the management fees as non-competition payments was a tax device to get the money set aside as tax-free in Canada.[7] There was no financial loss to the shareholders of the company and yet the jury was permitted to convict on the honest services fraud theory. It represented a persuasive rebuttal to Judge Posner's characterization of a pretty naked fraud.

The entire hearing ended in one hour and twenty minutes. With curt politeness his co-counsel informed Andrew Frey that he had done a "nice job." The mood was grim and there was some lingering tension from Frey's floundering argument. There was no pause to share a coffee or enjoy a parting lunch together before the lawyers departed to their respective law firms and cities. It was symbolic of a disjointed team.

The Court of Appeals released its opinion only twenty days after the hearing. The blade of the guillotine came down swiftly, and the executioner was Judge Richard Posner. He authored a sixteen-page opinion that ended with all of the existing convictions being affirmed and with a dissertation on the injustice to the reputation of the ostrich. Posner held that there was "compelling evidence" of the fraud, noting that the defence was "making a no harm, no foul argument, and such arguments usually fare badly in criminal cases." This ignored the fact there was nothing *usual* about the breadth of the honest services fraud statute that covered conduct that was not a crime.

What of Radler's professed belief that he had the approval of the audit committee for the management fee? The evidence of the audit committee was otherwise, Posner concluded, and it was open for the jury to accept it. Speculating about the jury's finding was hardly favourable to the government's position. It was equally open for the jury to believe David Radler's testimony about the surrounding circumstances of the payment.

Posner also included in his opinion that "although Hollinger is a large, sophisticated public corporation, no document was found to indicate that the $5.5 million in payments was ever approved by the corporation...."

Hollinger was the antithesis of a sophisticated company. As Ron Safer highlighted in his reply argument, "this was not your typical company." The incontrovertible evidence at trial was that the audit committee had approved $218 million in management fees without a piece of paper or being shown a single record.

The most glaring factual error in Posner's opinion was that Conrad Black was acting in his capacity as CEO of Hollinger when he ordered Kipnis to draft the covenants not to compete. The government and the defence were in complete agreement that it was David Radler who was directing Kipnis. There was no evidence at trial that Black had any dealings with Kipnis who was based in Chicago.

In relation to the obstruction conviction, Judge Posner held that there was ample evidence that the documents were concealed in order to make them unavailable in an official proceeding. According to Posner "there was evidence that Black knew that the alleged funds were being investigated by the grand jury and by the SEC."

Judge Posner also scorched the testimony of Conrad Black's secretary, Joan Maida. During argument, Posner observed that Maida's testimony hurt the defence. Her evidence was that Black intended to remove the documents to a temporary office that she planned to set up for him in her home because he would have to vacate his office at Hollinger in the next ten days. The clear evidence of Black moving the boxes into his own vehicle contradicted her trial testimony.

Andrew Frey's public statement the day that the appeal judgment was released was that "Black was a fighter" and that they were now looking at all of their options.[8] Black was resolved to move forward with a further appeal but it would be without Frey's representation. Black had received email summaries of the hearing in Chicago and read Posner's opinion and it was apparent that Frey had lost the appeal badly. It was time for a fresh start.

The parting with Andrew Frey was amicable and a search for a new lawyer began in earnest. Barbara Amiel interviewed several lawyers and Miguel Estrada was her recommended choice that Black settled upon. Estrada visited him in Florida at Coleman FCI. It marked the first of several visits by Estrada to the prison facility, which he later described as "an utterly dehumanizing environment."

THE JOURNEY TO THE SUPREME COURT

Early in January 2009, Conrad Black appealed his convictions to the United States Supreme Court. He had requested a commutation of his sentence from the departing American president, George W. Bush, but it was rejected. The Supreme Court represented Black's final opportunity to expunge his criminal convictions and to regain his freedom before the expiration of his sentence in 2013.

When the Supreme Court agreed to consider Black's appeal four months later, Estrada was ecstatic. "We've always maintained," he stated, "that what he [Black] was convicted of is simply not a crime." According to Ron Safer, if not for Miguel Estrada, the Supreme Court would not have granted certiorari to hear the petition. The story would have ended. It was Estrada's force, stature, credibility, and the substance of his argument that propelled the U.S. Supreme Court to act.[9]

Marc Martin had raised the question of honest services during Conrad Black's trial and asked the judge not to put the theory to the jury. He wasn't surprised that the Supreme Court had agreed to hear the appeal. There were some judges who were questioning the honest services fraud law and there were disagreements among the circuits on the underlying conduct required. "What is honest services in Chicago is not honest services in Iowa," he commented.

The honest services law hadn't registered as a big deal for the government at the trial. Eric Sussman was "for sure surprised" when the Supreme Court's decision to hear the appeal was reported. Sussman was pretty comfortable that the honest services law was on fairly solid ground and that the law in the Seventh Circuit was settled. He was aware that there were some issues with honest services and it was the reason that the government sought a special verdict, which would have specified the jury's basis of conviction. However, as a criminal law matter, he didn't expect any real questions to be raised on appeal about the honest services law.

According to Eddie Greenspan, the government never identified what the deprivation of honest services was in the case. The defence certainly discussed honest services fraud, but the big issues at the trial such as David Radler's testimony went well beyond it. For Ron Safer, honest services made a "huge difference" for his client. Mark Kipnis, he noted, was a perfect example of honest services fraud to the government.

The honest services fraud law was not a major issue for the jury during its lengthy deliberations. It was certainly reviewed by the jurors, but didn't resonate with them as a collective group. However, its possible impact on an individual juror couldn't be discounted.

Miguel Estrada was reasonably assured of receiving one favourable vote on the Supreme Court. Justice Antonin Scalia had written about honest services in a dissent from a denial of certiorari that "it invites abuse by headline-grabbing prosecutors in pursuit of local officials, state legislators, and corporate CEOs who engage in any manner of unappealing or ethically questionable conduct." It was such a vague law, Justice Scalia noted, that a prosecutor could charge a mayor for using the prestige of his office to get a table at a restaurant without a reservation.

The Supreme Court had taken the unusual step of hearing three separate appeals on the honest services fraud statute. The other appeals, which covered public corruption and boardroom corruption cases, included former Alaskan state legislator Bruce Weyhrauch and Jeff Skilling, the former chief executive of Enron. The Weyhrauch petition was scheduled to follow Black's on the same date.

THE SUPREME COURT HEARING IN WASHINGTON

On an early December morning in 2009 marked by peeks of sunshine, a row of people from across the United States and Canada gathered in front of the marble Ionic columns of the Supreme Court Building in Washington waiting for Conrad Black's appeal to unfold. Black's trial had largely been invisible in the U.S. outside of Chicago and New York, and as Dominick Dunne noted, "despite the rich people glamour, it never caught on with the American public."[10] Black's petition in the nation's capital had a national profile and was being closely monitored by the business and political communities as well as by law enforcement officials, prosecutors, judges, and the white-collar defence bar.

Miguel Estrada had argued about fifteen Supreme Court cases in his career. He found that he didn't sleep well for a couple of weeks before a big argument. He would be arguing on behalf of the four defendants in one synchronized voice. Estrada exhibited a degree of flexibility that was rare for someone of his intellect and stature. He was extremely inclusive with the written and oral presentations. The preparation Estrada demanded was exhaustive. Ron Safer described Miguel Estrada as being meticulously prepared in contrast to his predecessor Andrew Frey. Estrada came to Chicago to meet at Safer's law office to discuss and develop a strategy that was less fractured than the first appeal. Greenberg and Schachter participated by conference call. A number of mock hearings were also conducted before law professors and lawyers with Estrada insisting on playing his own part.

A key strategy decision that emerged from the moots and discussions was that Miguel Estrada would defend a component of the honest services fraud statute. During one of the moots he was asked: "Where do you draw the line?" Estrada candidly replied that he had no idea. After some discussion, Estrada was prepared to argue that the law was "too bad, period." A critical point was developed to keep the argument on track. For the law to be upheld, it required a limiting instruction that any honest services fraud prosecution must show that the defendant contemplated some identifiable economic harm to the victim. The Chamber of Commerce and the NACDL, by contrast, filed briefs in the petition arguing that the honest services law was unconstitutionally vague and could not be saved.

Moments before the formal hearing commenced at the Supreme Court, a familiar figure took her place in a reserved seat in the centre of the courtroom: Judge Amy St. Eve. Her presence surprised the lawyers. Judge St. Eve had brought her daughter for the hearing. She had earlier interviewed Justice Sonia Sotomayor in her chambers for a school project. Judge St. Eve later indicated that she wasn't the first judge who witnessed firsthand the Supreme Court's review of her craft, but acknowledged that it wasn't routine.[11]

Miguel Estrada was engaged in some friendly banter at the counsel table with the solicitor general, Elena Kagan, a friend and former law school classmate at Harvard. Kagan had high regard for her adversary. At her confirmation hearing for the nation's highest court several months later, she would describe Miguel Estrada as an extraordinary lawyer who was qualified to sit as a Supreme Court Justice.[12]

When Estrada rose to address the nine justices, he cited the relevant precedents relating to the honest services law with the ease of a master chef listing the ingredients of a complicated recipe. He agreed with Justice Sotomayor that the fraud statute could be constitutionally valid if it was limited to bribes or kickbacks. The benefit to Estrada's position was that the government hadn't alleged any bribes or kickbacks in Conrad Black's matter.[13] Estrada was equally comfortable supporting a textual interpretation advanced by Justice Scalia that the statute was bad law and unconstitutional.

Justice Samuel Alito asked Estrada for an explanation why any error in the honest services instruction wasn't harmless as applied to the Forum-Paxton transaction. He added that there was no evidence that the $600,000 payment was a recharacterized management fee.[14] Miguel Estrada answered in rebuttal that "you cannot say that you can uphold something as harmless when the entire theory on which the case was tried actually has been changed at the Supreme Court of the United States."

Deputy Solicitor General Michael Dreeben did an admirable job of defending the questionable fraud statute under an intense grilling by the panel of justices. Justice Steven Breyer observed that there were 150 million workers in the United States and that perhaps 140 million of them could be prosecuted under the government's interpretation of the law. Following a suggestion by Dreeben that the phrase "honest services" was a term of art, Justice Ruth Bader Ginsberg inquired: "How could it have been a term of art when the courts — the lower courts were massively confused?"

Barbara Amiel escorted Miguel Estrada as he hobbled gingerly down the series of steps of the Supreme Court Building. His foot was in a cast from a recent injury. Estrada paused for several minutes to answer questions at a media scrum and he appeared confident and buoyant. He would later describe to me that he was in a haze after the hearing concluded.

Estrada's law firm hosted a lunch after court at Morton's Steakhouse in the firm's office building on Connecticut Avenue. All of the lawyers in the case were present in a private dining room, including David Debold, Estrada's eminent co-counsel.[15] Black's wife and two of his children attended, as did the students from Gibson Dunn who had assisted with the research. One of them, a former marine, was set to clerk for Chief Justice Roberts in the coming term. The mood was good at lunch and there was a shared sense of cautious optimism. The Chief Justice's rebuke to the government during the Weyhrauch appeal was particularly encouraging: "I thought the principle was that a citizen has to be able to understand the law, and if he can't, then the law is invalid."[16]

Estrada began by asking everyone present at the oval-shaped table to introduce themselves. "What do you all think?" he asked. A lively debriefing ensued where everyone had an opportunity to contribute. The consensus was that there were four secure votes on the panel in their favour, possibly five. Ron Safer believed that at least seven justices had shown some antipathy to the honest services law.

Barbara Amiel ate sparingly at Morton's. At a small gathering the night before the hearing she continued to be troubled by her husband being badly treated and beaten up in the Court of Appeals. "But the Supreme Court granted him leave," she was reassured. She agreed that the hearing went well, but she appeared nervous. She made a point of telling Ron Safer at the table that she was impressed with his advocacy at trial, describing it as "wonderful," and expressed her regret that he hadn't defended her husband. It was a topic that made Safer uncomfortable and he avoided any disparaging comment about Conrad Black's trial team.

The Supreme Court's decision in Conrad Black's case was released at the beginning of the summer of 2009 and the news for Black was positive. His three mail fraud convictions were vacated. The decision was a sweeping 9–0 decision in his favour. None of the lawyers involved in the case had anticipated a unanimous ruling by the Supreme Court. The broad scope of the honest services law was confined exclusively to bribes and kickbacks. Three members of the court, including Justice Scalia, were prepared to strike down the law entirely.

Justice Ginsburg authored the eight-page opinion, and it was largely devoted to a procedural error in the lower court.[17] The Supreme Court adopted the analysis of honest services in the Skilling judgment, which was released the same day.[18] Black's mail fraud convictions were remitted back to the Court of Appeals for review. The lower court would be required to determine if the error of including an unlawful honest services theory was harmless to any of Conrad Black and his co-defendants' convictions.

The judgment also included a footnote that the court wasn't expressing an opinion on Black's contention that the spillover prejudice from the evidence on his mail fraud counts required reversal of his obstruction of justice conviction.

The attorneys in the Black legal team were extremely concerned with the remand order back to the Seventh Circuit. The same three-judge panel that heard the first appeal had the option to keep the case,[19] and it wasn't expected that Judge Posner would let Conrad Black's case slip from his judicial grasp. The Supremes, as Conrad Black described them, may have delivered him an illusory victory.

CONRAD BLACK'S FINAL APPEAL

A federal appeals court ordering him released on bail marked Conrad Black's continuing good fortune. It should have been expected, given the exceptional result in the Supreme Court, but it was widely viewed as a stunning achievement.[20] Conrad Black's legal team was enjoying a surge of confidence about Black's prospects on appeal. The most significant reason was that Judge Posner, along with the other two judges assigned to Black's appeal, had approved the bail order.

A bail hearing was scheduled a couple of days later before Judge St. Eve, and Marc Martin was brought in to assist on the ground in Chicago.

Martin was well liked and respected by everyone in the local courts. The list included Judge Amy St. Eve. During the trial in a discussion with the lawyers outside court, the judge made Ed Genson aware that she wanted Marc Martin to be involved in the trial and "not just the legal guy."[21]

Conrad Black was ordered released on bail on a $2 million bond. Roger Hertog, an affable American businessman who was previously involved with running the *New York Sun* with Black, was lined up to put up the cash bond. His selection was unopposed by the government. Hertog was instructed not to speak to the media and despite being harassed, avoided any comment. Hertog was eager to assist Conrad Black secure bail. He was a noted philanthropist who helped co-found the Shalem Center in Israel and had an abiding admiration for Black's steadfast support of the state of Israel with the *Daily Telegraph* in England.

At the urging of the government, a condition of the bail order was that Black was prohibited from leaving the United States. He was deemed a flight risk, which seemed fanciful given that Conrad Black had waived extradition and voluntarily returned to the United States for his trial over the course of several months. Judge St. Eve, however, was concerned about being publicly embarrassed if Black absconded to Canada. She was prepared to reconsider her position and allow Black to return to his home in Toronto after conducting a review of his finances.

Conrad Black left prison on July 21, 2010, with a spotless disciplinary record. Hundreds of inmates at Coleman lined up to wish him well and to hug him before he left the facility. Coleman was in a lockdown at the time of his release, and it prevented the throng of well-wishers from affectionately escorting Black to the front gates.[22]

Two days after gaining his freedom, Conrad Black appeared back in Judge Amy St. Eve's courtroom with his attorneys seeking to vary his bail to permit him to travel to Canada. He chatted amiably with some of the reporters who covered his trial and was in good spirits. He was observed outside court smiling with a radiant Barbara Amiel and holding her hand.[23] The judge read the terms of Black's bail as he stood at the front of the courtroom. A financial affidavit of Conrad Black was produced in court and it contained a number of careful qualifiers and estimates about the status of his finances. Black's corporate counsel from Toronto, Stan Freedman, contributed assiduously to the preparation of the affidavit and was available to testify about the worldwide freeze placed by a Canadian judge on his client's assets. Ultimately, the financial information provided by Conrad Black was determined by Judge St. Eve to be insufficient.

Miguel Estrada abandoned any further attempt to submit any additional disclosure of Black's financial records. Estrada believed that the government would pounce on any discrepancy in Black's sworn affidavit about his finances to revoke his bail. Black's trial prosecutors had employed the tactic in 2006 as they failed to convince Judge St. Eve that Black had lied about his finances. As one of Conrad Black's lawyers commented, his client didn't bother to look after the details of his financial affairs, and an itemized affidavit about Black's finances was a "veritable minefield."

The date for the second hearing before the Court of Appeals was scheduled for the early fall of 2010. In his written filing, Estrada suggested that the government had failed to address the Supreme Court's ruling in the case, and was wedded to the first Court of Appeals ruling. He described it as "the government's idiosyncratic version of *Groundhog Day*." The term "Groundhog Day" was only included after an email was circulated to the lawyers at Gibson Dunn to gauge the familiarity of the judges on the Court of Appeals with the comedy film.

There were three legal obstacles left for Miguel Estrada to overcome. They included the obstruction of justice conviction, the two APC mail fraud counts, and the Forum-Paxton mail fraud count. Mark Kipnis had the unique advantage of seeking to overturn only the Forum-Paxton conviction.

Within a half an hour of the hearing commencing, it was apparent that Black's obstruction of justice conviction would likely remain intact. The damaging videotape capturing him removing the boxes from his office on Toronto Street was the culprit. Judge Posner had already made his negative vote clear in his skeptical questioning of Estrada. Judge Sykes highlighted that there was visual evidence introduced at trial on the obstruction charge, "and visual evidence, as anybody who has tried a case knows, is powerful evidence."

The court's assessment of the APC counts was more favourable for Conrad Black and his three co-defendants. Edmond Chang[24] strenuously argued, on behalf of the government, that the prosecution's two legal theories merged into a single factual theory: that the defendants stole money. Judge Sykes noted that it was a complex four-month trial with sixteen counts where the jury was invited to base convictions on alternative theories. It was therefore extremely important how the government conceptualized the fraud. If a couple of jurors accepted that there wasn't stealing, but found a scheme and a breach of loyalty, that was sufficient to convict.

Judge Posner also expressed his problem with sustaining the APC counts. He suggested to Chang that the government never told the jury that that if it decided that the defendants didn't take anything, it shouldn't convict. He described it as the missing link.

In relation to the obstruction conviction, Edmund Chang noted in response to a question from the panel that "the defendant was on notice that the investigators had served document production requests on the defendant." This assertion by the government was entirely unsupported by the evidence.

Judge Posner reserved his harshest questioning for Miguel Estrada on the Forum-Paxton count. His basic contention was that since a non-competition payment agreement wasn't drafted for the $600,000 payment, the only viable finding for the jury was a simple theft. For Judge Posner the introduction of honest services was a harmless error when the evidence revealed that the defendants put money in their pockets without a contractual right to it.

Estrada countered that the jury could have found that the failure to have a written agreement in place for the Forum-Paxton transaction was an accidental oversight and not a theft.[25] Following the honest services theory, the jury could reasonably conclude that the later failure to inform the board of directors prior to approving the payment was a breach of a fiduciary duty, although it had nothing to do with fraud. It would have provided the jury with a path to convict on an invalid legal theory.

In response to a question from Judge Sykes, Estrada referred to counts two and three involving Hollinger Inc. and Forum-Paxton where the jury acquitted. The buyers in both transactions, Case and Paxton, had testified that they didn't have the slightest interest in the Hollinger Inc. non-compete contracts. If the jury had believed them, it would have convicted on these counts. It was therefore nearly impossible, Estrada contended, that it was safe to conclude that the jury could only have reached a verdict on the Forum-Paxton count favourable to the government.

At the conclusion of the hearing, Miguel Estrada had a telephone call with Conrad Black at his Palm Beach home. Black had been advised that it was better that he not to attend the hearing in Chicago to avoid creating any distraction and he readily agreed. Barbara Amiel was also notably absent after describing her husband's first appeal in the Seventh Circuit as "judicial murder" led by a shabby kangaroo court.[26] Marc Martin and Stan Freedman were present during the call with Black and offered their perspective of the argument in court. Estrada's assessment of the hearing was much harsher and he painted a very bleak picture for his client. Conrad Black accepted the news remarkably well.

Ron Safer invited the lawyers in the case to a buffet lunch in a private room at the Willis Tower.[27] Richard Greenberg asked if anyone was optimistic. Estrada replied, "Are you crazy?" Greenburg genuinely believed that his client, Jack Boultbee, would get time served on the Forum-Paxton count.

There was a consensus among the lawyers at the table that Conrad Black would get more prison time. Joan Maida's contribution to Black's predicament was discussed. It was Black's decision that she must be called as a witness. One lawyer noted that Maida had needed to humanize Black, but it didn't work.

The lawyer in the most enviable position after the hearing was Ron Safer. His client, Mark Kipnis, appeared secure in having his remaining convictions reversed. Safer, however, was cautious about the result. It was also clear to him that Judge Posner came to the argument (as with the first appeal) with his mind made up.

Michael Schachter reported that when he told Peter Atkinson that the hearing went well on APC, his unselfish reply was "good for Mark." Mark Kipnis felt genuine affection for Peter Atkinson. It was not a sentiment that he shared for Jack Boultbee.

A couple days after the appeal, Miguel Estrada and David Debold were panellists at a white-collar seminar at Fordham Law School. Estrada indicated that he slept well the night after the argument. Both lawyers were convinced that Black still had a chance to succeed with the Forum-Paxton count. Estrada believed that Judge Sykes was the key to persuading Judge Posner. Posner didn't want a dissent in the case.

Miguel Estrada expressed his view that it wasn't a fair hearing with Posner.[28] Estrada was resigned to losing the obstruction appeal based on Judge Sykes's comment about the powerful video evidence. The charge was lost at trial with the testimony of Joan Maida. Conrad Black had told Estrada for a long time what a poor job Ed Genson did at the trial.

Estrada ignored the comment until he read the transcript of Joan Maida's evidence. It was the worst he ever saw.[29]

Miguel Estrada had informed Black about a year earlier that he might be better off maintaining the obstruction conviction. Black was dismissive about it. Estrada believed that the government would retry Black if he won his full appeal. Julie Porter (formerly Julie Ruder) was still with the government and was the best lawyer on the case.

Exactly one month after the hearing in Chicago, the Court of Appeals released its judgment. Judge Posner wrote the opinion and the result was mixed for Conrad Black. The two mail fraud convictions for APC were "barely" reversed[30] because it was possible for the jury to convict the defendants of honest services fraud as a result of their failure to level with the board and the audit committee about the re-characterization of management fees. Black, Boultbee, and Atkinson's mail fraud conviction for Forum-Paxton was confirmed. The argument of spillover prejudice for the obstruction of justice was rejected and Conrad Black's conviction was affirmed.[31] The original sentences imposed were vacated and the matter was remanded to the trial judge for resentencing.

When Miguel Estrada reviewed Posner's opinion he was deeply offended. On the Forum-Paxton count, the defence evidence and arguments were referred to as "implausible," undermined by a fatal concession and "decisively unbelievable." The evidence of a "plain vanilla" pecuniary fraud was found to be compelling. In his analysis of Forum-Paxton, Judge Posner refuted the defence position that the jury could have believed that the absence of the non-compete covenants was an innocent mistake, but instead convicted them because they failed to disclose the payments to the board: "The failure to disclose is mentioned in passing in the information, but the evidence at trial, and the closing arguments focused on whether the absence of a written covenant was merely an oversight or instead proof of pecuniary fraud."

During oral argument, the government conceded that it presented the honest services fraud theory on each and every one of the mail fraud counts. Judge Sykes noted that the government did argue for conviction on a non-disclosure theory and that it was clearly part of the jury instruction to convict on that basis. Edmund Chang argued that those non-disclosures standing alone could not form the basis of a conviction. Judge Sykes then posed the following probing question: "How do we know the jury didn't convict on that basis?" The lingering concern was brushed aside in the decision of the Court of Appeals.

Judge Posner highlighted that it was the defendants' contention that the $600,000 payment was compensation for bona fides covenants not to compete. The owners of Forum-Paxton who testified that they didn't request such a non-compete covenant contradicted the defence position.

Judge Posner, however, overlooked the evidence that such non-competition agreements were conditions of closing in the transaction documents, and the validity of the non-competes didn't depend on what the buyers later surmised were personal feelings that they were unnecessary contract provisions. Professor Jinyan Li of Osgoode Hall Law School in Toronto[32] testified for the defence at trial that it made no difference who requested the non-compete payment or if it benefited the purchaser. It only mattered what the contract the parties entered into stated and whether the contract was legally enforceable.

The jury clearly didn't base its findings on the disinterested attitude of the purchasers because of the not guilty verdicts rendered for the Hollinger Inc. counts relating to Forum-Paxton. Judge Posner attempted to explain the acquittals for these similar counts:

> The jury acquitted the defendants on two other counts related to covenants not to compete with Forum-Paxton. But in those instances the fees went to Hollinger, and it is Hollinger that issued covenants not to compete, not the defendants, and Hollinger was a far more plausible entrant into Forum-Paxton's markets than the defendants, as individuals, were.

The evidence at trial was completely contrary to Posner's finding. Hollinger, Inc., a Canadian holding company, wasn't remotely situated as a more credible competitive threat to Forum-Paxton's markets than Conrad Black and the other defendants. Both Lloyd Case and David Paxton testified that they were not interested in non-competition agreements with Hollinger Inc., and their evidence was unequivocal.[33]

Judge Posner concluded his opinion by indicating that the government might judiciously decide to "wind up this protracted litigation," conserve its resources, and dismiss the APC counts. The matter could then proceed directly to resentencing. He issued a direct invitation to Judge St. Eve to consider the $5.5 million APC mail fraud counts at the resentencing hearing.

Ron Safer described the invitation for the Court of Appeals to weigh in about what they believe the district court should do as "extraordinary." Eddie Greenspan described it as gratuitous from a very mean-spirited judge. "It was an extraordinary interference by a judge in the process," he maintained.

Miguel Estrada would later refer to the lower court's decision as "not merely erroneous," but "a complete travesty."[34] Estrada's focus, however, was shifted to the resentencing of his client before Judge St. Eve. A return to Coleman FCI loomed as a realistic option for Conrad Black.

THE RESENTENCING OF
CONRAD BLACK

THE LAND OF
BILK AND MONEY

I never ask for mercy and seek no one's sympathy. I would never, as was once needlessly feared in this court, be a fugitive from justice in this country, only a seeker of it. It is now too late to ask for justice. But with undimmed respect for this country, this court, and if I may say so, for you personally, I do ask you to avoid injustice which it is now in your gift alone to do.

— An excerpt of Conrad Black's statement
at his resentencing hearing before Amy St. Eve

Conrad Black sold his mansion in Palm Beach in the spring of 2011 and relocated to the luxurious Mark Hotel in Manhattan. He left the "playpen of the rich" as he described his former posh neighbourhood, to be closer to family and friends. Black's daughter, Alana, lived in New York.

A few weeks before Black's scheduled resentencing hearing, the U.S. Supreme Court denied his second bid for a review of his case. The ruling ensured that Black's convictions for mail fraud and obstruction of justice remained intact and that he would be branded as a felon. He was also certain to be deported from the United States after his sentence was completed.

There had been a flash of good news as well. The government had announced in Judge St. Eve's courtroom that the two APC mail fraud counts would be dismissed, and therefore not retried. The total quantum of the fraud had instantly been reduced by over five million dollars with only the Forum-Paxton mail fraud conviction remaining.

The decision to drop APC marked the end of Mark Kipnis's legal woes and he was pleased when he learned of the outcome. For Ron Safer, however, the ultimate vindication for his client came too late. Kipnis's life had been dramatically altered by the case. He worked at a real estate company while other members of his family struggled to make a living at a sign shop. Kipnis's retirement savings were gone and his ability to practice law had realistically vanished. His principled choice to vigilantly assert his innocence and resist the seamless path of David Radler had been achieved with great personal sacrifice. Although he had ultimately prevailed, Mark Kipnis was arguably the biggest loser in the case.

The resentencing hearing for Conrad Black was scheduled for June 24, 2011. Judge Amy St. Eve was in the pivotal position of controlling Conrad Black's fate and determining whether he would return to prison after one year on bail. There was an acceptance on the part of Black's legal team that the judge's sentence would be unassailable, and an appeal futile. Any further sentence appeal would likely return to the coliseum of the imperious Judge Posner and the same panel of judges who presided over Black's previous two appeals. The Court of Appeals would invariably uphold any sentence imposed by Judge St. Eve.

Conrad Black's appeal team was initially pessimistic about its client's prospects for time served. By the time that the written sentencing submissions were filed, the outlook was less guarded. The most prominent reason for the shifting mood was that the highly influential presentence report of the probation department recommended a sentence of twenty-nine to thirty-three months, a range that coincided with the prison time already served by Black.

A second reason for a glimmer of hope for time served was that the government had decided to avoid any contested sentencing proceedings with Black's co-defendants, Peter Atkinson and Jack Boultbee. Atkinson and Boultbee served approximately eleven months in prison for the same $600,000 fraud that Conrad Black was confronting. Each of Black's co-defendants, including David Radler, served less than half of their original sentences. Extending Black's sentence beyond the twenty-nine months in prison that he had already served would create a harsh disparity that presumably wouldn't be tolerated by Judge Amy St. Eve.

Conrad Black arrived at the Dirksen Building holding hands with his wife and took his customary seat in Judge St. Eve's courtroom. He appeared paler and in poorer health since his trial concluded four years earlier. The bluster, however, hadn't dissipated. He appeared as the chairman of the board at the table as his team of four lawyers surrounded him. Black was privately confident of victory and walking out of court a free man. An interview was scheduled for the following day with *The National Post*.

Judge St. Eve entered court with a pencil tucked securely behind her ear. She announced that she had reviewed the written materials and expected the attorneys not to repeat their content. Black confirmed that he read the probation report that was filed and offered no further comment. The judge chronicled the history of the case and proceeded to rule in favour of the defence as she supported the probation officer's report that Black was to be sentenced exclusively for the $600,000 fraud and not for the other fraud counts. Miguel Estrada peered back and smiled at Barbara Amiel in the front row.

Judge St. Eve's next series of rulings were considerably less favourable to Black. She upheld the government's contention that the fraud involved "more than minimal planning" and "sophisticated means," both enhancements under the sentencing guidelines. Her findings were entirely contrary to Judge Posner's characterization of the "plain vanilla" nature of the fraud. It was now a frosty sundae. The presentence report had rejected the application of the same enhancements concluding that the Forum-Paxton fraud was a "single taking" without "any especially complex or intricate conduct … to commit or conceal the offence."

The Forum-Paxton mail fraud was achieved with such consummate sophistication and careful planning that Mark Kipnis, a non-participant in the fraudulent scheme, forgot to draft any non-competition agreements. As the defence had persuasively argued in its written materials, Kipnis's failure to write up, in the government's words, the "cover story," marked "the antithesis of planning."

The judge then signalled her intended sentence. She referred to the federal sentencing guidelines as "a framework, a starting point" and applied a guideline range in Conrad Black's case of fifty-one to sixty-three months. The lawyers immediately grasped that the gap between the judge's stipulated range and Black's actual time served in prison of twenty-nine months was unlikely to be bridged. Conrad Black would be returning to prison.

David Debold rose first to make the oral argument on Black's behalf. The original plan was that Debold would make all of the sentencing submissions. Eventually, Miguel Estrada decided to contribute. A third lawyer from Chicago, Carolyn Gurland, an intermittent member of Black's legal team, was also assigned a portion of the argument after she pushed for a role.[1]

Debold struck back at the prosecutors for their "open contempt" towards Conrad Black by their constant references to his absence of remorse. "A defendant can earn a lower sentence for an apology or receive a lower sentence for co-operating with the prosecutors. We are not seeking a lower penalty for accepting responsibility. Black is paying a price because of his failure to accept responsibility."

Debold added that Black "shouldn't be punished for taking a position" and for harbouring a foreign outlook of the American justice system. "When the full power of the federal government comes down on you, you can understand why someone would be skeptical of the system. As a foreigner, he can be forgiven for not having the same faith in the [U.S. Justice] system that we have. And still, he has sought to vindicate himself through the system."

Debold directed his next submission at the overly zealous tactics of his adversary. He accused the prosecution of "very aggressive methods" and using intimidation against Black. "This is not a case," he noted, "where someone is protesting in the face of vastly overwhelming evidence. There's enough room for doubt here to say that Black isn't being delusional."

Carolyn Gurland spoke passionately about Conrad Black's enlightening stay at the Coleman prison. She reviewed at length the glowing tributes to Black included in the written brief. The government wants to "vindicate their view of the case," Gurland observed, but the court "shouldn't allow for vindication to trump justice."

Julie Porter, on behalf of the government, mocked the defence's description of Black's behaviour in the court filings and during the hearing as an "exaggerated picture of his time there," and inelegantly accused Black of having "laid it on awfully thick." It was comparable to blasting the defence for presenting a catalogue of good deeds rather than a cursory, unimpressive account.

Porter also asked the judge to view the eighteen letters from prison inmates sent in support of Black "with a caution and a grain of salt." It was a subliminal message to the judge that this was a group of convicts who couldn't be trusted with providing the unvarnished truth.

The prosecutor also minimized Black's accomplishments as a tutor in prison. "Being a good tutor shouldn't be surprising because that's a good job for him," Porter stated. "He was a former corporate CEO who stole from his company. His crimes had a major impact. But he blames the government."

"His crimes had a major impact." Julie Porter was conflating Conrad Black's actual crime with the government's sweeping list of wishful crimes contained in the original indictment. It was a calculated tactic intended to influence the judge.

Porter referred critically to a statement made by Black via video link at the ideacity conference in Toronto a few days earlier. She described Black citing his remaining charges as the legal equivalent of reviewing your own expenses.[2]

Julie Porter referred to Black's "celebrity status in Coleman" and his presentence filings that "practically shriek with outrage" that he was convicted of fraud at all. "Fraud is stealing from shareholders, not a blip or clerical error. So after everything, we're back today to deal with a man who stole from the company and covered it up by obstructing justice," Porter advised the judge. She concluded by arguing that releasing Conrad Black for time served "would not be a just result."

Miguel Estrada countered the prosecutor's argument. "Black refused to see the government's case as it does. But this isn't China, you are not required to simply acquiesce." Estrada also noted that "Black stood his ground and was to a great extent vindicated. It is wrong-headed to impute arrogance on Black for doing nothing more than standing up for his rights."

Miguel Estrada described Black being re-incarcerated as "a huge demoralizing hardship." He turned to the prosecution table and claimed that he was once in their shoes and beseeched them to "keep in mind the aspects of the case, what he [Black] lost, his punishment, the hardships and those types of things you don't see everyday."[3]

In the defence peroration, Estrada told the court that singling Black out for further punishment, as the U.S. Government asked, was "a vindictive proposal and would not bring credit to our system of justice."

Judge St. Eve invited Conrad Black to address her before imposed the sentence. Black had consulted with Miguel Estrada during the hearing and realized that he was stranded on a sinking ship. Black stood before the judge and indicated that he had "only a few words," an estimate that was short by several thousand. Miguel Estrada had earlier urged his client not to speak and hadn't previewed any of the content of Black's speech to the court. Conrad Black spoke eloquently and without a note for the next twenty-five minutes. It was the most elaborate final statement by a defendant since the trial of Socrates.

Black thanked the judge for sending him to a prison with email access; a privilege that he was aware hadn't been afforded to his co-defendants, Boultbee and Atkinson. He offered a tepid defence to his "threadbare" convictions that he would have been "mad" and "barking, raving mad" to act improperly in the manner alleged by the government. His prosecutors were excused for being "victims" of Richard Breeden's lies and he expressed regret of being "too trusting of the honesty of one associate and the thoroughness of some others." David Radler's name didn't merit any mention in his grand moment.

Black quoted from Lord Denning of House of Lords fame, Cardinal Newman, Mark Twain, and Rudyard Kipling. The classic Kipling poem chosen, "If," was sent to him "by well-wishers from every continent except Antarctica." Rod Blagojevich inauspiciously referred to the same poem after his indictment in Chicago.

Black responded to Julie Porter's comment about the ideacity conference by assuring her that he didn't say on Canadian television that he was "like the person checking his own expense account." His explanation that followed was an ill-advised attack on the integrity of the panel of judges from the Court of Appeals involved in his case:

> I said that for the appellate panel that had been excoriated by Madame Justice Ginsburg on behalf of a unanimous Supreme Court, when assigned the task of assessing the gravity of its own errors, to resurrect these two counts after a gymnastic distortion, suppression and fabrication of evidence, was like someone reviewing his own expense account.

Judge St. Eve stared at Black with the bemused gaze of a shepherd watching a couple of his sheep mating in the field. If her mind was teetering about sending Conrad Black to prison, his brash display of denial, blame, and contrition for "tactical errors and mistakes of attitude" could only have eased his doomed fate.

Judge St. Eve sentenced Conrad Black to forty-two months, representing an additional thirteen months in prison. As soon as the sentence was announced, Barbara Amiel dropped with a loud thud as if she had been shot with a Taser. She had incorrectly interpreted the calculation of her husband's sentence as meaning an additional forty-two months in prison. The court bailiffs lunged at her as the judge, in a display of callous efficiency, resumed her reasons for sentence without a second of pause. Conrad Black stared rigidly at the judge, oblivious to his wife's fate behind him.

Judge St. Eve explained that the prison letters played a "significant" role in her sentence and bolstered her generous view that "you are a different person today having spent twenty-nine months in jail."

The prison sentence she imposed was intended to send a message to executives and other CEOs. The judge hadn't considered that a prison sentence of over two years delivered a sufficiently poignant message. Judge St. Eve ended her remarks with the following puzzling statement: "I still scratch my head as to why you engaged in this conduct. Good luck to you."

There is nothing mysterious about the reason that corporate executives steal and commit fraud. The obvious motivation is greed. The only head-scratching feature of the sentencing hearing was the questionable decision to return Conrad Black to prison.

Black's lawyers requested six weeks for Black to surrender to the prison authorities, and it was granted. A further request was made for Black to renew his British passport. Black didn't take the time to reflect on his sentence or consult with his lawyers. He rushed out of the courtroom to check on his wife's condition.

Conrad Black retreated to his hotel in Manhattan with his wife to await his self-proclaimed "victory lap" in prison. His surrender date was set for early September at the Coleman facility in Florida. His release date would follow in the spring of 2012. He received a return of the forfeited five and a half million dollars from the dismissed APC mail fraud convictions. Black's lawyers were occupied with securing his planned return to Canada as a temporary resident, where he was assured of a mixed reception of grace and hostility from the Canadian public.[4] Black was adamant that he would never seek Canadian citizenship again. Four days after his sentencing, Black informed a *Toronto Star* reporter that "his is a war and wars don't end until the fight stops."[5] Conrad Black was like a pummelled boxer lying flat on the canvas, refusing to recognize that the referee had stopped the fight. The trials of Conrad Black had ebbed without any surrender.

POSTSCRIPT:
FADE TO BLACK

My daughters came to Chicago for a brief visit and were understand-ably drawn to the Magnificent Mile on Michigan Avenue. As we strolled along the sidewalk, I suddenly realized that my oldest daughter was crying. "What's wrong?" I asked. She explained that she had watched in horror as a dishevelled man ran up to an older blind man playing his accordion on the boulevard and stole the change in his tray. The blind man mistook the brazen theft for an act of charity and uttered the words "thank you" as the thief ran off. The entire incident had taken only a matter of seconds but had deeply shaken my daughter.

I promptly reached into my pocket and gave both girls a few dollar bills. I instructed them to place the money securely in the blind man's hands. When they returned, my daughter's tears had subsided. I turned to them and said, "Whenever you witness an injustice, you must act to cor-rect it." If there is one enduring lesson that I can impart to my children, that is it.

I have come to the end of my journey regarding the trial of Conrad Black. It has been a richly rewarding experience covering it through the lens of a defence lawyer and legal analyst.

The trial has reminded me of another passion in my life — writing. It is as if I have taken a dusty old lamp from the basement and polished it. I owe a debt to the trials of Conrad Black for my renewed zeal for writing.

NOTES

INTRODUCTION

1. According to a member of Conrad Black's legal team, Marc Powers, Black spent about $30 million on his criminal trial, appeals, and related civil litigation. Michael Rothfeld and Chad Bray, "Loss Raises Questions Over Defense Strategy," *The Wall Street Journal*, May 12, 2011.
2. Adam Liptak, "Justices Offer Receptive Ear to Business Interests," *The New York Times*, December 18, 2010.
3. After Conrad Black appeared on local television, Genson was repeatedly told that his client was a "jagoff," a term most commonly used in Chicago to describe a jerk.
4. The third member of the team of prosecutors was Julie Porter (formerly Ruder). She was co-counsel for the government on the appeal. The final member of the Black prosecution team was Ed Siskel. Siskel had left the U.S. Attorney's Office to join the Justice Department as the Associate Deputy Attorney General.
5. James B. Stewart, *Tangled Webbs*, (New York: Penguin Press, 2011).
6. Liptak, "Justices Offer Receptive Ear to Business Interests." Many of these Supreme Court specialists had been part of the U.S. solicitor general's office, which acts for the federal government in court.
7. Richard A. Posner, *How Judges Think*, (Cambridge, MA: Harvard University Press, 2008), 6. Stephen Komie, a Chicago-based criminal defence lawyer, described Judge Posner as a professor with a robe who had no real life experience in the courtroom.
8. Judge Posner made the quip about Conrad Black in a dissenting opinion relating to the issue of jury identification during the former Illinois governor's first trial. At his retrial, Rod Blagojevich was convicted on seventeen of twenty corruption related charges.
9. Josh Gerstein, "Obama Backing Off Strict Crime Policy," *Politico*, September 11, 2010. The Dallas County District Attorney, Craig Watkins, described the mindset of prosecutors as "convictions, convictions, convictions." Watkins established a Conviction Integrity Unit in his office with the objective of expunging wrongful convictions. Eugene Robinson, "In Dallas: Defusing a Sociological Bomb: Wrongful Convictions," *The Washington Post*, January 7, 2011.

10. Brian W. Walsh, Tiffany M. Joslyn, "Without Intent: How Congress is Eroding the Criminal Intent Requirement in Federal Law," The Heritage Foundation and The National Association of Criminal Defense Lawyers, April 2010, 5. Gary Fields, John R. Emshwiller, "As Criminal Laws Proliferate, Most are Ensnared," *The Wall Street Journal*, July 23, 2011. After former presidential candidate John Edwards was indicted, one senior Washington litigator commented that "federal criminal laws are expansive enough that a clever prosecutor can recast almost any bad behaviour into a federal crime." "On Edwards Indictment, Am Law 200 Ranks Include Plenty of Skeptics," *The Am Law Daily*, June 3, 2011.

11. Jim E. Levine, written statement before the House Committee on the Judiciary Subcommittee on Crime, Terrorism, and Homeland Security, "Reining in Overcriminalization: Assessing the Problems and Proposing Solutions", September 28, 2010, 3. A federal judge in Orlando recently ruled that a state drug law in Florida was unconstitutional because there was no requirement to demonstrate a "guilty mind." John Schwartz, "Federal Law Ruled Unconstitutional," *The New York Times*, July 27, 2011.

12. Matt Welch, "The Ends Didn't Justify the Means," *Reason Magazine*, July 2011.

13. Chris Hedges, *Empire of Illusion* (Toronto: Vintage Canada, 2010), 49.

14. The retired Supreme Court justice, John Paul Stevens, referred in an earlier decision to the death penalty as "the pointless and needless extinction of life with only marginal contributions to any discernable social or public purpose." He authored a book review for *The New York Review of Books* ("On The Death Sentence," December 23, 2010) where he highlighted the finality of an execution including the risk that the state may put an actually innocent person to death. The state of Illinois abolished the death penalty in 2011.

15. "Rough Justice in America," *The Economist*, July 22, 2010. Driven by dropping crime rates and budgetary concerns, many states have reduced the severity of sentences, particularly for property and drug crimes. Some states have substituted treatment for incarceration for non-violent drug offenders and have reduced or eliminated mandatory minimum sentences. David Cole, "Hope and Betrayal on Death Row," *The New York Review of Books*, November 25, 2010.

16. Randall G. Shelden, "The Prison Industry," Centre on Juvenile and Criminal Justice, December, 2010. It is estimated that in the last quarter of the twentieth century, the criminal justice system in America grew five times more punitive. "The growth is not attributable to increased offending rates, but to increased punitiveness. Being 'tough on crime' became a political mandate. State and federal legislatures imposed mandatory minimum sentences, abolished or radically restricted parole, and adopted 'three strikes' laws that exact life imprisonment for a third offence, even when the offence is as minor as stealing a pizza." David Cole, "Can Our Shameful Prisons Be Reformed?" *The New York Review of Books*, November 19, 2009. See also Michael Gerson, "Michael Vick: Symbol of the Second Chance," *The Washington Post*, January 4, 2011.

17. Steve Chapman, "When Punishment is the Real Crime," *Chicago Tribune*, May 29, 2011.

18. *Brown v. Plata*, 12–13.

19. *Brown v. Plata*, 39.

20. Brad Heath and Kevin McCoy, "Prosecutors' Conduct Can Tip Justice Scales," *USA TODAY*, September 23, 2011. It was acknowledged in the series that the documented cases only represented a fraction of the total number of cases prosecuted. As well, under the direction of Attorney General Holder, prosecutors are receiving increased training in their duty to share the evidence with defendants, and every U.S. Attorney's Office is required to have a written discovery policy in place. Jim Lavine, the president of the NACDL, welcomed the changes but maintained that they hadn't halted prosecutors from concealing evidence.

21. Dahlia Lithwick, "Murder Conviction Most Foul: What Justin Wolfe's Case in Virginia Tells us About Death Row Cases Everywhere." *Slate*, July 14, 2011. Editorial Board, "A Deserved Rebuke in Prince William Murder Case," *Washington Post*, July 28, 2011. *Stinchcombe* upholds the principle that the search for truth is advanced rather than diminished by disclosure of all relevant material. In the subsequent case of *R. v. McNeil*, (2009 SCC3), the Supreme Court of Canada emphasized that relevance is to be regarded liberally and will include materials that have a reasonable possibility of assisting the person charged.

 In the doomed prosecution of Alaskan Senator Ted Stevens, the Attorney General sought dismissal of the charges because prosecutors had failed to disclose exculpatory evidence to the defence. At the pre-trial stage, the Stevens prosecutors had responded to the defence requests for discovery at a plodding pace, issue by issue, granting some and refusing others. Jeffrey Toobin, "Casualties of Justice," *The New Yorker*, January 3, 2011, 39.

22. The Supreme Court of Canada held in *R. v. Stinchcombe* (1991), 68 C.C.C. (3d) 1, that the right of an accused to make full answer and defence is a principle of fundamental justice under s. 7 of the *Canadian Charter of Rights and Freedoms*.

 Stinchcombe upholds the principle that the search for truth is advanced rather than diminished by disclosure of all relevant material. In the subsequent case of *R. v. McNeil*, (2009 SCC3), the Supreme Court of Canada emphasized that relevance is to be regarded liberally and will include materials that have a reasonable possibility of assisting the person charged.

23. Craig Horowitz, "The Defense Rests — Permanently," *New York Magazine*, March 4, 2002, 35.

24. Horowitz, "Defense Rests," 35.

25. "Rough Justice in America," *The Economist*, July 22, 2010.

26. Stuart Taylor Jr. & K.C. Johnson, *Until Proven Innocent: Political Correctness and the Shameful Injustices of the Duke Lacrosse Rape Case* (New York: Thomas Dunne Books, 2007), 177.

27. Ellen S. Podgor, written statement before the House Committee on the Judiciary Subcommittee on Crime, Terrorism and Homeland Security, "Reining in Over-criminalization: Assessing the Problems and Proposing Solutions," September 28, 2010, 3–4. Professor Podgor noted that a person charged with something called "mail fraud" may have no clue of the basis for the charge when no letter was mailed. The jury foreman in the first Blagojevich trial expressed his frustration with the prosecution's scattered list of charges: "Their shotgun approach — in hopes of

hitting something, they use a large-bore shotgun instead of finessing it with maybe an arrow — makes it harder on the jury." Bob Secter, Stacy St. Clair, "Blagojevich Jury's Advice: Keep it Simple," *Chicago Tribune*, August 28, 2010.

28. Carmen Hernandez is also a member of the U.S. Sentencing Commission's Practitioners Advisory Group. On the day after Conrad Black was sentenced, the United States Sentencing Commission voted to reduce sentences for crack-cocaine offences because the disparity to powdered cocaine was becoming "corrosive" to the justice system. The marked disparity was viewed as being racist, as crack-cocaine offenders were overwhelmingly black (*The New York Times*, December 16, 2007).

29. In *United States v. Booker*, 125 S. Ct. 738 (2005), the United States Supreme Court held that judges are still obliged to take the guidelines into account, but they are not required to impose them. Although Booker broadened the sentencing discretion of judges, the average sentencing length appeared to be unchanged since the Supreme Court decided the case. Posner, *How Judges Think*, 273. The sentencing guidelines are particularly harsh in major fraud cases. Economic crime offenders currently "easily face a prison term once reserved for murderers, terrorists, and serial rapists." James Feldman, Mary Price, "Out-of-Control Fraud Guidelines," *The National Law Journal*, July 25, 2011.

30. Ron Safer always believed that if he didn't put his client on the stand, he couldn't win the trial. In addition to the risk of the two-point enhancement, another factor was that Mark Kipnis had performed poorly in a simulated cross-examination.

31. Debra Cassens Weiss, "Why Casey Anthony Should be Glad She Won't Be Sentenced in Federal Court," *ABA Journal*, July 6, 2011.

32. Jenny Roberts, "Collateral Consequences: Who Really Pays the Price for Criminal 'Justice'?," *Howard Law Journal*, Vol. 54, 2011, 901.

33. Retired U.S. Supreme Court justice Sandra Day O'Connor denounced the election of judges adding that "[a]llowing cash in our courtrooms has the potential to erode the public's confidence in the impartiality and trustworthiness of the courts." Sandra Day O'Connor, "Why Michiganders Have Lost Faith in Judges' Impartiality," *Detroit Free Press*, June 12, 2011. See also the editorial "Can Justice Be Bought?" *The New York Times*, June 15, 2011.

34. Matt Welch, "The Ends Didn't Justify the Means," *Reason Magazine*, July 2011.

35. David Carr, "TV Justice Thrives on Fear," *The New York Times*, 22 May 2011.

36. Robert Fulford, "The Dangerous Spread of the Nancy Grace Virus," *The National Post*, July 9, 2011. In the Casey Anthony case, a highly publicized case involving a woman charged with murder of her young child, Grace lambasted the defendant's choice not to testify on her program: "That's right, Tot Mom refuses to take the stand, afraid of squaring off against veteran prosecutors. It's just not the same as a two-year-old little girl."

37. Carr, "TV Justice Thrives on Fear."

38. Tim Rutten, "For Some, Jackson Verdict is Already In," *Los Angeles Times*, June 11, 2005.

TITAN ON TRIAL

1. The evidence at trial demonstrated that Conrad Black learned of the sixth document request after the boxes of documents were removed. The initial contact about an impending document request came from a SEC lawyer one day before Black removed the thirteen boxes from his office in Toronto. The request was received by Jennifer Owens, an attorney with the law firm of Baker Botts based in Washington, D.C. Owens emailed Alex Bourelly, her supervisor at the law firm, and Dan Rosenthal, an attorney at Williams & Connelly who had previously worked for Black on the SEC matter. Owens, Bourelly, and Rosenthal testified at trial for the defence and they couldn't relate or recall a single in-person conversation, telephone call, or email with Conrad Black advising him of the imminent SEC document request.

2. Six production requests for documents appeared inherently excessive. Harry Markopolis, the private financial investigator who repeatedly contacted the SEC for nearly a decade with evidence of Bernie Madoff's fraud — only to be ignored, provided this pertinent insight about the SEC: "On Wall Street the real fear about the SEC was not that it would uncover hidden crimes, but rather that it would bury you beneath an avalanche of paperwork. That's what it was best at. SEC audits consisted primarily of confirming that a checklist of documents existed, not necessarily that these documents were accurate, not even that they reflected real trades — just that you had the proper papers in your file." Harry Markopolis, *No One Would Listen*, (Toronto: John Wiley & Sons, 2010), 62.

3. The colour chart represented the various levels of risk for a terrorist attack: severe, high, elevated, guarded, and low. If the alert level was elevated, it indicated a "significant risk of terrorist attack."

4. Prior to the commencement of Conrad Black's criminal trial, Ravelston Corp. pleaded guilty to one count of fraud and agreed to pay a $7-million fine. The fine was imposed by Judge St. Eve on November 28, 2007. A further order for $6 million in restitution was added.

5. Tom Wolfe, *The Bonfire of the Vanities* (Avenel, NJ: Wings Books, 1994), 267.

6. Stuart Taylor Jr. & K.C. Johnson, *Until Proven Innocent: Political Correctness and the Shameful Injustices of the Duke Lacrosse Rape Case* (New York: Thomas Dunne Books, 2007), 367. Vague and undefined charges cast a wide net of potential criminality.

7. Nicholas Stein, "Judgment Day," *Men's Vogue*, November 2007, 150.

8. Stein, "Judgment Day," 155.

9. Craig Horowitz, "The Defense Rests — Permanently," *New York Magazine*, March 4, 2002, 36.

10. Jane Kelly had worked on a number of criminal cases with Greenspan before the Black trial, including the successful defence of former Nova Scotia premier Gerald Regan. She was appointed to the Ontario Superior Court after the trial.

11. Canadian courts have traditionally resisted importing the influence of American practices in the challenge process for jury selection. The underlying concern is that

"[t]rials should not be unnecessarily prolonged by speculative and sometimes sus-pect challenges for cause." *R. v. Cameron* (1995), 22 O.R. (3d) 65 (Ont.C.A.), at 72. See also David M. Tanovich, David M. Paciocco & Steven Skurka, *Jury Selection in Criminal Trials: Skills, Science, and the Law* (Concord, ON: Irwin Law, 1997).

12. Romina Maurino, "Conrad Black's Tale has Drama but Lacks Victims who get a lot of Sympathy," *The Brooks Bulletin*, March 11, 2007.

13. This point was made to me by Mark Sandler, a highly regarded Canadian human rights and criminal lawyer in Toronto. Reference should be made to *Mugesara v. Canada (Minister of Citizenship and Immigration)*, 197 C.C.C. (3d) 233 (S.C.C.). The case sets out the history of the conflict in Rwanda between the Hutu and the Tutsi that led to genocide and crimes against humanity. In the view of one American expert, Dr. Alexander Tsesis, the hateful stereotyping of the Tutsis was an essential link to the Rwandan genocide, which led to more than 300,000 children being killed. See *Warman v. Lemire*, Canadian Human Rights Tribunal (February 26, 2007) at 3486; Romeo A. Dallaire, *Shake Hands With the Devil: The Failure of Humanity in Rwanda* (New York: Carrol & Graf, 2004), 510.

14. *R. v. Keegstra* (1990), 61 C.C.C. (3d) 1 (S.C.C.). The concept of an open "mar-ketplace of ideas" as justification for permitting all forms of offensive speech is expressly rejected in the decision. It is Dr. Tsesis's view that the United States "has maintained an antiquated notion of free speech, when it comes to hate speech" and that Canada's laws "are very much in accord with other democracies, and the United States is out of step" (*Warman v. Lemire*, Canadian Human Rights Tribunal [February 26, 2007], 3475). I represented the Friends of Simon Wiesenthal Center for Holocaust Studies at the hearing. The matter is currently under appeal before the Federal Court.

THE PROSECUTION

1. Greenspan made this remark in a presentation at the Advocates' Society Annual Fall Convention in the Bahamas on November 17, 2007.

2. Barbara Shecter, "Prosecutors Have 'Erred' in Black Case," *The National Post*, March 27, 2007.

3. *R. v. Gardiner*, [1982] 2 S.C.R. 368 at para 110. The case marked my first appearance in the Supreme Court of Canada as an articling student at the Crown Law Office in Ontario.

4. Dominick Dunne later related to me that he had made a special effort to thank Mohammed for his special act of kindness at Gibsons. As for Eddie Greenspan, Dunne later appeared on *Larry King Live* where he described Greenspan as a "Toronto defence attorney who is the toughest guy I ever saw in my life."

5. John F. Harris, *The Survivor* (New York: Random House, 2005).

6. Harris, *The Survivor*, 291–93.

7. Hon. Justice Michael Moldaver, Court of Appeal for Ontario, "Address" (Sopinka Lecture on Advocacy, delivered at the Criminal Lawyers' Association Annual Fall Conference, Toronto, October 21, 2005).
8. Greenspan reported seeing the same photo in the judge's chambers during the trial and realized that the *Toronto Star* photo was dated.
9. Jennifer Lee, "Who Needs Giacomo? Bet on the Fortune Cookie," *The New York Times*, May 11, 2005.
10. Jacquie McNish, "Torys Reaches $30-Million Settlement with Hollinger," *The Globe and Mail*, November 29, 2005.
11. The Honourable Patrick T. Galligan, *Report to the Attorney General of Ontario on Certain Matters Relating to Karla Homolka* (March 15, 1996), 161–62.
12. *Report of the Kaufman Commission on Proceedings Involving Guy-Paul Morin*, vol. 1 (Toronto: Ontario Ministry of the Attorney General, 1998), 565. I served as counsel to the Ontario Crown Attorney's Association at the public inquiry.
13. In *R. v. Barrow* [1987] 2 S.C.R. 694, the Supreme Court of Canada held that it was reversible error for the trial judge to address the jury panel "out of earshot of all counsel and the accused."
14. The Supreme Court of Canada in *United States v. Burns*, [2001] 1 S.C.R. 283 (hereafter cited as *Burns*) ruled that, as a condition of extradition, the Minister of Justice must obtain an assurance that the death penalty will not be imposed. Referring to a series of Canadian cases in which DNA evidence was eventually used to overturn wrongful convictions, the court asserted (at para. 102) that "had capital punishment been imposed, there would have been no one to whom an apology and compensation *could* be paid in respect of the miscarriage of justice … and no way in which Canadian society with the benefit of hindsight could have justified to itself the deprivation of human life in violation of the principles of fundamental justice." See also Fernando Santos, "Vindicated by DNA, but a Lost Man on the Outside," *The New York Times*, November 25, 2007. DNA testing has exonerated more than 250 people in the U.S. since the late 1980s. Seventeen were sentenced to death for crimes they didn't commit, and the average time spent in prison was thirteen years. Jeffrey Rosen, "The Wrongful Conviction as Way of Life," *The New York Times*, May 26, 2011.

    The resort to the death penalty may be dissipating as the direct result of DNA. According to Joshua Marquis, the vice-president of the National District Attorneys Association, there are fewer executions and fewer people being sentenced to death in America. "People really do question capital punishment," he noted. "The whole idea of exoneration has really penetrated popular culture" (Adam Liptak, *The New York Times*, December 26, 2007).
15. In *Burns*, the court acknowledged that DNA evidence only helps redress the plight of the convicted innocent in a narrow class of cases. (See footnote 38 at para 109.) The other concern relates to the wrongfully charged. In one case that I defended, my client Ken was charged with two counts of threatening death after calling a crisis centre out of fear that he might act on his thoughts of killing his wife and her lover, whose affair he had just discovered. I was retained in the case (after my client spent

several days in jail) by my client's employer, Ernest Singer. Singer was a survivor of the Auschwitz concentration camp and stood resolutely by his employee until his charges were ultimately withdrawn.

16. The rest of the team consisted of Austin Cooper, QC, David Harris, David McCombs, and Ted Minden.

17. Geoffrey Robertson, *The Justice Game* (London: Vintage, 1999), 353.

18. Stuart Taylor Jr. & K.C. Johnson, *Until Proven Innocent: Political Correctness and the Shameful Injustices of the Duke Lacrosse Rape Case* (New York: Thomas Dunne Books, 2007), 366.

19. Michael Miner, "Big Jim Testifies at Conrad Black Trial," *Chicago Reader*, May 3, 2007.

20. William Glaberson, "Many lawyers rebuffed at Guantanamo Bay," *The New York Times*, May 5, 2007.

21. *Vetrovec v. The Queen*, [1982] 1 S.C.R. 811.

22. Tom Bower, *Conrad & Lady Black: Dancing on the Edge* (London: HarperCollins, 2006).

23. Steve Bogira, *Courtroom 302* (New York: Alfred A. Knopf, 2005), 190.

THE DEFENCE

1. In *R. v. Rose*, [1998] 3 S.C.R. 262, the Supreme Court of Canada upheld the right of the Crown to address the jury last in a case where defence evidence was called. However, in Canada, the prosecution has no right to address the jury both before and after the defence closing argument.

CLOSING ARGUMENTS AND JUDGE'S INSTRUCTIONS

1. Crown counsel is a "*quasi*-judicial officer of the court and agent of the Attorney-General." Michael Code, "Crown's Responsibility Advising Police," *Criminal Law Quarterly* 40 (1998): 326, 338.

2. For example, in the *Regan* case (see note 11 of "Titan on Trial") jury members were permitted to leave their hotel during deliberations for a day trip, but all newspaper boxes along the planned route were carefully covered.

3. In *R. v. Krieger*, [2006] 2 S.C.R. 501, the Supreme Court of Canada held that the trial judge usurped the jury's power when he directed the jurors to return from their deliberations with a guilty verdict. Once an accused elects a jury trial, the jury has complete province over the determination of a defendant's guilt or innocence.

4. Matthew Hutson, "Unnatural Selection," *Psychology Today*, Mar/Apr 2007.

5. I was prominently featured on Michael Jackson's website during the Jackson trial (April 25, 2005) with my claim on *Canada AM* that Michael Jackson wasn't "just winning the case, but winning it by a lot." The jury's verdict was entirely justified in the case.

Notes

THE VERDICT AND SENTENCING

1. In a letter to the *Globe and Mail* prior to his sentencing, Black's lack of remorse continued unabated: "The media preoccupation with my lack of remorse seems to assume that I should go from protesting my innocence, as was established on most of the charges, to protestations of guilt and shame because a jury found against me on a quarter of the counts. On to appeal." Tara Perkins, "Black Defends his Rant Against U.S. System," *The Globe and Mail*, December 3, 2007.

2. Rick Westhead, "Bungles that Helped Topple Black," *The Toronto Star*, December 8, 2007.

3. Adam Liptak, "Serving Life for Providing Car to Killers," *The New York Times*, December 4, 2007.

4. Adam Liptak, "Lifers as Teenagers, Now Seeking Second Chance," *The New York Times*, October 17, 2007. The United States Supreme Court struck down the death penalty for juveniles only a few years earlier. In Justice Anthony Kennedy's majority opinion, it was recognized that the United States stood alone in a world that turned its face against the juvenile death penalty. See Jeffrey Toobin, *The Nine* (New York: Doubleday, 2007), 193–99, for a fascinating account of the Supreme Court's decision.

5. Marc Martin pointed to two concepts that emerged from this law-and-order agenda that would be particularly perplexing to the man on the street. A defendant can be reprosecuted for conduct that he had been acquitted for as long as a different sovereign (state or federal court) is involved. A defendant can also be sent to jail for conduct that he was acquitted for in a multiple count indictment where there is at least one finding of guilt by the jury. As Martin noted critically, it "fails to show proper respect and recognition to the jury's verdict."

6. Tom Wolfe, *The Bonfire of the Vanities* (Avenel, NJ: Wings Books, 1994), 327.

7. Theresa Tedesco, "At the End, a Win for the Defence," *The National Post*, December 11, 2007. In an editorial in the *Globe and Mail* (December 11, 2007), prosecutors in the Conrad Black trial were described as securing "a Phyrrhic victory on the conviction." It went on to say, "In the context of the resources the United States threw at the prosecution, and the accompanying overwrought rhetoric, the government must view the results as a failure."

8. It is difficult to adequately capture the brittle tension in the courtroom at the time that a verdict or sentence is pronounced. My close friend Tim Lipson recounted the close of a murder case he was involved with in Stratford, Ontario, where his client had just been convicted of murdering a twelve-year-old boy he had earlier kidnapped from a shopping mall. As he exited from the dark oakwood courtroom, Tim was forced to pass the young victim's sobbing parents. The father suddenly reached out, grabbed Tim's arm, and addressed him in a doleful tone: "I'm sorry we couldn't have met under better circumstances. We respected the way you conducted the case."

9. *United States v. Gall*, 552 U.S. (2007).

10. *Gall*, at 8. However, a cautionary note for judges about the significance of the sentencing guidelines was also part of the majority decision (at 7–8):

337

It is also clear that a district court judge must give serious consideration to the extent of any departure from the Guidelines and must explain his conclusion that an unusually lenient or an unusually harsh sentence is appropriate in a particular case with sufficient justifications. For even though the Guidelines are advisory rather than mandatory, they are … the product of careful study based on extensive empirical evidence derived from the review of thousands of individual sentencing decisions.

11. Mark Kipnis focused exclusively on the APC transaction in his statement because Judge St. Eve had earlier acquitted him of one count of mail fraud relating to the Forum and Paxton non-competition payments. Kipnis's co-defendants were less fortunate. All of their motions to set aside the jury's verdict were denied.
12. Mike Medavoy, *You're Only as Good as Your Next One* (New York: Pocket Books, 2002), 262.
13. I sat beside Michael Miner during the sentencing hearing of Mark Kipnis. Miner wrote a profoundly moving account of the hearing, which he ended with these stirring words: "Euphoria doesn't last long, and when Kipnis adds everything up, he'll be confronting the fact that he's middle-aged, disbarred, broke, and a convict, and for the next five years of probation his life won't be his own. But to enter prison is to die. To go home is to live" (*Chicago Reader*, December 11, 2007).
14. The common law recognizes a "long-standing and entirely pragmatic convention" that criminals should receive lower sentences than they deserve because of their co-operation (see *R. v. P; R. v. Blackburn* [2007] EWCACrim 2290; Court of Appeal, Criminal Division, October 22, 2007). Conrad Black's prosecutors sought a sentence for him that was literally eight times longer than David Radler's proposed joint submission. This marked an indefensible gap devoid of any sense of proportionality or principle.

THE APPEAL-GO-ROUND

1. Janet Whitman, "Black Brings In a Big Gun For Appeal," *New York Post*, July 28, 2007. Andrew Frey had argued sixty-five cases before the U.S. Supreme Court.
2. Barbara Amiel, "Conrad and I Were Betrayed," *The Sunday Times*, August 10, 2008.
3. Conrad Black's submission in response to updated presentence report and in aid of resentencing. (The submission is relied upon extensively for background information about Black's confinement at Coleman FCI.)
4. James Warren, "The Conrad Black Style of Doing Time," *The New York Times*, May 8, 2010.
5. Conrad Black remained loyal to his assistant despite her damaging testimony at trial. Maida regretted her disastrous role as a witness, but Black refused to attribute any blame to her.

6. Court documents were filed by the government for the resentencing, outlining that Conrad Black demanded special treatment from prison staff, was a complacent tutor, and gathered inmates who acted like servants as they cooked, mopped the floor, and ironed his shirts. Theresa Tedesco, "Unflattering Profile 'Lies': Black," *The National Post*, June 6, 2011. Black was depicted as thinking that "the privileges of nobility extended to prison." Ameet Sachdev, "Affidavits: Conrad Black Lorded Over Captive Audience in Prison," *Chicago Tribune*, June 7, 2011. Conrad Black's lawyers were steaming about the fresh allegations and viewed the government's material as a malicious attempt to poison Judge St. Eve's view of Black. In a subsequent filing by the defence, prosecutors were accused of orchestrating a "drive-by disparagement of Conrad Black" with "shameful" affidavit material that was "demonstrably false." Sunny Freeman, *Canadian Business*, June 9, 2011.

7. Under Canadian law, the re-characterization of management fees as non-competition payments was entirely proper.

8. Paul Tharp, "Appeal Lost, Black Eyes Another," *New York Post*, June 26, 2008.

9. Jacob Frenkel's differing view was that the Skilling case was crying out as an opportunity for clarification on honest services and that but for Skilling, Conrad Black would never have been at the Supreme Court.

10. Email from Dominick Dunne to Susan Berger, July 12, 2008.

11. Michael Miner, "His Father's Honor," *Chicago Reader*, December 17, 2009.

12. Nathan Koppel, "On Kagan, Miguel Estrada and Chinese Food on Christmas," *Law Blog, Wall Street Journal*, June 29, 2010.

13. Professor Alschuler filed a "friend of the court brief" in the Weyhrauch petition, advancing the position that the honest services statute should be limited to bribes and kickbacks. The Supreme Court referred to his brief approvingly. Alschuler suggested that Conrad Black was fortunate that the Supreme Court relied upon Miguel Estrada's "very clever point" in his written brief that there weren't any bribes or kickbacks in Black's case. "There's no reason that kickbacks couldn't be disguised as non-competes," Alschuler contended. Ron Safer agreed that the government should have argued kickbacks.

14. It was instructive that Andrew Frey had never made any reference to the Forum-Paxton conviction during oral argument in the Court of Appeals.

15. The group of attorneys from the trial also attended the lunch at Morton's with the exception of Benito Romano, Eddie Greenspan, and Ed Genson. Conrad Black did not seek Greenspan and Genson's active involvement after the trial.

16. The lawyers had remained in court to follow the argument in the Weyhrauch appeal.

17. Justice Ginsburg's opinion held that the defence didn't forfeit the right to challenge the jury instructions on appeal because there was an objection to the special verdict form requested by the government.

18. Jeff Skilling's case was sent back to the Fifth Circuit Court of Appeals, and in April 2011 his appeal was dismissed. Bruce Weyhrauch was also successful with his appeal in the U.S. Supreme Court on the honest services fraud issue. In March 2011, the government dropped his federal corruption charge and Weyhrauch pleaded guilty to a state misdemeanor.

19. According to Marc Martin, there was nothing irregular or unusual about the same panel of judges being assigned to Black's appeal after the remand from the Supreme Court.

20. Two days before the bail order was issued, my article, "Bail May Be Possible for Conrad Black," was published in *The National Post*.

21. When Ed Genson was advised of the trial judge's view of Marc Martin, he informed Greenspan that Martin should take the lead on the obstruction count. "Shouldn't I do this, if not you?" Greenspan asked. Genson insisted it be Martin because he wanteded to please Judge St. Eve. As a result, Joan Maida was supposed to be prepared and called as a witness by Marc Martin. However, a scheduling conflict prevented Martin from meeting with Maida in advance of her testimony. Ed Genson was brought in as a late replacement and called Joan Maida without extensive preparation.

22. Conrad Black's submission in response to updated presentence report and in aid of resentencing.

23. Laura Bleakinsop, Paul Waldie, "'A More Upbeat Lord Black than We've Seen Before,'" *Globe and Mail*, July 23, 2010.

24. A few months after arguing the Black appeal for the government, Edmund Chang became the first Asian-American federal judge in Illinois.

25. Ed Genson had worried about winning the Forum-Paxton count from the beginning of the case.

26. Barbara Amiel, "Conrad and I Were Betrayed," *The Sunday Times*, August 10, 2008.

27. The Sears Tower had changed ownership and was renamed.

28. During oral argument Miguel Estrada asked Judge Posner if he could get in three sentences, but Posner only permitted him to complete the first sentence before interrupting him again.

29. Eddie Greenspan believed that the blame attributed to Genson was unfair. His cross-examination of Paul Healy was instrumental in Black winning the perk count involving the Park Avenue apartment. Ed Genson could have devoted fifty hours preparing Maida, a loyalist to Black and not overly astute, but it would have been futile. Either Conrad Black or Joan Maida needed to testify, and calling Black would have been a recipe for disaster. Earl Cherniak had devoted three days in Chicago to prepare Black for cross-examination. Greenspan could only stand to watch for an hour before leaving.

30. George W. Bush *barely* won the presidency over Al Gore, but that didn't prevent him from running the country for four years.

31. Judge Posner's description in the first appeal of there being *evidence* that Black was aware that his alleged fraudulent conduct was being investigated by a grand jury and by the SEC was elevated by Posner to *compelling evidence* in the second appeal. In fact there was no evidence that Conrad Black knew about a grand jury investigation. In relation to the SEC investigation, the incontrovertible evidence was that Black complied fully with the five document requests that he was made aware of. He wasn't advised of an imminent sixth document request prior to the boxes of documents being removed from his office.

32. Jinyan Li was also a Visiting Scholar at Harvard Law School and served as the Interim Dean at Osgoode Hall Law School from July 1, 2009, to June 30, 2010.

33.	Government:	"Would you have been willing to close that deal [Forum] without any non-compete agreement from the Canadian company Hollinger Inc.?
	Lloyd Case:	"Yes." Case also testified that if someone volunteers a non-compete, "it would be silly not to take it."
	Government:	"Did you want Inc. included in the non-competition agreement [Paxton]?"
	David Paxton:	"We did not feel we needed Inc. included in the non-competition agreement."
	Government:	So why didn't you ask them to take it out?"
	Paxton:	"It was not important to us, so it was their proposal. It was easy to accede to their proposal."

34. Greg Stohr, "Conrad Black Rejected by U.S. High Court Over Fraud Conviction," *Bloomberg*, May 31, 2011.

THE RESENTENCING OF CONRAD BLACK

1. The fourth member of the defence team was Marc Martin.
2. Conrad Black was repeatedly instructed by his lawyers not to comment publicly about his case while his appeals and resentencing remained outstanding. There were instances, however, where, according to one of his attorneys, "the duct tape fell off."
3. There was some tension in Black's defence team about the approach that should be taken in the written filings towards the conduct of the government. One side urged a tempered and measured assessment, while the other side, supported by Black, was prepared to engage in a strident attack on the prosecution's tactics. A compromise was eventually reached.
4. The blogs were replete with tirades against Black and condemned his possible return to Canada. As an example, one blogger wrote: "It's too bad they couldn't find a hell hole for him to rot in since that is what he deserves."
5. Mitch Potter, "Black Crusades Against U.S. Legal System," *Toronto Star*, June 28, 2011.

ABOUT THE AUTHOR

S teven Skurka is a respected criminal defence lawyer with a law practice in Toronto. He is a certified specialist in criminal litigation and a former adjunct professor at Osgoode Hall Law School. He has extensive experience with cross-border work dealing with the United States and is a life member of the National Association of Criminal Defense Lawyers. He is also a member of the Criminal Lawyers' Association in Ontario.

Steven has been involved in a number of high-profile cases in Canada, including the landmark Dee Brown racial profiling case, the Maple Leaf Gardens sex abuse scandal, the Guy Paul Morin wrongful conviction inquiry, and the test case of the country's anti-gang laws.

He has defended complex and lengthy white-collar fraud cases as well as representing athletes, entertainers, lawyers, police officers, and politicians. He has co-authored a book on jury selection and is regularly invited to appear on educational panels for lawyers and judges.

Steven is the legal analyst for the CTV national television network and is a frequent guest on television and radio to provide expert commentary on a variety of legal topics. He covered the trial and appeals of Conrad Black for CTV.

INDEX

Index

OF RELATED INTEREST

Under Arrest
Canadian Laws You Won't Believe
by Bob Tarantino

9781550027037
$24.99

Did you know that Canada's Criminal Code still has provisions outlaw-ing the practice of witchcraft and "crafty sciences"? Did you know that blasphemy is a crime in Canada? And did you know that putting a picture of a red poppy on your website could get you in trouble with the Royal Canadian Legion?

Lawyer and author Bob Tarantino takes readers on an entertaining and informative romp through Canada's legal labyrinths in a book that spot-lights the country's past and present strange-but-true laws and legal history.

Justice Miscarried
Inside Wrongful Convictions in Canada
by Hélèna Katz

9781554888740
$24.99

Behind the proud façade of Canada's criminal justice system lie the shattered lives of the people unjustly caught within its web. *Justice Miscarried* tells the heartwrenching stories of twelve innocent Canadians, including David Milgaard, Donald Marshall, Guy Paul Morin, Clayton Johnson, William Mullins-Johnson, and Thomas Sophonow, who were wrongly convicted and the errors in the nation's justice system that changed their lives forever.

Available at your favourite bookseller.

www.dundurn.com

What did you think of this book?
Visit www.dundurn.com for reviews, videos, updates, and more!